DATE DUE

DEMCO 38-296

Contents

Editorial Advisory Committee

Chairman: Professor Stanley H. Hoffmann, Chairman, Center for European Studies, Harvard University

Mr. John C. Bierwirth, Professor, SUNY-Stony Brook; Retired Chairman, Grumman Corporation

Ms. Carole Dale, Project Director, Mershon Center, The Ohio State University; Great Decisions Coordinator, Columbus, Ohio

Mr. Earl W. Foell, Editor in Chief, *World Monitor*

Dr. Arnold Shore, President, Council for Aid to Education

Dr. Richard L. Smoke, Research Director, Center for Foreign Policy Development, Brown University

Dr. Allen Weinstein, President, The Center for Democracy

Staff for Great Decisions 1990: Editor in Chief: Nancy L. Hoepli; **Senior Editors:** Nancy King Bernstein, Ann R. Monjo, Lawrence G. Potter, K. M. Rohan; **Associate Editor:** Mark Vaughan; **Assistant Editor:** Gaiti Ali; **Consultant:** J. Owen Zurhellen Jr.; **Consultant on Opinion Ballots,** Helmut Norpoth; **Typography and Design:** K.M. Rohan. Printed by Dartmouth Printing Co., Hanover, New Hampshire

© Copyright 1990 by Foreign Policy Association, Inc., 729 Seventh Avenue, New York, New York 10019

A Special Message from the President of FPA

The Foreign Policy Association welcomes you to GREAT DECISIONS 1990. This is the 36th year that you and other concerned individuals across this country join with FPA in the belief that an enlightened public is the basis for an enlightened U.S. foreign policy.

We are proud of GREAT DECISIONS and the service this program performs for the American people and the democratic process. But as we look ahead, I also wish to share with you serious concerns that FPA must confront.

Over the years, FPA has subsidized the actual cost of the annual GREAT DECISIONS briefing book from other income. For some time we have faced rising publishing and related costs. In order to deal with this situation, we must seek additional income.

This year, we found it necessary to increase the price of the briefing book by one dollar. This still does not begin to cover the cost of the book or the supplementary GREAT DECISIONS publications and community outreach costs that FPA must bear. Other increases may be needed in the future.

Last year, many of you responded to our request for financial support. As you take part in this year's GREAT DECISIONS program, we ask that you send FPA a contribution by using the special envelope inserted in this book.

We thank you again for your past support and for your participation in a program that makes all of us better prepared to deal with foreign policy issues of vital importance to our future.

If the envelope in this book has already been used, kindly make your check payable to the Foreign Policy Association and mail it to:

Great Decisions Fund
Foreign Policy Association
729 Seventh Avenue
New York, N.Y. 10019

John W. Kiermaier

Vox Pop: Flame to the Gasoline

LAST OCTOBER the editor of the most popular Soviet newspaper, the weekly tabloid *Argumenty i Fakty,* came in for a tongue-lashing by Mikhail Gorbachev for publishing a readers' poll indicating that the four most popular members of the Supreme Soviet were all liberal critics of Gorbachev.

Opinion polls—not to mention press criticism—are new to the Soviet Union, products of Gorbachev's own policy of *glasnost,* or openness. What was not new or surprising to Westerners was Gorbachev's reaction to the unfavorable poll: anger and frustration. "When you read the newspapers," he complained, "you get the impression you're standing up to your knees in gasoline. All it takes is a spark." (The editor of the offending paper was asked to resign—but refused.)

American Presidents have frequently been scorched by unflattering opinion polls. But polls cut two ways, and more than one President has cited opinion polls (or even commissioned his own) to prove his popularity or that of his policies. Only last September, Secretary of State James A. Baker 3d, rebutting criticism that the Administration was slow to respond to Gorbachev's policy of accommodation, reminded the press that the President was "rocking along with a 70 percent approval rating on his handling of foreign policy...." Nevertheless, the grumbling continued and within a month Secretary Baker signaled a major change in the tone if not the substance of U.S. policy toward the Soviet Union in an address to the Foreign Policy Association.

In a democracy, public opinion counts. Informed public opinion counts even more, and that is where the GREAT DECISIONS program of the Foreign Policy Association comes in. GREAT DECISIONS "has helped shape our national dialogue on international issues," former Secretary of State George Shultz wrote FPA. It has done so in two ways: through discussion and

National security adviser Brent Scowcroft (r.) studies the Great Decisions 1989 National Opinion Ballot Report presented to him by FPA's president, John W. Kiermaier (l.), and Leonard H. Marks, chairman of the executive committee of FPA's Board of Governors.

exchange of views and through the National Opinion Ballot Report. The report summarizes the views of those GREAT DECISIONS participants who fill in the opinion ballots at the back of the book (see pages 93–96) and mail them to FPA for tabulation. The report is circulated to key policymakers in the White House, the State and Defense departments, Congress and the media. Rep. Lee H. Hamilton (D-Ind.) called the 1989 report "the most in-depth survey" of the views of community leaders as well as the attentive public. "Your annual Report is an important aid to the Committee on Foreign Affairs in its work."

Many discussion groups like to review the ballot results at each meeting. You can duplicate the ballots to circulate to your discussion group, but be sure to mail in your completed ballots to FPA by June 30.

This year, for the first time, the three states submitting the largest number of ballots will receive, free of charge, a tabulation of their state opinion ballot results to compare with the national report.

While Gorbachev wades up to his knees in free speech, help keep your own policymakers knee-deep in informed opinions.

—*Nancy L. Hoepli*
Editor in Chief

How to get more out of GREAT DECISIONS

❖ **TELEVISION...** As GREAT DECISIONS 1990 goes to press, plans are under way for a series of eight, half-hour television programs on the 1990 topics. Coproduced with the Georgetown University School of Foreign Service, the series will present differing perspectives on each of the topics by recognized experts, and Peter F. Krogh, dean of the School of Foreign Service, will anchor the series. For details contact Great Decisions Media, Foreign Policy Association.

❖ **BIBLIOGRAPHY** for GREAT DECISIONS 1990 ...This annotated bibliography by FPA's editors provides further reading suggestions on the eight topics. Send for your copy (20 pages, $2.00 plus $1.75 for postage and handling, prepaid).

❖ **1990 ACTIVITY BOOK...**The *Great Decisions 1990 Activity Book* (48 pages) has been prepared by Dr. Mary E. Soley, FPA's Vice President for National Programs and the association's social studies specialist, and Learning Design Associates of Columbus, Ohio.

Designed to be used with the GREAT DECISIONS 1990 briefing book, it provides learning objectives, teaching strategies, decisionmaking exercises, role-playing activities and handouts that can be reproduced for classroom use. It reinforces important concepts, promotes critical thinking skills and provides 16 student activities. It also includes questions, summaries and glossaries for each of the eight topics.

Although the *Activity Book* is invaluable for teachers who use the GREAT DECISIONS 1990 briefing book with their students, it also can help discussion leaders plan stimulating group participation around the 1990 topics ($9.95 plus $1.75 for postage and handling, prepaid).

❖ **LEADERSHIP HANDBOOK...** This FPA guide discusses the need for citizen involvement in foreign policy and includes strategies for establishing and maintaining world affairs programs. A how-to manual as well as a ready reference book ($15.00 plus $2.75 for postage and handling, prepaid).

❖ **WORLD MAP...** A specially designed 18″ by 24″ four-color map, based on the projection by Arthur H. Robinson, is available from FPA. Two years ago, the National Geographic Society adopted the Robinson projection for all its world maps. One free copy of the map is available per request, plus $1.75 for postage and handling, prepaid. Additional copies of the map are $1.95 each, plus $1.75 for postage and handling, prepaid.

TO ORDER FPA MATERIALS, PLEASE MAKE CHECKS
PAYABLE TO FOREIGN POLICY ASSOCIATION AND
ORDER FROM:

Foreign Policy Association
729 Seventh Avenue, New York, NY 10019
For information call: (212) 764-4050

1.

U.S.S.R. AND EASTERN EUROPE
END OF AN ERA?

I
T WAS AN UNBELIEVABLE scene: thousands of East and West Germans celebrating together in the early hours of November 10, 1989, many atop the Berlin Wall chipping away pieces of it as souvenirs of the night the East German government lifted all restrictions on travel to the West. Nearly 200 East Germans had been shot trying to cross that wall since it was built in 1961.

It was not the first amazing picture to emerge from Eastern Europe. Ever since 1985, when Mikhail S. Gorbachev came to power in the Soviet Union, the headlincs coming out of Moscow have made jaded Soviet-watchers sit up and take notice. Instead of Communist propaganda, they were reading uncensored complaints about the Soviet system by Soviet citizens. By 1987, Gorbachev's ambitious plans for restructuring the Soviet economy and democratizing the political system had optimistic Western analysts predicting radical change in the U.S.S.R.

By the end of 1989, even many diehard skeptics were confessing to astonishment. The first contested elections in Soviet history had been held in March, complete with noisy campaigning and upset losses by some of the party's handpicked candidates. At the new Congress of People's Deputies, delegates criticized one major government or Communist party institution after another—including Gorbachev himself—while an estimated 200 million Soviets sat glued to their sets watching the televised proceedings. By the end of the first session of the Congress, the U.S.S.R. had its first embryonic opposition group, the Inter-Regional Group of People's Deputies.

In Eastern Europe (see map, p. 11) the Communist bloc's first non-Communist government took office in Poland in August 1989.

Reuters/Bettmann Newsphotos
Dismantling the Iron Curtain: Hungarian soldiers on the Austrian border, May 1989.

Hungary's Communist party dissolved itself two months later, declared the country a republic and rewrote its constitution. Hungary had already started tearing down the barbed-wire Iron Curtain along its border with neutral Austria in May; East Germany completed the job six months later.

It is impossible to overestimate So-viet leader Gorbachev's personal importance to all of these changes. Skepticism about his motives has given way to a widespread sense that why he is encouraging reform matters less than how those reforms are transforming the U.S.S.R., Eastern Europe—and relations with the U.S. "Today," says *Foreign Policy* editor Charles William

Maynes, "the debate is not about whether he is for real, but about whether he will succeed, whether we can, or should, help him, and most of all, whether even if he disappears tomorrow the reforms that he has initiated can ever be rolled back."

The New York Times has pronounced the cold-war era ended; others think such a watershed is at least within reach and are calling on the U.S. to adjust its Soviet policy accordingly. Still others warn that Gorbachev's political future is by no means certain. In the past year, he has had to deal with worsening economic conditions, paralyzing strikes and violent unrest on the Soviet periphery. If his reforms fail, a conservative backlash could lead to renewed repression within the U.S.S.R. and Eastern Europe and a more dangerous period in U.S.-Soviet relations.

How should the U.S. respond to the changes in the Soviet Union and Eastern Europe? How can it take advantage of the historic opportunities Gorbachev has presented without running unacceptable risks?

A society on the ropes

"Economic restructuring," Gorbachev has written, is "an urgent necessity." The Soviet economy had ground almost to a halt by 1985, leaving a country with the military credentials of a superpower and the internal workings of a Third World nation: "Upper Volta with rockets," as one saying goes.

This was not always the case. Joseph Stalin achieved rapid growth for a while by centralizing all economic activity in the 1930s, enabling him to direct all available resources into heavy industry as the first step in a crash modernization program. While much of the world was mired in the Great Depression, the Soviet gross national product (GNP) grew 8–9% a year, and economic growth continued at impressive rates well into the 1950s. Thereafter the growth rate slowed, and by the end of Leonid I. Brezhnev's 18-year rule in 1983, it was down to less than 2% a year. Soviet farmers (20% of the Soviet Union's 289 million citizens, more farmers than in all the Western industrialized countries and Japan combined) produce less than one quarter of what Western farmers do. A third of Soviet produce rots in the fields every year because of inadequate roads, transportation and storage facilities. Only heavy government subsidies keep food prices low, and chronic shortages of even the most basic daily necessities are a fact of Soviet life.

Outside of military and space programs, most goods and services produced in the U.S.S.R. are of poor quality and outmoded. (In a single month, exploding Soviet-made televisions caused 90 apartment fires.) Industrial equipment and machinery are old; raw materials such as coal and oil are becoming more costly to extract and are used wastefully. There is little technological innovation: the world revolution in computers and telecommunications of the 1970s and 1980s has bypassed the Soviet Union, where personal computers and even hand calculators are still rarities.

What Soviet citizens do have is a system that guarantees the majority a job, a place to live and subsidized food. But the poor quality and meager choice of consumer goods has created what Gorbachev has called "a gradual erosion of the ideological and moral values of our people." Soviet consumers are sitting on piles of rubles, worth $30 billion by some estimates, because there is nothing to spend them on. Social and physical ills have multiplied. Alcoholism afflicts an estimated 17 million, most of whom are men. Related to this is a high divorce rate. Life expectancy is declining and the infant mortality rate is among the highest in the world—four to five times that in the West—due largely to the poor state of health care. Some 30% of Soviet hospitals do not have sewage systems; many lack running water. Health problems are aggravated in many places by polluted air and contaminated water.

Glasnost

Gorbachev has staked his career on reversing these trends without destroying the economic security that the Soviet system provides for its citizens. At the 27th party congress in late February 1986 he laid out a plan to achieve "a new quality of growth: an all-out intensification of production on the basis of scientific-technical progress." He promised to double Soviet industrial output and GNP by the end of the century.

To accomplish this, his first task was to energize the Soviet people and enlist their help. This required changing the "party line" which for years claimed that all was well, suppressing facts that proved otherwise. Gorbachev believes the "discrepancy between the reality and the proclaimed policy" had "bred public passivity and disbelief in the slogans being proclaimed." This situation had to be changed before he could restart the stalled economy. With *glasnost,* meaning roughly openness or public airing, Gorbachev widened the limits of permissible debate in the Soviet Union to levels unimaginable a few years ago. Newspapers and television report the news rather than party propaganda. Reporters attend weekly press briefings on levels of crime (which had not been reported since 1933), alcoholism and poverty—social ills that Communist society was supposed to have eliminated. Government critics voice their opinions on subjects that would have meant a jail sentence not long ago. Soviet citizens—and the rest of the world—have also been given their first look at official statistics on the size of the army and the defense budget, until now closely guarded state secrets.

The official version of Soviet history is being reexamined. Blame for the country's problems has been publicly heaped on Communist party officials, both living and dead. Brezhnev is in posthumous disgrace for sending the U.S.S.R. into its "years of stagnation." Nikita S. Khrushchev, Brezhnev's reform-minded predecessor who had been a "nonperson" since his 1964 ouster, has been restored to a place of honor. Stalin, whose economic success was achieved through terror and the murder of millions during the forced collectivization of agriculture and the purges of the 1930s, is accused of "enormous and unforgivable" acts of lawlessness. Even Vladimir I. Lenin, the founder of the revolution, has come in for some criticism (though not yet by the top Soviet leadership). The rewriting of history is moving so fast in the U.S.S.R. that spring history exams had to be canceled in 1988 because Soviet textbooks had not caught up.

Books, films and plays critical of the Soviet government, banned for years, are being published, and a number of imprisoned dissidents have been released and encouraged to participate in the growing debate. Physicist Andrei D. Sakharov, back from exile in Gorki, now represents the Soviet Academy of Sciences in the Congress of People's Deputies.

Glasnost has gained Gorbachev the enthusiastic support of many intellectuals, who have stumped for his reforms. But the resulting debate over means and ends has led to challenges to the authority of the Communist party and Gorbachev himself. One well-publicized letter, printed in the daily paper *Sovietskaya Rossiya* in 1987, harshly attacked Gorbachev and glasnost for undermining authority and demoralizing the Soviet population, especially its youth. In the fall of 1989, Gorbachev himself lashed out at a prominent editor for adding to discord by giving too much coverage to his radical critics.

Economic reform

During the first two years of the reform program, Gorbachev cracked down on laziness and inefficiency in the workplace. He stiffened penalties for absenteeism and drinking on the job, and made vodka harder to find and more expensive to purchase.

In 1987, Gorbachev turned to the structure of the economy itself. In the Soviet system, the central planning agency passes party directives to scores of different economic ministries, which tell the tens of thousands of local enterprises what and how much to produce. The emphasis is on quantity; there are few incentives for improving quality. State-set prices bear no relationship to actual value, so supply and demand are continually out of balance.

Perestroika, or restructuring, is intended to free the Soviet economy from the stranglehold of central planning. Since the Law on the State Enterprise went into effect in January 1988, the Soviet Union's 37,000 largest factories (which produce about 60% of total output annually) have, in theory, been self-financing and self-administering. Managers who turn a profit can in principle decide how to spend it; managers who fail lose raises and bonuses; and plants that consistently lose money may be shut down.

The plan has not worked as advertised, and output has fallen throughout the Soviet Union as factories try to adjust to new rules and old supply prob-

AP/Wide World Photos
Mikhail Gorbachev

lems. Plants that lost money gave out raises and bonuses anyway, adding to deficits and driving up inflation, now running at 6–8%.

The 1988 Law on Cooperatives, encouraging the creation of a legal private sector to meet consumer needs, has been more successful. By the end of 1988, roughly 2 million Soviets were working for some 50,000 nonstate businesses, which accounted for about 1% of GNP.

Gorbachev is also betting on privately run farms to eliminate some of the inefficiencies of Soviet agriculture. New legislation will let farmers lease land from the state for 50 years or more, retain their profits in return for paying a tax, and pass their holdings on to their children. As an incentive to produce more, farmers are now paid in foreign currency.

The quality of goods and services cooperatives turn out is higher than that of state enterprises, and so are their prices. Their handsome profits, even after being taxed at rates of up to 90%, have provoked intense resentment. Gorbachev has not been able to talk most Soviets out of this "wage-leveling mentality," despite his insistence that "work, and work alone, should be the criterion for determining a person's value, his social prestige and his material status."

Sticker shock

People are tired of waiting for Gorbachev to keep his promise that reforms will make things better. "Brezhnev brought us to the edge of the abyss," goes one joke, "and Gorbachev is taking a giant step forward." U.S. estimates show that the Soviet economy grew by only 1.5% in 1988, and short-

ages of consumer goods are worse than they have been in 30 years.

Gorbachev announced in 1989 that he would cut Soviet defense spending 14.2% and put the money toward the production of consumer goods. He warned of "unpopular, probably tough and even painful measures" ahead—possibly wage controls and rationing. But he has postponed price reform until at least 1991, and most Western economists do not believe perestroika can succeed without it: unless prices accurately reflect costs and give people an incentive to produce, there will always be shortages and bottlenecks in the economy. If those shortages continue to worsen, warns Soviet economist Nikolai Shmelev, "in two to three years there will be complete destruction of the consumer market."

Democratizatsiya

Gorbachev does not believe economic reforms will work without the "wholesome, full-blooded functioning by all public organizations....In short, we need broad democratization of all aspects of society. That democratization is also the main guarantee that the current processes are irreversible."

Democratizatsiya has already produced revolutionary results. In March 1989, the country elected delegates to the new Congress of People's Deputies in the first secret-ballot, multicandidate elections in Soviet history. In one Leningrad district, 34 candidates campaigned for one seat. In more than 20 cases, prominent candidates running unopposed failed to receive the 51% vote required for election.

The new Congress met two months later to elect a president and 542 representatives to the revamped Supreme Soviet. In proceedings that lasted a week instead of an anticipated few days, delegates grilled Gorbachev and attacked sacred cows like the army and the secret police (KGB). The Congress elected party chief Gorbachev to the presidency but only after one delegate, "to set a precedent," nominated himself for the job. Under the new rules, the president has sweeping powers but is limited to two five-year terms.

The Supreme Soviet, formerly a rubber stamp for the party leadership, is now the U.S.S.R.'s main legislative body. One of its first moves, in July

1989, was to reject six of the party's proposed candidates for top ministerial jobs.

The party in trouble

The upshot of all this has been a decline in the influence of the traditional power centers, the Politburo and the Communist party itself. The party's humiliation in the March elections and the delegation of many of its powers to elected bodies have weakened its authority. Enrollment of new members fell by 20% in 1988; membership in the All-Union League of Communist Youth, the Komsomol, has dipped even more sharply, as thousands of young Soviets have joined independent political groups. Gorbachev cannot have meant glasnost to undermine his power base, but he has been unable to stop it. Many Soviets are beginning to call publicly for amending the constitution, which gives the party a "leading role" in Soviet society, and for a multiparty system.

The dangers inherent in the combination of expanded freedom to protest and worsening economic conditions were graphically illustrated last summer when almost 500,000 miners walked off the job in the U.S.S.R.'s two largest coal-producing regions, angered by shortages of soap and decent food, poor housing and dangerous mine conditions. It cost the Kremlin an estimated $8 billion in concessions to get the miners back to work. More miners walked off the job in October, defying a 15-month strike ban.

As unrest spread last summer, even supporters of reform were urging Gorbachev to decree emergency powers. "If a person is seriously ill," said Deputy Prime Minister Leonid I. Abalkin, "he needs certain healing methods. He has to be calmed, be put to bed, he has to change his diet, he has to be forbidden to run barefoot in the streets."

Gorbachev's innovations have produced stiff opposition among those with a strong vested interest in the old system, notably bureaucrats and party and military leaders. Although Gorbachev has replaced opponents with allies in the Politburo and Central Committee, there is no such thing as job security in the Kremlin—especially for a leader undertaking the kind of radical changes Gorbachev is attempting.

The Soviet empire

GORBACHEV has preached his gospel of glasnost and perestroika to help "the Soviet peoples" achieve "a single destiny." But the Soviet Union is a multiethnic state, and as Moscow has loosened controls from the center and encouraged the expression of grievances, many of the different groups within Soviet borders have used the new atmosphere to pursue their own agendas. Between the beginning of 1988 and mid-1989, violence due to ethnic unrest had claimed well over a hundred lives, and Moscow's control appeared to be slipping.

Before the founding of the Soviet state in 1918, the Russian empire had grown over 400 years to embrace a wide variety of peoples. Many of the more than 100 nationalities that make up the Soviet Union have preserved their histories, cultures, religious traditions and languages to a significant extent. Soviet Central Asians, especially in the south, are mostly Muslims. Estonians may pretend not to understand if they are addressed in Russian. The Catholic Church in the Ukraine and Lithuania retains ties to Rome whereas most Soviet Christians in this officially atheistic state are Eastern Orthodox.

Every Soviet leader since Lenin has had to deal with the "national question." To enlist the minorities' support against the czars, Lenin talked of national self-determination. Once in power, he declared the new nation a "federation of Soviet republics founded on the principle of a free union of the peoples of Russia." The republics were divided along national lines, but, despite a clause in the constitution guaranteeing republics the right to secede, there was nothing "free" about the union: all were brought under Moscow's control between 1918 and 1922.

While keeping a tight rein on the non-Russian republics politically, Lenin encouraged them to preserve their languages and cultures. Over the years, this policy tended to produce educated elites who could articulate minority interests.

During the Stalin years, many of those pressing for fuller autonomy for the republics were killed or sent to Siberia. Entire national groups, such as the Meskhetian Turks who were moved from Georgia to Uzbekistan, were forcibly relocated.

Brezhnev's way of dealing with the nationality problem was to declare it solved and to leave local party leaders pretty much to their own devices. With Moscow's controls loosened, corruption ran rampant.

Gorbachev has cracked down on corruption and has adopted the formula of "a strong center and strong republics," hoping to gain the support of the republics for perestroika. But Gorbachev's political reforms have encouraged regional leaders to vent their grievances openly. Says Yulian Bromley of the Institute of Ethnography at the Soviet Academy of Sciences, "Perestroika destroyed the old mechanisms of keeping people quiet, but it hasn't created a mechanism of its own to prevent turning democracy into anarchy."

The national groups' demands are as varied as their circumstances and histories. Some want greater autonomy or even independence from Moscow; others want more economic help. Some are involved in age-old ethnic feuds with neighbors; others want to return to the homes Stalin forced them to leave. A common grievance is environmental pollution.

The Baltics—Estonia, Latvia and Lithuania—were absorbed by the U.S.S.R. in 1940 as a result of a secret protocol to the 1939 Nazi-Soviet pact, the existence of which Moscow denied until mid-1989. The Baltics have a strong West European orientation, highly developed economies and the country's most sophisticated independent political organizations, known as popular fronts.

Hoping to secure the Baltics' cooperation on perestroika, Moscow legalized the Popular Front of Estonia in 1988. It became the model for similar fronts in Latvia and Lithuania, which have spearheaded fast-growing nationalist movements. All three republics have been promised a significant degree of economic autonomy effective January 1990.

Not content with these concessions, many in the Baltics are demanding full independence. On August 23, 1989, the 50th anniversary of the Nazi-Soviet pact, thousands of people linked hands to form a 400-mile-long chain across the three republics. Local elections, scheduled for 1990, are expected to result in a rout for local Communist parties by popular-front candidates.

The Caucasus is home to Georgians, Armenians and Azerbaijanis, as well as many smaller groups. Clashes between mostly Muslim Azerbaijanis and Christian Armenians in the autonomous region of Nagorno-Karabakh have cost over 100 lives and created a flood of refugees. Last summer, the extremist Azerbaijani national front blockaded the railway that is Armenia's lifeline. To end the blockade, the Azerbaijani Communist party was forced to grant the front unprecedented concessions, including the right to secede from the U.S.S.R.

Georgia has also been the scene of violent nationalist and ethnic unrest. On April 9, 1989, Soviet troops killed 20 nationalist demonstrators and injured hundreds more in the capital, Tbilisi. And in July 1989, 20 more people died in clashes between Georgians and Abkhazians, who want to secede from Georgia. There have also been tensions between Georgians and Azerbaijanis living in Georgia.

Soviet Central Asia has the largest and fastest-growing minority in the Soviet Union, some 50 million Muslims. Unemployment is high, there are chronic food shortages and the infant mortality rate is twice the nation's average. Overirrigation from the Aral Sea—once the fourth largest lake in the world—and pollution from chemicals used in growing cotton, the region's largest crop, have caused serious environmental deterioration and related

Nationalism in the Soviet Union

0   Miles   500

Arctic Ocean

ESTONIA 1.6
LATVIA 2.6
LITHUANIA 3.6
BELORUSSIA 10.1

Moscow

RUSSIAN REPUBLIC 145.3

UKRAINE 51.2

MOLDAVIA 4.2

SOVIET UNION
Figures show population in millions, 1987

GEORGIA 5.3   Caucasus Mts.

KAZAKHSTAN 16.2

ARMENIA 3.4

Aral Sea

MONGOLIA

AZERBAIJAN 6.8

TURKMENISTAN 3.4

UZBEKISTAN 19.0

KIRGIZIA 4.1

TADZHIKISTAN 4.8   CHINA

Ural Mts.

Baltic Sea

Black Sea

Caspian Sea

NORWAY   SWEDEN   FINLAND   POLAND   ROMANIA   TURKEY   IRAQ   IRAN   AFGHANISTAN

Robert Mansfield

The U.S. government has not recognized the incorporation of Estonia, Latvia and Lithuania into the U.S.S.R.

health problems. Organized corruption and violent crime are rampant.

Already the poorest region in the U.S.S.R., Central Asia is growing poorer and blames its backwardness on Moscow's neglect. Alma-Ata, Kazakhstan's capital, exploded with rioting and looting in 1986 when Gorbachev added insult to injury by replacing a Kazakh party leader with a Russian as part of his anticorruption drive. Economic grievances also sparked rioting by Kazakh youths in June 1989.

Just a week earlier in Uzbekistan, Uzbeks and the Turkish Meskhetian minority, moved there by Stalin in 1944, clashed, resulting in nearly 100 deaths, 1,000 injuries and the destruction of 400 homes. Some 16,000 Meskhetians had to be evacuated for their protection.

Closest to home

In the heartland of the U.S.S.R. live the **Ukrainians, Belorussians** and **Moldavians.** Moldavians have been agitating to have Moldavian adopted as

their official language. The Ukraine, the second most populous of the U.S.S.R.'s republics and the most important agricultural and industrial region, now has a fast-growing nationalist movement, known as Rukh (Ukrainian for movement). By the time its first congress met last September, Rukh already had 270,000 members, many of whom were calling for independence.

Ethnic **Russians** account for just over 50% of the Soviet population. Although they still dominate the U.S.S.R. politically, culturally and socially, they fear they are on the verge of losing their cultural dominance along with their majority status, and resent Moscow's attentions to the non-Russian republics. Russians moved to other republics by Stalin also feel discriminated against by local authorities. In August 1989, thousands of Russians in Estonia staged a series of strikes protesting a local law that would have prevented many of them from voting or running for office. Under pressure from Moscow, Estonia repealed the law two months later.

At the far right of the Russian movement is an organization called Pamyat (Russian for memory), notorious for its Russian chauvinism and strong anti-Western, anti-Semitic views.

Although Gorbachev has called for "profound reform" of the Soviet federal structure, he has not said what he means—beyond ruling out secession—and the Kremlin continues to respond to

crises on an ad hoc basis. If Moscow's control of the republics continues to weaken, many worry Gorbachev may feel compelled to crack down. That could mean the end of political reform.

Eastern Europe

The events that are now taking place in the countries of Eastern Europe concern the countries and peoples of that region. We have no right, moral or political right, to interfere in events happening there.

—Mikhail Gorbachev,
October 25, 1989

WITH THESE WORDS, Gorbachev officially reversed the Soviet Union's expressed right to use force to maintain its East European empire. That policy was articulated by Brezhnev in 1968, after the Soviet Union invaded Czechoslovakia to halt its liberalization program.

Soviet control of Eastern Europe dates from the end of World War II, when the Soviet Red Army drove Adolf Hitler's forces back from Soviet territory and across Eastern Europe. Agreements reached with the U.S., Britain and France in effect recognized Soviet dominance in the region, but called for free elections. Moscow reneged on those and instead converted Bulgaria, East Germany, Hungary, Poland, Romania and Czechoslovakia into "people's democratic republics" under tight Soviet control.

Along either side of the Iron Curtain that sealed Eastern Europe off from non-Communist Western Europe, the cold war hardened into a military standoff. Fearful of further Communist expansion, the Western countries—the U.S., Canada, Belgium, Britain, France, Luxembourg, the Netherlands, Norway, Denmark, Iceland, Italy and Portugal—banded together in 1949 in the North Atlantic Treaty Organization (NATO), a military alliance paralleled by Moscow when it created the Warsaw Pact in 1955. (Its members are Bulgaria, Czechoslovakia, the German Democratic Republic [GDR], Hungary, Poland, Romania and the Soviet Un-

ion.) The U.S.S.R. reinforced its leadership of the "socialist commonwealth" through the Council for Mutual Economic Assistance (CMEA, or Comecon), founded in 1949.

Maintaining control of Eastern Europe has been Moscow's primary foreign policy goal ever since. The Soviet-led bloc provides the U.S.S.R. with a buffer zone between it and potential Western aggressors. It keeps ethnic tensions that had caused innumerable wars in the region over the centuries in check. And the presence of other Communist regimes modeled after the government in Moscow and loyal to it gives the Soviet state legitimacy.

Until Gorbachev, the Soviet Union generally did not tolerate political liberalization in Eastern Europe that threatened either the dominance of national Communist parties or their participation in the Warsaw Pact. (The exceptions were Yugoslavia, which broke with Moscow in 1948, and Albania, which formally withdrew from the Warsaw Pact in 1968.)

Eastern Europe has witnessed recurring rebellion against Communist rule, often sparked by economic hardship. On two occasions, Soviet troops invaded to restore order: in Hungary in 1956 and Czechoslovakia in 1968.

Today Eastern Europe's socialist economies suffer from many of the same maladies that afflict Soviet socialism—low productivity, consumer-goods shortages, inefficient industries. In recent years, the quality of the manufactured goods Eastern Europe sells to the Soviet Union has declined while the cost of Soviet energy and raw materials needed to produce them has skyrocketed. Increasingly, the bloc has become a burden to Moscow.

Gorbachev is gambling that if he gives East European governments the freedom to experiment with their eco-

nomic and political structures, they can revive their listless economies and become an asset instead of a liability to the Soviet Union.

The vanguard

Leading the charge toward change are Poland and Hungary. At the start of the Gorbachev era both were in serious economic trouble, with declining standards of living, inefficient industries and heavy national debt. Today, while still facing daunting economic problems, both are on the road to a multiparty political system and a market economy.

Poland has always been the most troublesome member of the Communist bloc. The crisis that ended with the imposition of martial law in 1981 was sparked by the deterioration of the Polish economy after 1976. Workers, backed by the powerful Catholic Church and liberal intellectuals, banded together to create the independent trade union Solidarity, representing some 10 million Polish workers and headed by Lech Walesa. The union forced the party into concessions during a wave of strikes in 1980, but was outlawed a year later when martial law was declared. Solidarity went underground, and the economic situation continued to worsen.

Today, Poland has an inflation rate of over 100%, a debt of nearly $40 billion and, in the words of *The Economist* (London) magazine, "an archaic industry remarkable mainly for its capacity to pollute." Store shelves are nearly empty.

In early 1989, facing economic disintegration, labor unrest and growing pressure from Solidarity leaders, the Communist party agreed to hold semi-free elections in the spring. It also restored Solidarity's legal status in exchange for a promise that the union would help secure popular cooperation for economic reforms.

In the June 1989 parliamentary elections, the Communist party lost almost every seat open to contest, retaining control of a majority in the lower house only because of pre-agreed election rules that guaranteed it a majority. It was nevertheless unable to form a government when two smaller parties defected to the Solidarity side in August. To break the deadlock, the party asked Solidarity to form a government, and it became the first Communist party to permit itself to be turned out of office.

Poland's new non-Communist prime minister, responsible for the day-to-day running of the government, is Solidarity leader Tadeusz Mazowiecki. Gen. Wojciech Jaruzelski (who barely won the parliamentary vote needed) is president, which among other things gives him the power to dissolve parliament and call for new elections at any time. The rules specify that his successor be chosen by a fully popular vote. The Communist party still controls the defense and interior ministries, and therefore the country's army and police.

The new government is carrying out a radical plan to turn Poland rapidly into a market economy, through subsidy cuts to reduce the deficit, privatization of industry and, eventually, a currency fully convertible with that of other nations. It has devalued its currency to soften the impact of sudden price rises and has appealed to the International Bank for Reconstruction and Development (World Bank), the International Monetary Fund (IMF) and Western countries for considerable financial help and emergency food aid to cushion the effects of these reforms, which are bound to make a bleak economic situation even worse before things begin to get better.

Most affected by the austerity measures is the working class, Solidarity's main base of support. Workers can afford fewer basic goods as inflation spirals upward, and many will lose their jobs as the new government moves to close down unprofitable businesses. Some analysts have suggested that economic hardship will cost Solidarity its support and pave the way for the party to regain control of the government.

Hungary's 1956 rebellion was triggered by government inaction in the face of a slide in the Hungarian standard of living. János Kádár, who took over after the Soviet tanks withdrew, recognized the need for economic reforms to prevent future explosions. His solution, known as "goulash communism," was the first experiment with a partially decentralized economy by a Communist country. Limited private enterprise was encouraged, and the government by and large stayed out of the private lives of individuals.

Hungary's economy prospered, compared with much of the bloc, until the mid-1980s, when it began to feel the crunch of a mounting debt to the West and rising consumer shortages. Hungary today has a 20% inflation rate, rising unemployment, a debt of $21 billion—Europe's highest per capita—and a falling standard of living. Today one out of three Hungarians lives below the official poverty line. It has the highest suicide rate in the world, and has among the highest rates of alcoholism, divorce, abortion and heart attacks.

Much of the blame for Hungary's economic troubles was heaped on Kádár, who was ousted in May 1988. Political and economic changes since then are pointing Hungary in the direction of a democratic, free-market country. The 1988 Law on Economic Association permits anyone to set up a joint-stock company, limiting risk to individual entrepreneurs, and Hungary has

---

East Germany

Richest, strongest bloc member. In November 1989, new government under Egon Krenz opened borders to West, and promised free elections in attempt to stop flight of best and brightest of 16.6 million population.

Czechoslovakia

Once a major industrial power, economy stagnant, although food shelves still well stocked. Anti-reform party chief Milos Jakes forced out in November 1989. Of 15.6 million population, 63% Czech, 31% Slovak.

Hungary

East-bloc reform leader, with Poland. Moving toward multiparty system with free parliamentary elections in 1990 and more-market-oriented economy. Now a republic; Communist party remodeled on social democratic lines.

Eastern Europe

Poland

First bloc country to oust Communist government. Tadeusz Mazowiecki, Solidarity leader, counting on West to cushion effects of economic reforms. With 38.2 million, most populous bloc nation, second poorest.

Romania

Nicolae Ceaușescu, most repressive East-bloc leader, presides over poorest of the six. Independent foreign policy, persecution of minority Hungarians, opposition to reforms have antagonized Moscow.

Bulgaria

Over the years, the most loyal, docile Soviet ally. Todor Zhivkov, 78, hard-line leader for 35 years; announced plans for cosmetic economic and political reforms during 1989; ousted that November.

"...LOOK FOR PARTIAL CLEARING IN POLAND WITH SCATTERED UPRISINGS ACROSS THE BALTIC STATES... FURTHER SOUTH, CONTINUED FLASH FLOODS OF HUMANITY RUSH FROM EAST GERMANY CLEAR ACROSS CZECHOSLOVAKIA AND HUNGARY INTO AUSTRIA WITH EXPECTED HIGHS IN THE THOUSANDS AND A 35% CHANCE OF CONTINUED GLASNOST..."

Reprinted by permission: Tribune Media Services.

opened the first stock exchange in Eastern Europe.

In October 1989, the Communist party renamed itself the Hungarian Socialist party. It has rewritten the country's constitution, transforming it from a socialist state run by the Communist party to a democratic, constitutional republic with "the values of both bourgeois democracy and democratic socialism." The new constitution legalizes opposition parties, guarantees human and civil rights and confers separate powers on the judiciary, executive and legislative branches of government. The Republic of Hungary's first multiparty parliamentary elections are scheduled for early 1990.

The antireformers

Not all East European countries were enthusiastic about reform. The governments of the GDR, Bulgaria, Czechoslovakia and Romania resisted change and suppressed opposition; but three out of four had buckled by late November 1989.

Although the **GDR** enjoys Eastern Europe's highest standard of living, that has not prevented large numbers of East Germans from wanting more. By early November 1989, 167,000—1% of the population—had left the country; some estimate that a full 10% of all East Germans has applied to leave.

Many emigrants told reporters they

were seeking political freedom. But the East German economy has also become a factor: East German economic growth in real terms (accounting for inflation) has dropped to 1% a year, despite some $2 billion a year in trade and aid from West Germany.

The population is well educated and knows, thanks to West European television (which East Germans alone among Communist East Europeans see), that its neighbors to the West are much better off. Experts say that the mass emigration to the West has hurt East Germany's economic prospects badly: most who are leaving are young and skilled, and there are estimates that they may cost the GDR the equivalent of about $179 million in lost productivity. Hundreds of thousands of East Germans who stayed behind staged huge demonstrations in the days following East Germany's 40th anniversary, demanding reforms. The unrest led to a government shake-up in East Berlin, the GDR's capital, in mid-October, when Erich Honecker (77) was retired and fellow hard-liner Egon Krenz took over. On November 9, Krenz lifted all restrictions on travel to the West; some 40,000 East Germans crossed the Berlin Wall that weekend, though most returned home afterward.

In **Bulgaria,** it is said, there is no word for "pluralism." Traditionally the U.S.S.R.'s closest ally, the government

of Todor Zhivkov (78) had difficult relations with Moscow during the Gorbachev years because of Zhivkov's opposition to reform. He was forced out of office on November 10, 1989.

Bulgarian debt is not large—$6.3 billion—but debt-servicing absorbs 36% of its export earnings a year. Bulgaria, too, is plagued by food and energy shortages and a declining standard of living. The government in Sofia has come under fire not only in the West but from its bloc neighbors for its campaign of forced assimilation and religious repression of its Turkish minority, some 300,000 of whom were either driven out of the country or fled during 1989.

After the Soviets invaded in 1968, ending the reform program under Alexander Dubček known as the Prague Spring, **Czechoslovakia** offered its citizens what they call "salamis for submission": a relatively high standard of living in return for political submissiveness. It worked well until the Czechoslovak economy, too, began to slow down and the pace of change in neighboring countries overwhelmed the hardline Czechoslovak leadership under party chief Milos Jakes.

On November 14, 1989, the government lifted restrictions on travel to the West. Three days later, it responded brutally to a peaceful demonstration by some 25,000 students in Prague. That sparked a week of daily protests involving hundreds of thousands of Czechoslovaks from all walks of life, and on November 25, Jakes and the rest of the party leadership resigned.

Elated but not satisfied, millions of Czechoslovaks shut down the country two days later in a nationwide strike, calling for democratic reforms. The party gave in almost immediately to two central demands: that it give up its monopoly on power and admit non-Communists to the government.

The opposition, small and tightly repressed until the Jakes regime fell, is short on leaders and experience: best known is playwright Vaclav Havel. Karel Urbanek, Jakes' successor, is no radical reformer. The speed of the November events has made everyone gun-shy about predicting the future, but many are hopeful that Czechoslovakia's relative economic health will help it make the transition to democracy.

Romania is headed by Nicolae Ceauşescu (71) and his family. It is one of the most repressive regimes in the world, and its people live in Eastern Europe's most miserable conditions. Ceauşescu paid off all of Romania's heavy foreign debt—$21 billion—in 1989, but at the expense of its citizens, who have lived with severe food and fuel rationing for years. In a country that used to export agricultural products, a common Romanian joke runs, "If we had a little more food, it would be like wartime." The low and still-falling standard of living provoked rioting in the city of Brasov in November 1987 that the government crushed.

Romania's leadership considers it "unnecessary to restructure." It has denounced Gorbachev's reforms and censored all references to glasnost and perestroika. The government has plans to raze whole villages and force inhabitants to move into "agro-industrial centers," allegedly to increase agricultural efficiency. Critics suspect the policy is part of a pattern of discrimination against Romania's Hungarian and German minorities. Such policies have earned Romania not only Western criticism lately, but that of its East European neighbors, especially Hungary. Romania rejects any "inadmissible interference" in its affairs by outsiders.

Prospects

Gorbachev's pledge of noninterference in Eastern Europe has encouraged reformers there, but they caution that their efforts will fail without Western help. They need aid to offset the impact of austerity measures on strapped consumers and to buy their new governments time to make reforms succeed.

The U.S. and Western Europe have expanded their economic relations with Hungary and Poland, as well as the U.S.S.R. Joint ventures with Western firms are now legal in those countries, and the number of such enterprises is climbing, especially in Hungary, where terms are most favorable. Lending, by individual countries as well as the IMF, has begun to increase again, after falling off during the 1980s when East Europeans found themselves unable to pay their debts from the 1970s. During their economic summit meeting in Paris in the summer of 1989, the seven major non-Communist industrialized powers agreed to have the European Community coordinate food aid for Poland as a reward for political reforms and as encouragement to move further toward a market economy. West Germany has pledged the most—$1.9 billion.

End of an era?

FOR 40 YEARS, East-West relations have been on a roller coaster, alternating between periods of tension and relaxation. Stalin's death in 1953 was followed by a thaw, when the Korean armistice was signed and Soviet troops withdrew from a neutralized Austria. The thaw ended abruptly with the Soviet invasion of Hungary in 1956. That period of serious tensions culminated in 1962, when the U.S.S.R. placed nuclear missiles in Cuba, within striking distance of the U.S. The crisis brought the superpowers to the brink of nuclear war. Both sides recognized the importance of avoiding a repeat performance and relations improved. They signed the hot-line accord, guaranteeing rapid communication during a crisis, a treaty to ban nuclear testing in the atmosphere, underwater and in outer space (1963), and an agreement to prevent the spread of nuclear weapons to other countries (1968).

Détente, or a lessening of tensions, picked up speed during the 1970s, as West Germany and the Soviet Union signed treaties on the status of the divided city of Berlin and other issues that had periodically threatened the peace. The superpowers negotiated two treaties on strategic nuclear weapons (1972 and 1979), and 35 nations signed the Helsinki Final Act of the Conference on Security and Cooperation in Europe in 1975, in which the West agreed to accept the existing postwar boundaries in Europe in return for Communist promises to make improvements in human rights.

Détente foundered in the late 1970s on the divergent views of Washington and Moscow on the arms race, Soviet involvement in the Third World and Soviet human-rights policies at home and in Eastern Europe. It died when the Soviets invaded Afghanistan in December 1979; the coup de grace was Soviet support for the imposition of martial law in Poland two years later.

Soviet policy changes

Some Western observers of Gorbachev's "smile offensive" worry that today's thaw may prove as transitory as its predecessors. But a growing majority is beginning to think this thaw may last. Faced with the imperative of getting his Soviet house in order, Gorbachev appears to have decided to eliminate as many bones of contention with other states as possible, both to save money and perhaps convince the West to pitch in with economic, technical and managerial help for perestroika.

On military issues, Moscow has pushed for arms-control agreements with the U.S. that will make it safe for the Soviets to shift funds away from defense into other areas that need it desperately. In the process, he has made concessions that would have been unimaginable a few years ago. In the treaty eliminating intermediate-range nuclear forces (INF), signed by Gorbachev and President Ronald Reagan in December 1987, Moscow said yes to much that it had previously rejected in U.S. proposals, including visits by U.S. experts to Soviet military bases to verify compliance with a treaty. For nearly 40 years, the Kremlin had adamantly opposed on-site inspections.

After signing the INF treaty, Moscow kept up the peace offensive by announcing in December 1988 that it would unilaterally cut its active military forces by 500,000 troops and 10,000 tanks. Of these, 50,000 men and 5,000 tanks would come from Eastern Europe, where Soviet strength in manpower, tanks and artillery has long been the major concern of Western defense planners. Gorbachev began pulling troops out of Hungary and East Germany in April 1989.

Agence France-Presse

Bush and Walesa in Poland, July 1989. Solidarity would take power within the month.

On regional issues, the Soviets have also surprised the West. Not only did the Soviets withdraw their last troops from Afghanistan in 1988, after nine years' occupation, but they now admit the invasion was illegal. Almost certainly under pressure from Moscow, Vietnam promised to pull its forces out of neighboring Cambodia (see Topic 4). Moscow also participated in talks during 1988 that led Cuba to withdraw its troops from Angola. And Gorbachev has supported a strengthening of the role of the United Nations in solving regional conflicts, and backed up his rhetoric by paying $225 million of the debt owed to the UN since the early 1960s.

On human rights, Moscow has also allayed many U.S. concerns. It has freed many political prisoners and allowed increased emigration over the past few years. American officials expect as many as 250,000 Soviet émigrés to request entrance to the U.S. in 1990.

The Soviet Union has also adopted new laws governing psychiatric hospitals, which were routinely used in the past to warehouse political prisoners. In 1989, 30 American observers who were allowed to visit Soviet mental hospitals to interview patients concluded that "the transition to a more humane regime has just begun." Also in early 1989, 35 nations, including the U.S.S.R. and all its Warsaw Pact allies

except Romania, signed an accord promising more religious freedom, travel and rights for minorities. So far, however, most of these rights have not been been incorporated in the laws of any of the Communist signatories.

'New thinking'

There is still a good deal of discussion in this country about Gorbachev's true motives. Clearly his major concern is economic: Soviet military spending has been eating up roughly a quarter of the annual budget and monopolizing the U.S.S.R.'s best brains and resources. Regional adventures have also proved expensive: by 1980, Moscow's Third World clients were costing somewhere between $36 billion and $45 billion annually.

Moscow badly needs Western economic, technical and managerial assistance to make perestroika succeed. Until now, U.S.-Soviet trade has suffered because of the Jackson-Vanik and Stevenson amendments to the 1974 Trade Act, which punish Moscow for restricting Jewish emigration. The amendments deny most-favored-nation status to the Soviet Union and limit Export-Import Bank credits to finance Soviet purchases of U.S. goods. In the wake of increased emigration, there is now growing support in the U.S. for waiving the provisions of these laws, at least for a year.

Many Western analysts believe that economic considerations only partially explain Gorbachev's foreign policy. Robert Legvold, director of the W. Averell Harriman Institute for Advanced Study of the Soviet Union at Columbia University, believes Gorbachev's actions also reflect a new Soviet perception of national security in the modern world, where military power has limited applications. "Security," Gorbachev declared at the 27th party congress, "is increasingly a political function that can be accomplished only by political means." He is the first Soviet leader to talk about the relationship of national security to "mutual security." "Less security for the U.S. compared to the Soviet Union," he said, "would not be in our interest since it could lead to mistrust and produce instability." The Soviets are also downplaying the importance of the struggle between capitalism and socialism—ending with socialism's triumph—as the main dynamic of international affairs.

Other analysts remain doubtful that much has changed beyond Moscow's desire to rescue its economy. Deeds, they claim, have not so far matched words. They say support to client states has not fallen off appreciably (Moscow still spends some $10 billion a year supporting its friends in Central America); defense spending is still high, and, by some estimates, if arms production continues at present rates, Moscow will still be outproducing the U.S. in weapons well into the 1990s. Soviet espionage, including the pirating of Western technology, has actually increased, according to the Administration. Some conservatives conclude from the above that Moscow is only seeking a breathing space (*peredyshka*) before it returns to its aggressive ways.

U.S.-Soviet relations

President George Bush approached U.S.-Soviet relations cautiously. More than three months elapsed before Bush made his first major policy statement, in which he declared that "the U.S. now has as its goal much more than simply containing Soviet expansionism—we seek the integration of the Soviet Union into the community of nations." Bush also said that "promises are never enough" and that Moscow would have to earn a new relationship with the U.S.

Over the ensuing months, Moscow's proposals, combined with the political unrest within the U.S.S.R. and the measured Soviet reactions to it, led to an evolution in Administration thinking. At two meetings between Secretary of State James A. Baker 3d and Soviet Foreign Minister Eduard A. Shevardnadze, significant progress was made on arms control, and Bush believes that agreements on strategic nuclear weapons and conventional forces in Europe are possible within a year. The U.S. and U.S.S.R. have also signed an agreement on "The Prevention of Dangerous Military Activities," designed to forestall military maneuvers, such as border crossings, from accidentally triggering a war, and to block its spread should one break out. The two countries have also made progress on a treaty to ban chemical weapons (see Topic 5).

By the time Baker addressed the Foreign Policy Association in October 1989, the Administration had dropped its cautionary tone and welcomed "a historic opportunity with the Soviet Union…to leave behind the postwar period with the ups and downs of the cold war…to make the change toward better superpower relations more secure and less reversible." To help perestroika succeed, Baker said that the U.S. stood ready to provide Moscow with technical and other assistance.

The Bush Administration's policy toward Eastern Europe has also changed, partly in response to congressional pressure. When Bush visited Poland and Hungary in July 1989, he promised $100 million in seed money to start private businesses—1% of the $10 billion Solidarity leader Walesa requested—and another $15 million to help clean up the environment. Since then, the Administration has raised its offer to $455.5 million and is pushing the World Bank to approve a $325 million loan and debt restructuring. Hungary will get $25 million for private enterprise and $5 million for the environment.

Baker also quietly assured Shevardnadze that, although it supports the right of all people to self-determination, the U.S. would do nothing to add to the unrest in Eastern Europe and the Soviet republics. The speed of change in those areas persuaded Bush to meet with

Sean McCloud
Secretary of State James A. Baker 3d.

Gorbachev before the planned 1990 summit, in early December 1989.

Options

Michael Mandelbaum, director of the Project on East-West Relations at the Council on Foreign Relations, has written that "the master key to ending the cold war is the process of internal reform that Gorbachev has begun in the Soviet Union." Liberalization is the best guarantee that the changes taking place in Eastern Europe and in Soviet foreign policy as a whole will continue, he believes, because it is harder for a government to renege on international commitments if it has to contend with public debate.

What, if anything, can the U.S. do to ensure that the process of liberalization continues? Some of the ideas currently being floated follow.

❐ **1. Make economic concessions to help give Gorbachev and East European reformers time to get reforms working.** The U.S. can lower the risk of a political explosion due to falling standards of living when reforms are first implemented and a repressive backlash by offering substantial loans and favorable trade terms. These would enable governments to cushion the impact of austerity measures by buying consumer goods to tide people over during the transition period. As a first step, the U.S. could waive the provisions of the Jackson-Vanik and Stevenson amendments.

❐ **2. Treat the U.S.S.R. and East European countries the way we would any other country.** Western investors should "pursue profits, not politics," says Sen. Bill Bradley (D-N.J.). The U.S. should not subsidize the Soviet or East European efforts to provide consumer goods past the point of sensible

economic risk; nor should it deny the U.S.S.R. or East European countries loans or deals that would be profitable for U.S. firms. The credit rating of East European borrowers has dropped because they fell behind on debt-service payments on loans made in the 1970s. On the other hand, the Soviet Union has an excellent credit rating, making it a prime candidate for loans were it not for political objections.

❐ **3. Tie economic aid to economic and political reforms.** "The pressure of foreign debt has been one of the main things pushing Poland and Hungary toward freer markets….It would be foolish for Western governments to relax the pressure while most of the reforms remain on paper," says *The Economist* (London) magazine. Without making further free-market reforms, East European governments will not be able to put Western funds to any better use than they did previously. By the same token, rewarding economic and political liberalization should enable the U.S. to retain the economic leverage that will encourage further change, suggests Rep. Don J. Pease (D-Ohio).

❐ **4. Tie economic concessions to cuts in the Soviet armed forces.** The U.S. should not increase the flow of funds to Warsaw Pact countries without explicit guarantees that Moscow will not spend the money on its military establishment and that it will reduce its defense budget, argues Judy Shelton of the Hoover Institution. Otherwise, the U.S.S.R. could well emerge in time with a stronger economy, a stronger military and an increased appetite for world aggression. With such assurances, the U.S. can expand trade and loans to the U.S.S.R. and its allies; it can also feel more secure about reducing its own defense budget, says former defense official Richard N. Perle.

★ ★ ★

Are the changes taking place in the Soviet Union and Eastern Europe irreversible? How can the U.S. help make sure the current trends in Moscow and in East-West relations prove more lasting than previous thaws?

Opinion Ballot
||➡ **on page 93** ||➡

FOR DISCUSSION

1. Suppose you are the secretary of state, trying to decide on whether or not to make fundamental changes in the approach underlying U.S. policy toward the Soviet Union. What factors would convince you that it was safe to do so? What factors would convince you that to do so would pose unacceptable risks in the event that Soviet policy abruptly changed course?

2. The U.S. has never recognized the absorption of the Baltic republics into the Soviet Union, and it favors self-determination for all peoples. Should it encourage the Baltics in their quest for autonomy or even independence? Why or why not?

3. What, if anything, do you think could prompt the Soviet Union to renege on Gorbachev's pledge not to interfere in the affairs of Eastern Europe? What role can the U.S. play, if any, in preventing such an occurrence?

4. Some in the Soviet Union are urging Gorbachev to give himself emergency powers to help the Soviet Union through its current economic troubles and related political unrest so that reforms have a chance to take effect. What do you think of that idea?

5. Should the U.S. waive provisions of the Jackson-Vanik and Stevenson amendments? Why or why not?

6. What seems to you to be the biggest obstacle to reforming the Soviet economy?

7. What seems to you to be the issue with the most potential to topple Gorbachev from power?

SUGGESTED READINGS

Baker, James A., 3d, "Excerpts from Baker's Remarks on Soviet Union." **The New York Times,** October 17, 1989, p. A14. Taken from a speech before the Foreign Policy Association in which U.S. secretary of state declares U.S. wants perestroika to succeed, and offers U.S. technical and managerial assistance.

Cockburn, Patrick, "Dateline U.S.S.R.: Ethnic Tremors," **Foreign Policy,** Spring 1989, pp. 168–84. Overview of nationalities issue by former Moscow bureau chief of the **Financial Times.**

Diehl, Jackson, "Dismantling Communism." **The Washington Post,** April 16–18, 1989. Three articles covering the changes in Poland and Hungary and the problems they face.

"East Europe, 1989." **Current History,** November 1989. Entire issue. Articles on arms control in Europe, Poland, Soviet-East European relations, Hungary, East Germany, Czechoslovakia and Yugoslavia.

Gati, Charles, "Eastern Europe on Its Own." **Foreign Affairs** Vol. 68, No. 1 (America and the World 1988/89), pp. 99–119. Good background on the changes that have swept Eastern Europe since the beginning of 1989.

Gorbachev, Mikhail, **Perestroika: New Thinking for Our Country and the World.** New York, Harper & Row, 1987. 254 pp., $8.95 (paper). Soviet leader makes his case for change to Western readers.

Harries, Owen, "Is the Cold War Really Over?" **National Review.** November 10, 1989, pp. 40–45. Editor of **The National Interest** is skeptical.

Legvold, Robert, and The Task Force on Soviet New Thinking, "Gorbachev's Foreign Policy: How Should the United States Respond?" **Headline Series** No. 284. New York, Foreign Policy Association, April 1988. 64 pp. $4.00 Analysis of Gorbachev's "new political thinking" and implications for the U.S.

Mandelbaum, Michael, "Ending the Cold War." **Foreign Affairs,** Spring 1989, pp. 16–36. Prospects for change in U.S.-Soviet relations by Council on Foreign Relations expert.

"Retreat from Communism." **World Press Review,** October 1989, pp. 13–23. Views of the changes in Poland from newspapers around the world.

"The New U.S.S.R." **Time,** April 10, 1989, pp. 46–134. Special issue devoted to the panoply of changes in the Soviet Union.

"The Soviet Union, 1989." **Current History,** October 1989. Entire issue. Articles on U.S.-Soviet relations, Soviet "new thinking," economic reform, politics, military policy and nationalities question.

Taubman, William, and Taubman, Jane, **Moscow Spring.** New York, Summit Books, 1989. 301 pp. $18.95. Account of the first six months of 1987 spent by two Amherst College professors in the U.S.S.R.

For further in-depth reading, write for the Great Decisions 1990 Bibliography (see page 4).

2.

THE U.S., EUROPE AND JAPAN
GLOBAL ECONOMY IN TRANSITION?

Balancing the budget will always remain a goal of any Administration that believes as much as we do that the soundness of our money must be assured, and that an unbalanced budget has a very bad effect on it.
—President Dwight D. Eisenhower

IN HIS FAREWELL address to the American people, President Ronald Reagan listed what he considered to be the two greatest triumphs of his Administration: the recovery of the U.S. economy and the recovery of American morale.

"America," said President Reagan, "is respected again in the world, and looked to for leadership."

In his inaugural address, President George Bush struck a more pessimistic note when speaking of the U.S. economy. "… We must bring the Federal budget into balance," said the new President, "and we must insure that America stands before the world united: strong, at peace and fiscally sound. But, of course, things may be difficult."

Between the optimism of Ronald Reagan and the cautiousness of George Bush lies an America confused about its position in the changing global economy and its ability to compete in a world that seems increasingly to be drifting in the direction of economic superblocs.

The 1980s did bring some impressive changes in the U.S. economy. After one of the most severe recessions since the Great Depression of the 1930s, the nation experienced seven years of strong economic growth (1983–89), the longest peacetime expansion in U.S. history.

As economists C. Michael Aho and Marc Levinson have noted, President Reagan was able to leave Bush "both an unusually low unemployment rate and a relatively low and stable rate of infla-

tion, perhaps the most welcome gifts of all."

On the other hand, the Reagan era was also marked by record budget and trade deficits. In less than six years, the U.S. went from being the world's largest creditor (lender) nation to its biggest debtor (borrower), and from exporting more goods than it bought to importing more than it sold. The annual Federal budget deficit tripled during the decade, peaking in 1986 at $221 billion. Just to keep the government afloat, the U.S. must now sell $10 billion in Treasury bonds each month.

Some American economists warn that unless the U.S. tightens its belt, consumes less and saves more to invest in education, training, infrastructure improvements (roads, bridges, etc.) and research and development, the country will not remain competitive in the inter-

national arena. They foresee high debt and deficits restricting the nation's economic performance well into the next century.

Others are more optimistic, citing reductions in both the budget and trade deficits as evidence of the nation's ability to adapt to a changing economic environment. They point out that the U.S. production of goods and services, the gross national product (GNP), is nearly twice that of any other nation and that the U.S. is still the world's single largest market.

Most economists, however, agree that the role of the U.S. in the global economy is changing. Rapid improvements in the economies of other developed nations and the newly industrializing countries, coupled with greater regional cooperation—particularly in Western Europe and the Far East—

Comparison of the U.S., the European Community (EC) and Japan

	U.S.	EC	Japan
Population (mid-1987, in millions)	244	325	122
GNP (1987, in trillions)	$4.5	$4.1	$2.9
Per capita GNP (1987)	$18,530	$12,732	$15,760
Unemployment rate	5.5%	10.25%	2.5%
U.S. exports (in billions)		$75.9	$37
EC exports (in billions)	$84.9		$24
Japanese exports (in billions)	$89.8	$47	
U.S. direct foreign investment (in billions)		$126	$17
EC direct foreign investment (in billions)	$194		NA
Japanese direct foreign investment (in billions)	$53	$6.6	

All figures are for 1988 and in U.S. dollars unless otherwise noted.

Sources: *World Development Report 1989; Business Week,* 12/12/88; *U.S. Dept. of State Bulletin; Background Notes* (Japan); U.S. Commerce Department; Bank of Tokyo.

have greatly diminished U.S. influence on the world's economic course. As Japan's former Prime Minister Noboru Takeshita put it, the U.S. is no longer number one in the world economy, but rather "first among equals."

For the average citizen, an economically stronger U.S. translates into more jobs, better public services and security for the future. On the other hand, continued high debts, chronic trade and budget deficits, and a deteriorating infrastructure could lead to a drop in the U.S. standard of living.

Do "Japan, Inc.," and "fortress Europe" present a real or imagined threat to the prosperity of the U.S.? If the era of U.S. dominance of the global economy is coming to an end, then what lies ahead? For older Americans in particular, the past holds lessons for the future.

The U.S. economy: a brief history

INTERNATIONAL COMMERCE has always played an important part in U.S. economic development. Before independence, agricultural trade with Europe and the West Indies helped to make the American colonies the richest and most materially comfortable colonies in the world. The Industrial Revolution of the 19th century brought a shift in the U.S. economy away from agriculture and toward manufacturing. By 1860 the value of U.S. manufactured products was surpassed only by that of Britain.

In the early 20th century, World War I created a surge in demand for U.S. agricultural and industrial products abroad. The U.S. economy expanded at a rapid pace, with America forging ahead of Europe in the manufacture of industrial products and consumer goods, such as steel, automobiles and refrigerators. After the stock market crash of 1929, however, U.S. economic expansion came to an abrupt halt.

In 1930, to insulate domestic industry and farming from foreign competition, the U.S. Congress passed the Hawley-Smoot Tariff Act, a trade bill that placed high tariffs on all sorts of imported products. Many U.S. trading partners retaliated with stiff protectionist measures of their own. As the Great Depression spread across the globe between 1929 and 1932, U.S. foreign trade dropped 70%. The outbreak of World War II brought another boom to the U.S. economy. Unemployment sank to negligible levels while farm and industrial output set record highs.

The postwar period

In 1944, as the war was winding down, President Franklin Delano Roosevelt took the first step toward reconstructing the postwar economy by sponsoring a meeting between representatives of the U.S., Britain and 42 other nations at Bretton Woods, N.H. The purpose of the talks was to reorganize the international monetary system in order to promote world trade and economic cooperation.

The Bretton Woods delegates established the International Bank for Reconstruction and Development (or World Bank) and the International Monetary Fund (IMF). The institutions were funded by member-country contributions, with voting rights allocated according to contribution size. Since the U.S. was the largest single contributor, it held veto rights in both the World Bank and the IMF. In 1947, the General Agreement on Tariffs and Trade (GATT) was drawn up and became a forum for liberalizing trade among nations and settling trade disputes.

To stabilize the international monetary system, a standard of fixed exchange rates was set up at the Bretton Woods meeting. Under this standard, the price of gold was fixed at $35 per ounce, and the U.S. dollar became the measure for setting the value of all other currencies.

U.S. lead narrows

The Bretton Woods system remained intact for nearly three decades. During that time, the U.S. became the world's economic "locomotive," assisting recovery in Western Europe and Japan and development in the Third World. As Asia and Europe rebuilt their economies, the U.S. economic lead began to narrow. Between 1952 and 1968, for example, the U.S. share of global exports in manufactured goods shrank by 50%. During the 1960s, President Lyndon Baines Johnson's Great Society welfare programs and the escalating war in Vietnam placed a growing strain on the Federal budget. By 1968, the Federal government deficit had reached $25 billion, alarmingly high for peacetime, though less than half of what it was in 1943 at the height of World War II.

The 1970s were marked by economic turbulence around the globe. In 1971, faced with rising inflation, unemployment and a flood of red ink in the trade balance, President Richard M. Nixon ended the Bretton Woods arrangements by suspending the convertibility of the dollar into gold, which ended the system of fixed exchange rates, and for the first time in U.S. peacetime history imposed temporary price and wage controls. The economy, however, continued to limp along. Due to their large dependency on energy imports, the U.S. and other industrialized countries were hit hard by the Arab oil embargo of 1973–74 and the quadrupling of the price of oil.

During the Administrations of Presidents Gerald R. Ford and Jimmy Carter, a growing demand abroad for agricultural products and machinery helped promote a U.S. economic recovery. Nonetheless, by the time President Carter left office in January 1981, the continued need to import oil, together with the oil price hike of 1979, contributed to a $30 billion trade deficit, a $79 billion Federal budget deficit and an annual inflation rate of 13%.

Reaganomics

When Ronald Reagan was elected President in 1980, he promised to "reverse our nation's economic decline." President Reagan based his plan for economic recovery on a controversial theory known as supply-side economics. The supply-side economists believed that across-the-board cuts in personal and business tax rates would bring a higher level of savings and a more efficient allocation of investments. This in turn would lead to greater economic activity, creating more jobs and thus broadening the tax base and bringing higher government revenues.

Using supply-side economics, President Reagan hoped to eliminate the budget deficit while increasing military spending to counteract a perceived Soviet military threat. Though there were deep cuts in some nondefense domestic programs, the most expensive ones, such as Social Security entitlement payments, were left intact.

Just how successful supply-side economics has been is still being debated. According to Harvard economist Benjamin Friedman, Reagan's program simply led to increased consumer spending. Says Friedman, "By now we should realize that being in favor of saving and investment or work effort or competitiveness is not the same as actually advancing these objectives."

Beryl Sprinkel, chairman of President Reagan's Council of Economic Advisers, sees things differently. He points to the decline in inflation, the large number of jobs created, the low level of unemployment, and the long period of economic expansion as evidence that the supply-side program has worked.

"I'm rather pleased with the results," Sprinkel told *The Washington Post* in December 1988. "Yes, there are challenges ahead, but given the conditions we faced when we came [to office in 1981], we have done well."

Borrowing from abroad

The Reagan era set two post-World War II records simultaneously: for highest peacetime budget deficits, and for highest government spending. At the same time, high consumer spending caused the personal savings rate to fall to its lowest level in 40 years—from an average of 7.2% of after-tax income during the 1950s through the 1970s, to just 3.7% in 1987, a reduction of more than 50%. Since domestic savings normally provide capital for both public and private-sector investment, which is essential for economic growth, the low savings rate due to both high personal

©1988. Reprinted with permission of United Feature Syndicate, Inc.

consumption and government spending during the 1980s forced the U.S. to look abroad for funds.

The U.S. Treasury now relies heavily on foreigners to buy a big share of the $10 billion in bonds it issues each month in order to finance Federal expenditures for defense, education and other programs (Japan currently buys about 40% of the bonds). By the end of 1988, the total U.S. foreign debt was estimated at $500 billion, more than that of all the Latin American countries combined. (Some economists dispute these figures, contending that official statistics grossly underestimate the value of U.S. assets abroad and therefore are misleading.) Dividends and interest on the foreign debt cost U.S. taxpayers between $40 billion and $50 billion each year.

Foreign ownership on rise

The most visible sign of the growing foreign presence in the U.S. economy is the rapid increase in foreign-owned companies and real estate. The perception of the U.S. as a safe place to invest, combined with high interest rates and liberal investment policies, has attracted foreign investors. Foreigners, especially the British, Japanese and Dutch, now own such stalwart U.S. corporations as Standard Oil of Ohio, Firestone and Carnation. Foreigners also own roughly 25% of all office space in Washington, D.C., and nearly half of downtown Los

Angeles, as well as substantial holdings in many other U.S. cities.

Much of the rise in foreign investment in the U.S. stems from measures taken by the Federal Reserve Board to curb the nation's double-digit inflation. In 1979, newly appointed Federal Reserve Board chairman Paul Volcker raised the interest rate on loans to banks, known as the prime rate. The theory behind the move was that higher interest rates would encourage savings and discourage borrowing, slowing the demand for homes, automobiles and other consumer goods, and thus check inflation.

By January 1981, interest rates had hit a historically high 21%, bringing the U.S. economy to a standstill and throwing the world into a deep recession. The combination of worsening economic conditions abroad and high interest rates in the U.S. made dollar investments extremely attractive to foreigners.

As Volcker's policy took hold and the inflation rate fell to just 4% in 1982, interest rates also began to decline. By the end of 1984, with the nation's economic recovery well under way, the prime lending rate was lowered to 10.75%. However, real interest rates—adjusted for inflation—remained at unusually high levels, keeping the dollar attractive to foreign investors.

The Reagan Administration welcomed the dollar's rise, seeing it as a sign of foreign confidence in the U.S. economy. The strong dollar, however, created two major problems for U.S. industries. First, it led Americans to buy more and more foreign goods, because they could get more for their dollars than they did buying domestic products. Second, it raised the price of U.S. products abroad in terms of foreign currencies, making it more difficult for U.S. firms to compete in the international market.

Trade deficits

The net result was that Americans bought far more goods and services abroad than they sold to foreigners. This led to a dramatic deficit in the U.S. current account (which represents trade in goods, services and investment) of $156 billion in 1986, in contrast to a surplus of $6.9 billion in 1981.

When the U.S. imports more than it exports, this imbalance can affect the economy in many ways. First, a decline in exports can contribute to unemployment, especially in manufacturing. By one calculation, each $1 billion drop in exports equals 25,000 fewer jobs. Second, a rise in imports can put U.S. firms out of business or discourage them from expanding production. Finally, recurring large trade deficits can undermine the nation's status as a global leader by making it appear that the economy is out of control. On the other hand, imports can benefit consumers by providing a larger choice of lower-priced goods and services. They can also create jobs in sales, distribution and other services, and they can stimulate domestic industries to be more in-novative and to raise their productivity.

In September 1985, worried over the growing current-account deficit and a rise in protectionist sentiments in the U.S. Congress, then Treasury Secretary James A. Baker 3d called a meeting of the economic policymakers from the so-called Group of Five (G5) nations—France, West Germany, Britain, Japan and the U.S.—at the Plaza Hotel in New York City. The purpose of the meeting was to develop a policy that would force the value of the dollar down and thus stabilize the world currency markets. At the same time, a cheaper dollar would help the U.S. expand its export markets and become more competitive at home against foreign imports.

The Plaza Accords

The Plaza Accords called for an orderly depreciation of the dollar against other major currencies. The G5 countries expressed their willingness to intervene in the currency markets by selling large amounts of dollars to force the value down. It was also agreed that West Germany and Japan would stimulate economic growth at home (creating a greater demand for imports) by lowering their domestic interest rates.

To a certain extent, the Plaza Accords were a success. Between 1985 and 1988, the dollar lost nearly 50% of its value against all other major currencies. It was not until 1988, however, that the U.S. current account improved. That year, the deficit fell to $127 billion from the 1987 high of $160 billion, almost a 21% drop. Since then the current-account deficit has continued to decline, but the strong dollar and the mid-1989 deficit in the service sector, the first in 30 years, could reverse the trend. A service surplus has traditionally helped offset the deficit in goods.

Some economists point to low unemployment rates, steady investment in American productive capacity and the continued (if slower) economic expansion as evidence of the country's robust economic health. They see no cause for alarm in the latest trade figures. But others, among them William R. Cline, a senior fellow of the Institute for International Economics, believe there is urgent need for a change in U.S. policy—namely cutting the budget deficit and further lowering the dollar's value against other major currencies.

Servicing the debt

The growing national debt also worries many economists. Though they admit that the size of the debt relative to GNP may have been higher in the past, the percentage of Federal funds necessary to service the debt, they say, has never been greater. In 1945, interest paid on the Federal debt was $3.8 billion, or about 4¢ of every $1 in revenue the government collected; in 1988, the interest paid was $151.7 billion, nearly 15¢ of every revenue dollar.

Since the U.S. government is now highly dependent on financing from abroad, how the economy is perceived from outside the country is as important as how Americans view it themselves. Many foreigners are worried that in the long run financing the U.S. deficit will place a great strain on the international financial system.

'Japan, Inc.'

MANY ANALYSTS believe that the global economy is poised between the era of U.S. dominance and the age of Japan. From the depths of their World War II defeat, the Japanese have come roaring back, the new lions in the realm of international trade and finance. Today, their economic strength is second only to that of the U.S., and if current trends persist, they will soon be in first place.

"The American century is over," says Clyde Prestowitz, a former U.S. Commerce Department official and author of *Trading Places: How We Allowed Japan to Take the Lead.* "The big development in the latter part of the [20th] century is the emergence of Japan as a major superpower."

Asia-watchers have been captivated by the spectacular rise of Japan, a country with a population about half that of the U.S., living in an area slightly smaller than California. Until a little over a century ago, Japanese society was based on a feudal structure, largely unchanged for 500 years. In 1852, President Millard Fillmore commissioned Commodore Matthew C. Perry to sail into Tokyo Bay and force Japan to sign trade agreements with the U.S. This began a lasting commercial relationship between the two nations. In

1868, the Japanese adopted an aggressive modernization program, designed to bring the country into the contemporary industrial world.

During the first half of the 20th century, Japan followed an expansionary, imperialist policy toward its Asian neighbors. The stunning defeat of the Russian navy in the Russo-Japanese War (1904–5) left Japan in control of Korea and parts of China. In World War I, Japan sided with the allies against Germany, sending large quantities of munitions to Europe and attacking and occupying German possessions in the Pacific. After the war, a rapidly growing population led Japan to emphasize manufacturing and foreign trade as a means to provide employment.

The economic hardships of the Great Depression of the 1930s helped to strengthen imperialist sentiments within Japan. In 1931, the Japanese military seized Manchuria from China, setting up a puppet state under Japan's control. The move was condemned by the League of Nations, prompting Japan to be the first major country to withdraw from the organization.

In 1937, Japan's continued aggression in China put an end to friendly relations between Japan and the Western democracies. In 1940, Japan entered into an alliance with Nazi Germany and Fascist Italy, greatly expanding its military operations throughout the Far East. In 1941, Japan took the fateful step of bombing the U.S. Navy at Pearl Harbor, Hawaii, bringing the U.S. into World War II.

The postwar period

The war left Japan in ruins. Massive bombing raids throughout the country, including the dropping of two nuclear bombs, had obliterated its industrial base; total casualties reached 1,850,000, including 700,000 civilians. The U.S. postwar occupation policy called for reconstructing Japan as a free, peaceful, medium-sized economic unit with a standard of living no higher than those of its East Asian neighbors.

This policy changed radically after the outbreak of the Korean War in 1950, when the U.S. Army began to place large orders for armaments and other equipment with Japanese manufacturers. Between 1950 and 1955, such vital industries as coal mining, iron and steel works, textiles and machine tools were restored to their pre-World War II production levels. The new U.S. aim in rebuilding Japan became the creation of an economy that would fuel development throughout Southeast Asia, and thus work as a hedge against the encroachment of world communism.

Double-digit growth

In the 1950s and 1960s, Japan experienced phenomenal economic expansion, with its GNP growth rate averaging 11% a year. Even during the tumultuous 1970s, when high prices for oil and other commodities sent shock waves through the developed world, Japan's economy continued to expand at a rate nearly double that of the U.S. and Western Europe.

Despite its prosperity, Japan lacked both economic and political clout in the global sphere. During the 1960s, Japanese officials at times experienced difficulties in getting appointments to see foreign heads of state. As late as 1978 Japan failed to gain the Asian seat on the UN Security Council, which went instead to Bangladesh.

All this changed radically during the past decade. With its high per capita income and enormous foreign reserves, Japan has rapidly become a major international player. Under its postwar constitution, fashioned by the U.S., Japan renounced forever its right to wage war and pledged not to maintain military forces. It was, however, allowed to establish "Self-Defense Forces," which slowly grew in number until they reached a peak of 250,000 personnel.

Until 1987, defense spending in Japan was maintained at a self-imposed 1% of GNP, as compared with 3.3% for most Atlantic alliance countries, and 6.2% for the U.S. Now the 1% cap has been breached and defense spending is increasing at about the same rate as the economy. Even at this modest level, though, Japan's military budget is the third largest in the world, after the U.S. and the Soviet Union. Japan now pays 40% of the annual $6 billion cost of keeping 60,000 U.S. troops on Japanese soil, and has taken responsibility for protecting sea-lanes out to a distance of 1,000 miles south and east of Tokyo.

The U.S. would like Japan to take on even more responsibility for international security, perhaps through picking up a higher percentage of the cost of maintaining U.S. troops in Japan and by increasing its aid to countries such as the Philippines. The U.S. Congress has repeatedly suggested such moves as a fair way of strengthening U.S.-Japanese security cooperation while easing the strain on economic ties.

U.S. pressure has also prompted Japan to contribute more aid to developing countries. In 1989, Japan was expected to become the world's largest aid donor, exceeding the U.S. by more than $500 million. Tokyo currently gives more assistance than Washington to such crucial countries as China, India and the Philippines. It is even showing a greater interest in areas outside its traditional sphere of influence, especially in Latin America.

Political power

As Japan's role in defense and international development has increased, so has its share in the international power equation. There has been talk, for instance, that the next president of the World Bank should be Japanese. At recent economic summit meetings, Japan has asserted American-style authority by taking the initiative on such important issues as the Third World debt. Japanese officials have even expressed their desire to enter into a special power-sharing pact with the U.S. that would harmonize strategies on trade negotiations and other sensitive international issues.

Much of Japan's wealth and newfound political power undeniably results from its long and prosperous relationship with the U.S. America is Japan's number one trading partner, absorbing 36% of all Japanese exports, while Japan is America's second-largest foreign customer (Canada is the largest). In 1988, U.S.-Japanese trade totaled $127 billion, with Americans buying almost 2.5 times more goods from Japan than they sold to it.

To a large measure, the Japanese can take credit for their own economic success. In the 19th century, foreign visitors to the U.S. often remarked on the industriousness of the American people; today, many Westerners react in much the same way to the Japanese. During the postwar years it was not

Sheila Phalon

A member of Japan's expanding senior citizenry, which faces economic hardships in the later years, checks for change in a cigarette dispenser.

uncommon for Japanese factory workers to labor 70 hours a week. Even now, they work an average of five hours more per week than do Americans.

Japan also leads America in a number of other important areas. For example, it spends nearly twice as much as the U.S. on nondefense research and development, and employs nearly five times as many industrial robots. Its primary and secondary education is much more rigorous. Illiteracy is virtually nonexistent in Japan, while it afflicts 1

in 5 American adults and is on the rise. The personal saving rate in Japan is currently three times as great as that in the U.S.

Of course, the Japanese economy is not trouble free. For one thing, the country suffers from a rapidly aging population. Japan does not have a Social Security program comparable to the U.S. program, and savings are expected to shrink drastically as more and more people use up their nest eggs to finance retirement and old-age needs. Another major problem is a chronic dependence on imported materials, making Japan susceptible to even minor changes in the global trade environment. Japan imports 95% to 100% of its oil, iron ore, copper, tin, aluminum and nickel, and 80% of most other raw materials, including coal, natural gas and lead. Also, although Japan ranks second in the world in per capita income, it ranks fifth in purchasing power. The Japanese, living on some of the most crowded real estate on earth, spend 25% more on housing than do Americans and their food costs are nearly twice as high.

Japan bashing

Many Americans are worried by Japan's growing economic influence. Japanese direct investment in the U.S. totals more than $53 billion and some 250,000 U.S. workers are employed by Japanese firms in jobs ranging from finance and food processing to biotech, electronics and automobile manufacturing. According to some predictions, as many as one million Americans will be working for Japanese firms by the end of the century.

Is Japanese direct investment in the U.S. an asset or a threat? For Americans working for Japanese firms, who might otherwise be unemployed or working in low-paying jobs, it is obviously an asset. According to Daniel Burstein, author of *Yen! The Japanese Financial Empire and Its Threat to America,* the U.S. simply is not in a position to refuse investment from any quarter.

Burstein believes that the real issue is not whether Japanese investment is good for the U.S. economy, but, "Why are the Japanese building the most efficient factories in America? Why is it that American automakers are reducing payrolls while Japanese in this country add to theirs?"

The Japanese have become increasingly sensitive to what they consider to be unfair "Japan bashing" in the U.S. For the 22-year period between 1961 and 1982 Japan's total trade surplus with the U.S. was $35 billion, or an average of just $1.5 billion per year. However, during the 1980s, the U.S. trade balance with Japan deteriorated rapidly. In 1983, the annual trade deficit jumped to $21 billion; in 1984 it hit $35 billion; and by 1986 it had reached $60 billion.

Many Japanese point to the enormous U.S. budget and trade deficits as the real source of the economic problems now plaguing Japan-U.S. relations. Former U.S. Deputy Secretary of State John C. Whitehead seems to agree. "The U.S. trade balance can strengthen only if our domestic savings rise relative to our domestic investment spending," Whitehead said in a speech to the United Nations Association of the United States of America.

European integration

DEVELOPMENTS on the other side of the globe from Japan are also being closely watched by U.S. policymakers and economic analysts for signs of their impact on the U.S. and global economies. In 1992, the European Community (EC) of 12 nations (Belgium, Britain, Denmark, France, Greece, Ireland, Italy, Luxembourg, the Netherlands, Portugal, Spain and West

Germany) is scheduled to complete the first stage of its economic integration program. By 1993, over 325 million Europeans are expected to become not only the industrialized world's largest single trading bloc, but also a single lucrative market whose size and diversity will clearly surpass that of the U.S. and Japan.

This new Europe will have a com-

bined GNP of approximately $4.1 trillion, 140% greater than Japan's and only slightly less than that of the U.S. in 1987. It will enjoy a highly educated and diverse work force, including millions of engineers and scientists; a technologically advanced industrial base, producing some of the world's most sophisticated products; and in many of its member countries, state-of-the-art communication and travel facilities. All barriers to internal trade will disappear, allowing goods, services and labor to cross borders at will. The move is expected to produce as much as a 6% jump in Europe's GNP, and to create as many as 5 million new jobs by the end of the decade—not to mention an expanded market for the U.S.

United States of Europe

Many Europeans also envision a time when Europe will be managed under a federal system similar to that of the U.S., with a single monetary unit. In fact, plans for a European central bank that would resemble the U.S. Federal Reserve system are under consideration, and use of the European Currency Unit (ECU), already employed for some transactions, is expected to be greatly expanded.

Bringing these integration plans to fruition has become the primary concern of the EC. A sense of unity and optimism for the future is sweeping the Continent. In the words of one French industrialist, "No one talks about Europe as a broken economic machine anymore. Just that psychological change gives Europe a real chance to go forward."

Stronger ties

As in the case of Japan, World War II left much of Europe in ruins. Once the initial shock of the mass devastation began to recede, Europe's leaders took steps to organize the Continent into a more cohesive political and economic unit. In 1949, to assure their mutual defense against a threatening Soviet Union, most West European countries joined the U.S. and Canada in forming the North Atlantic Treaty Organization (NATO). That same year, 10 European countries formed the Council of Europe, an organization designed to promote political harmony.

The seeds of economic cooperation were first sown by the Marshall Plan, when American dollars helped finance the rebuilding of Europe. Under the plan, named for its chief architect, Secretary of State George C. Marshall, the U.S. provided $13 billion in direct foreign aid—most of which did not have to be repaid—to European public and private industry in the period 1948–52. The philosophy behind the plan was

EURO MAN

As 1992 approaches, the Old World takes on a new look

● **A German head**
for business and for managing the EC's inflation policy

● **A Belgian ear**
for languages, which despite wars between the country's own French and Dutch speakers, enables it to be host to the EC's major institutions

● **Danish eyes**
for design, which often set the EC's high-tech standards

● **A Portuguese nose**
sniffing enviously at richer partners as it hopes to smell more of the benefits of 1992

● **An Irish mouth**
using blarney to extract money for farmers

● **An English stiff upper lip**
to fight off the "socialist" tendencies on the Continent

● **A Dutch finger**
in the dike against the dreaded flood of Japanese imports

● **Italian hands**
capable of talking rings around EC rules without speaking a word

● **A French chest**
deflated by adapting many French business customs to more rational German ones

● **The deep pockets of Luxembourg,**
the EC's tax haven, which hopes to keep its privileged status despite cries for reform

● **A Greek heel,**
the Achilles' heel of the EC, in that Greece is the least willing to pay the price for benefits of the Community

● **Spanish feet**
doing a nimble flamenco to adapt to modern EC standards while remaining Spanish

Dan V. Romer

that an economically prosperous Europe would be better able to fight communism while providing a healthy trading partner and a strong market for American goods.

The EC

In 1951, with the economic recovery of Europe well advanced, six nations (Belgium, France, Italy, Luxembourg, the Netherlands and West Germany) formed the European Coal and Steel Community to promote cooperation in the trading of those commodities. In 1957, the Six established the European Economic Community (EEC) and the

European Atomic Energy Community (Euratom). In 1967, the three organizations were united in the European Community, and all tariffs between the members were abolished. Britain, Denmark and Ireland joined the EC in 1973; Greece became a member in 1981; and Spain and Portugal joined in 1986, resulting in the current EC Twelve.

Today, the EC includes four major institutions: the Parliament, which consists of 518 members elected by popular vote; the Commission, whose 17 members represent the interests of the EC as a whole and recommend policy;

the Court of Justice, which plays a role similar to that of the U.S. Supreme Court; and the Council of Ministers, composed of ministers from each member state, which approves all EC legislation and drafts the EC budget for Parliament's consideration.

Economic integration

The decision to seek greater economic integration within the EC grew out of a perceived threat to the community's international competitiveness. By the early 1980s, it was obvious to many of the EC's leaders that Europe had fallen behind the U.S. and Japan in such important fields as computers, telecommunications, aerospace, energy and biotechnology. According to Jacques Delors, the current president of the EC Commission, the time had come for the community to work toward a "common objective which would enable us to surmount our everyday problems, concentrate our strengths and combine our energies."

The stage was set for the integration program when the EC Commission, under the direction of Delors, issued a white paper in 1985 that identified 300 directives necessary to remove remaining trade and economic barriers among the members. The EC also moved to strengthen its laws in order to enforce an integrated market. In 1987, the European Parliament passed the Single European Act, providing for a majority rather than unanimous vote on most issues in the Council of Ministers. Since then, the EC has concentrated on working out the technical aspects of integration, such as health and industrial standards, communications, and transportation.

'Fortress Europe'

The U.S. shares broad economic interests with the EC. In 1988, two-way trade between the U.S. and Western Europe totaled more than $160 billion, and combined direct investment in each other's markets is estimated at nearly $320 billion. The U.S. purchases 20% of all the EC's goods and services sold abroad, while two of the three countries with the largest direct investment in the U.S. (Britain and the Netherlands) are EC members.

Throughout the postwar period and until recently, the U.S. maintained a flexible attitude toward European trade practices. U.S. policy has always called for fair treatment abroad for American exports, but trade disagreements were never allowed to interfere with NATO security relations. During the 1980s, the U.S. attitude stiffened. Plagued by growing trade deficits and under pressure from domestic exporters, Washington began to push for equal access to the EC's markets. Agricultural trade, which is heavily subsidized on both sides of the Atlantic, was a particular bone of contention.

Trade war

In 1981, the extension of EC tariffs to Greece, its new member, provoked strong protests from the U.S. In 1986, when Spain and Portugal became EC members, the curtailment of U.S. access to those markets nearly sparked a full-scale trade war. A mini-war of sorts did erupt briefly in 1989, when the EC imposed a ban on $130 million worth of beef from hormone-treated cattle.

Many policymakers have expressed fears that a single internal market in Europe will lead to increasing discrimination against U.S. products. In a 1988 speech in Washington, D.C., then Deputy Treasury Secretary M. Peter McPherson warned the EC that the creation of a single market that reserved "Europe for the Europeans" would be "bad for Europe, bad for the U.S. and bad for the multilateral economic system."

Open for enterprise

The Europeans deny they are planning to establish a fortress Europe, with high trade barriers to keep out foreign competition. They argue that though protectionist pressures remain strong in some European countries, notably France and Italy, the EC as a whole is dedicated to the principle of liberal trade. According to Corrado Pirzio-Biroli, the deputy head of the EC delegation in Washington, Europe is more dependent on world trade than is the U.S. "European companies," says Pirzio-Biroli, "would not survive if we created a 'fortress Europe.'" It would be "economic suicide." Adds British Ambassador to the U.S. Sir Anthony Acland, the motto for Europe in 1992 should be, "Open for enterprise."

Partly as a hedge against the possible emergence of a fortress Europe, the U.S. government has worked to strengthen ties with its North American neighbors, Canada and Mexico. In 1988, the Reagan Administration signed a historic agreement with Canada calling for the elimination of all trade barriers between the two countries by 1999. Since Canada is already the largest trading partner of the U.S. (the U.S. trades more with the province of Ontario than with Japan), the free-trade agreement is expected to intertwine the two countries' economies at every level.

Over the past few years, the U.S. has also been holding low-key discussions with Mexico about putting their trade relations on a more formal basis. Mexico, the third-largest trade partner of the U.S., is its largest foreign supplier of oil. In 1987, the Reagan Administration announced a tentative agreement with Mexico on a "framework" for future trade.

Superblocs

Some economic analysts have expressed concern over what they see as a trend toward the formation of regional trade superblocs. In recent years, Japan has forged much stronger ties with its Asian neighbors, especially the highly successful newly industrialized economies of Singapore, Taiwan, Hong Kong and South Korea. Trade within the EC already surpasses trans-Atlantic commerce, while the U.S., Canada and Mexico account for the majority of each other's exports.

According to Jeffrey E. Garten, a trade analyst who served in the Administrations of Presidents Nixon, Ford and Carter, the danger with establishing superblocs is that they discourage international cooperation on economic, political and other issues, and they weaken multinational institutions, such as GATT, the World Bank and the IMF. Furthermore, superblocs could tend to exclude most Third World nations from the markets they so desperately need.

Decline or renewal?

Will the U.S. thrive or fall behind in this rapidly changing global economic environment? The answer to that question, many analysts believe, lies in the country's ability to shrink its trade and budget deficits, manage its burgeoning national debt, slow consumption, promote savings, increase productivity and improve its crumbling infrastructure. While the rest of the industrialized world moves ahead, they say, the U.S. is in danger of being stuck in an economic quagmire of its own making.

These economists offer a number of disturbing statistics to support their argument: every two days a bridge collapses somewhere in the U.S.; an estimated 20% of American 18-year-olds are now functionally illiterate while one quarter of today's high-school students drop out before graduation; government spending on commercial research and development has declined 95% over the past two decades; and savings and investment rates as a percentage of GNP are the lowest in the industrialized world. This, these analysts argue, is evidence that the nation is facing a serious decline in its ability to compete in the global marketplace.

Other analysts point to a different set of statistics to support their claims that the U.S. is entering a period of economic renewal: during the 1980s, 17 million new jobs were created in the U.S., bringing the unemployment rate to 5.5%, its lowest level in nearly two decades; productivity growth in manufacturing has picked up considerably, rising at an average pace of 4% a year since 1981; exports have grown by as much as 30% annually in recent years; and the budget deficit, though still high, is shrinking steadily.

Policy options

In planning for the future, U.S. policymakers are faced with decisions affecting a range of economic issues, from international trade to investment in infrastructure and education. Two of the more controversial issues concern U.S. savings policy and Federal subsidies for U.S. industry.

❏ **1. Should the U.S. encourage savings and discourage spending?** Many analysts argue that the U.S. cannot continue to pile up large deficits and debts indefinitely. They believe American consumers must tighten their belts and save more—even if it means a drop in the standard of living of most Americans. Otherwise, the debt will be passed along to the next generation and its living standard will suffer.

Danziger in *The Christian Science Monitor.* ©1989 TCSPS.

One way the government could encourage personal savings is by offering tax breaks for long-term investments, much as it did under the individual retirement account (IRA) program of the early 1980s.

Critics argue that a drop in consumption would lead to a general economic slowdown, sparking a recession and bringing higher unemployment rates and, consequently, lower government revenues. They maintain that the government should both tax less and spend less, while letting consumption fuel economic growth. They point to the continued economic expansion and the steady, if slow, improvement in the trade balance as evidence that current Federal policies are working.

❏ **2. Should the government subsidize high-technology research and development and selective export industries?** There is rising concern that the Federal government is not doing enough to promote development of consumer-oriented technology. Unlike Japan, where government agencies are involved at nearly every level of development of such innovations as high-definition television, U.S. government-sponsored research is nearly all concentrated in the defense industries.

Advocates of government subsidies for commercial research claim that such programs are necessary in order for the U.S. to remain competitive abroad and to insure adequate employment opportunities at home. They maintain that the development of new technologies such as high-definition television requires resources that are too diverse for commercial industries to provide on their own.

Opponents of such programs claim that it would be difficult for the government to pick winning technologies that would eventually enjoy commercial success. They say it is the marketplace, not the government, that should determine which products are eventually developed. They point out that the already low unemployment rates in the U.S. are a sign that subsidizing research is unnecessary. In addition, they say, current budgetary restraints call for reducing the existing Federal subsidies, not adding new ones.

★ ★ ★

Since World War II, the U.S. has been the undisputed leader of the global economy. Today, that role appears to be changing. Is the U.S. prepared to meet the challenges of a changing global economy? Will the American century be followed by global economic growth or by trade wars among the superblocs?

Opinion Ballot
➡ on page 93 ➡

FOR DISCUSSION

1. You are an American consumer in the market for a new car. Will you a buy a Toyota, a Volkswagen or a Ford? On what will you base your decision? Jobs for U.S. workers? Quality? Price?

2. The U.S. has long been an advocate of free trade, yet in recent years has run up large trade deficits, especially with Japan. Are U.S. trade policies too liberal? Should American workers be protected from foreign competition?

3. Japan's Sony Corporation bought Columbia Pictures in 1989 with dollars earned from sales to the U.S. How do you feel about this investment? Do foreign investors hurt or help the U.S.

economy? Should the government restrict direct foreign investment?

4. The Japanese save a much higher percentage of their personal income than Americans. The current U.S. savings rate is the lowest in 40 years. Are Americans spending too much and saving too little? Should the government offer tax incentives to increase savings?

5. In the mid-1980s, the U.S. became the world's biggest debtor nation, owing more to foreigners than it has invested abroad. Is this cause for concern? Will being a debtor nation lead to a drop in the U.S. standard of living? Should lowering the national debt be a

priority for the Bush Administration?

6. The U.S. has been nagged by persistent budget deficits for many years. Do you think this is a serious problem? If so, how would you balance the Federal budget: by raising taxes, cutting spending on defense and/or social programs, or some combination of the two?

7. Does the U.S. have anything to fear from a "fortress Europe" or a "Japan, Inc."? Will a stronger Europe and a stronger Japan translate into a weaker U.S.?

8. Has the U.S. century come to an end, or is it just beginning?

SUGGESTED READINGS

Aho, C. Michael, and Levinson, Marc, **After Reagan: Confronting the Changed World Economy.** Council on Foreign Relations, 58 East 68th Street, New York, N.Y. 10021, 1988. 245 pp. $11.95 (paper). An overview of the changing global economy.

Brimelow, Peter, and Scheer, Lisa, "Is the Reagan Prosperity for Real?" **Forbes,** October 31, 1988, pp. 85–90. A discussion of U.S. economic trends during the Reagan Administration.

Friedman, Milton, "What Is the 'Right' Amount of Saving?" **National Review,** June 16, 1989, pp. 25–32. A symposium in which seven eminent economists and businessmen express a wide range of opinions on the U.S. national savings rate.

Greenwald, John, "Knitting New Notions." **Time,** January 30, 1989, pp. 46–48. An essay on the new economic theories that developed during and after the Reagan years.

Huntington, Samuel P., "The U.S.—Decline or Renewal?" **Foreign Affairs,** Winter 1988/89, pp. 76–96. The author argues that the U.S. faces no real danger of going into decline.

Laurent, Pierre-Henri, "The European Community: Twelve Becoming One." **Current History,** November 1988, pp. 357–60+. An overview of events leading to European economic integration and the benefits and concerns surrounding the move.

Maidment, Paul, "The Yen Block." **The Economist,** July 15, 1989 (special survey). 20 pp. A detailed report on Japan's economic influence in East and Southeast Asia.

Mann, Thomas E., and Schultze, Charles L., "Getting Rid of the Budget Deficit: Why We Should and How We Can." **The Brookings Review,** Winter 1988/89, pp. 3–17. The authors argue that the budget deficit is the most pressing economic problem for the U.S.

McNeil, Francis, and Sato, Seizaburo, **The Future of U.S.-Japan Relations.** Council on Foreign Relations, 58 East 68th Street, New York, N.Y. 10021, 1989. 31 pp. $8.95 (paper). The report of a conference convened by the Council on Foreign Relations and The Asia Pacific Association.

Niskanen, William A., **Reaganomics: An Insider's Account of the Policies and the People.** New York, Oxford University Press, 1988. 363 pp. $22.95. A former member of President Reagan's Council of Economic Advisers describes in detail the formulation of the Reagan economic program.

Rauch, Jonathan, "Is the Deficit Really So Bad?" **The Atlantic Monthly,** February 1989, pp. 36–42. A look at the current Federal budget deficit in its historical context.

Whitehead, John C., "Toward a Stronger International Economy." **Vital Speeches of the Day,** July 1, 1988, pp. 552–55. The deputy secretary of state outlines recent changes in the global economy, detailing international trade relations.

For further in-depth reading, write for the Great Decisions 1990 Bibliography (see page 4).

3.

NICARAGUA AND EL SALVADOR

WAR OR PEACE IN CENTRAL AMERICA?

ON JANUARY 20, 1989, the day George Bush was sworn in as President of the U.S., thousands of Nicaraguans poured into the streets of their capital, Managua, to celebrate the end of President Ronald Reagan's term in office. The cause of their jubilation was proclaimed on national television and radio and from billboards in the streets: "Reagan is gone, and the revolution is still here!"

For the Sandinistas, Nicaragua's governing party, surviving the Reagan presidency was a hollow victory. A decade of civil war has left their country in a state of near chaos. The annual inflation rate for 1988 reached an incredible 36,000%, causing the government, which can no longer afford such minor luxuries as light bulbs for most public-school classrooms, to slash its 1989 budget by half, putting some 35,000 public employees out of work. Even for those Nicaraguans lucky enough to have a job, the average salary of $8 per month does not come close to meeting basic needs. As tragic as the situation in Nicaragua may seem, in the context of Central America as a whole it is not unusual.

Central America, the narrow isthmus bridging North and South America, which includes Costa Rica, El Salvador, Guatemala, Honduras and Nicaragua (but traditionally not Panama), is a region in crisis. In El Salvador a 10-year civil war has claimed an estimated 70,000 lives and displaced 500,000 people. In Guatemala and Honduras, fledgling democratic governments have been frustrated in their attempts at economic and political reform by well-entrenched military establishments and members of the upper class who oppose change. And in Costa Rica, the only Central American country where democracy has gained a sure footing, worsening economic conditions have

T.R. Lansner

Salvadoran FMLN rebel stands guard with captured U.S.-made M-16 rifle.

seriously eroded the standard of living.

U.S. involvement in Central America has a long and pervasive history. The frequent intervention of the U.S. in the economic and political life of the region has caused most Central Americans to view North Americans with a mixture of resentment and esteem. Though many admire the U.S. for its high standard of living, democratic tra-

ditions and respect for basic human rights, others resent Washington telling them how to run their countries.

Brief history

Central America was once the home of a highly developed Indian society. During the classic Mayan period (A.D. 300–900), large urban centers boasting towering pyramids and populations in the tens of thousands thrived in what is now southern Mexico, Guatemala and Honduras.

When the Spanish arrived in 1501, those great urban centers had been abandoned and the old Mayan Empire was gone. In its place, the Spanish found isolated groups of Indians living in the mountain highlands, with little knowledge of their own past. The Spanish established the Kingdom of Guatemala as part of the viceroyalty of New Spain, which ruled the isthmus during the entire 300-year colonial period (1520s to the 1820s).

In 1823, Central America declared its independence from Spain and formed a federation. Bickering soon broke out between two major political factions, the Liberals and the Conservatives. The Liberals, who represented commercial, urban and intellectual circles, favored restrictions on the power of the Roman Catholic Church, free trade, the abolition of slavery and the promotion of economic development. The Conservatives—representing mainly large landowners, rural areas and the Church hierarchy—were suspicious of change, supported the Church, and argued against free trade and other economic reforms. The battle between Liberals and Conservatives brought the destruction of the federation and the establishment of five independent states in 1838.

Outsiders originally intervened in Central America's political affairs at the request of internal opposition parties, who sought help in settling disputes with those in power. The most infamous case came when frustrated Liberals in Nicaragua turned to an American adventurer for help in ousting the Conservative government. In 1855, the Liberals contracted William Walker, a well-educated Tennessee mercenary, to hire a small army and invade Nicaragua. This he did, winning a quick victory and declaring himself head of the armed forces and chief of state. Walker, who attempted to expand his control into Honduras and Costa Rica, was driven out of power by Conservative forces in 1857. When he attempted to return to Nicaragua in 1860, he was caught and executed.

From its earliest days, Central America's economy has been closely linked to agriculture. Spain encouraged the development of crops in demand in Europe, such as cocoa and indigo, a natural dye. Under the export-promotion policies of 19th-century Liberal governments, agriculture continued to dominate the region's economy.

Coffee, not native to the isthmus, was the first modern cash crop introduced there. Costa Rica and Guatemala began serious production in the 1830s, and by the end of the century, El Salvador, Nicaragua and Honduras had all joined the coffee trade. Today, Central America accounts for approximately 15% of the world's coffee production, selling primarily to the U.S. and West Germany. Coffee is the number one export of Guatemala, El Salvador, Nicaragua and Costa Rica.

Because of the industry's size and its need for a large labor pool at harvesttime, coffee workers have traditionally been kept idle during much of the year, with neither enough land nor money to provide for their own subsistence. Tensions centered around coffee plantations have erupted into major confrontations between workers and governments. In 1932, coffee workers in El Salvador joined a Communist-led rebellion which ended with the massacre of 30,000 peasants.

Banana republics

It is the banana, however, which is most closely associated with Central America. Because of the importance of the fruit to their economies, the region's countries are often derogatorily referred to as banana republics.

Bananas were first exported from Central America in the 1870s. In 1889, a group of U.S. entrepreneurs formed the United Fruit Company. Known as El Pulpo (the octopus), United Fruit soon acquired an unsavory reputation for meddling in the internal affairs of the countries where it operated. Because of its close association with members of the U.S. government, U.S. policy in Central America through the first two decades of the 20th century often reflected company interests.

During the 1920s, United Fruit and another U.S. firm, the Standard Fruit and Steamship Company, its major banana competitor, expanded their investments to develop the region's principal utilities, railroads, ports and communication systems.

Between 1950 and 1970, agriculture in Central America was diversified, first into cotton and sugar production, and later into beef and nontraditional crops, such as flowers and vegetables. Nonetheless, coffee and bananas remain the region's two largest export commodities, making it dependent on external trade and vulnerable to changes in the global market.

Common market

In 1960, the region's leaders created the Central American Common Market, or CACM. The organization was meant to stimulate industrial development by promoting free trade among the Central American countries, and initially it met with enormous success.

Between 1960 and 1978, trade among CACM's member countries jumped from $32 million to over $900 million. By the mid-1970s, intraregional trade accounted for 25% of total exports, and included flourishing electronic products, prepared foods, paper products and other consumer-goods industries.

The same period brought a boom in economic growth to Central America. In the late 1970s, however, the price of coffee, bananas and other commodities on the international market began to decline as the global economy took a downturn, and by the early 1980s the boom had turned into a bust.

Shattered hopes

Because of the region's dependency on imports, especially oil, and the drop in the value of its exports, Central America soon began to run increasingly high trade deficits. In 1980, for example, its trade deficit reached $1 billion; by 1982, it had doubled to $2 billion. To finance the growing disparity between imports and exports, Central America's leaders began to borrow heavily from international banks. In 1981 alone, the region's combined debt increased by more than 30%. Today, the region owes nearly $25 billion, or around $1,000 for every man, woman and child, far more than an entire year's income for most Central Americans.

Today, only Guatemala, with the region's most diverse economy, and El Salvador, sustained by huge infusions of U.S. economic aid, are in a position to service their debts on a regular basis.

(For a discussion of the debt crisis see GREAT DECISIONS 1989, Topic 3.)

During the economic boom of the 1960s and early 1970s the standard of living of many Central Americans improved. However, the wealthiest 20% of the region's inhabitants continued to receive over 65% of all income while just 7% of the region's landowners held title to 75% of the arable land. According to the United Nations Economic Commission for Latin America and the Caribbean, over 60% of the population lived in poverty during the boom years. In El Salvador, Guatemala, Honduras and Nicaragua, 1 out of 10 children died before reaching the age of 5, and an estimated 52% of all children suffered from malnutrition. Moreover, economic growth was not accompanied by any increased participation in the political process. This alienated the middle classes, professionals and small entrepreneurs, especially in Nicaragua.

The economic crisis of the 1980s shattered the rising hopes of many Central Americans for a better life. Since 1979, the region's combined gross domestic product (GDP) has fallen by about 15%. In Nicaragua, the most severe case, per capita GDP in 1988 was less than half of what it was in 1976. In El Salvador, per capita income has fallen to the levels of the 1960s. Unemployment and underemployment, traditionally high, now stand at over 50%, and chronic hunger and malnutrition are estimated to affect 70% of the population.

Central America: bullets or ballots?

Nicaragua's revolution

On July 20, 1979, a group of battle-weary revolutionary leaders representing all sectors of the population, especially the middle class, drove triumphantly through the streets of Managua. They were celebrating the downfall of the country's dictator, Anastasio Somoza Debayle, and the end of the long-ruling Somoza family dynasty.

The broad-based popular uprising toppled a regime that had maintained an iron grip on the country's economic and political life since 1937. During their decades in power, the Somozas had acquired huge fortunes at the expense of their fellow countrymen. When he was overthrown, Somoza's family wealth was estimated at $1 billion.

The coalition government that replaced the dictator included leaders of the Sandinist National Liberation Front, or Sandinistas, a Communist rebel group that takes its name from the 1920s anti-U.S. national hero, Augusto Sandino. Before long the Sandinistas were in charge. They took over a country in ruins: 50,000 dead, 100,000 wounded and an estimated $1.3 billion in war damages. Some 25% of Nicaragua's factories suffered damage to plant and inventory, and over 90% closed completely during the last stages of the war. Before they fled the country, the Somozas plundered the national banks, leaving only $3.6 million in the treasury and a debt of $1.6 billion.

At first, the new government enjoyed considerable international support. Its recovery program was assisted by nearly $600 million in foreign loans and grants, including $118 million which the U.S. provided. In 1980, Nicaragua's GDP increased by 10.7%, one of the highest growth rates in the world, and unemployment fell to pre-war levels. The government initiated an aggressive literacy campaign, improved health care and began a sweeping agrarian reform program.

The economic recovery and the concept of a democratic government were short-lived. By 1981 it was apparent that the Sandinistas intended to transform the political and military structures along Marxist-Leninist lines. National elections that were to have been held immediately were postponed indefinitely as the Sandinistas shifted their focus toward military preparation. The army grew from 20,000 troops in 1981 to a current strength of over 70,000, one of the largest forces in Latin America. Military aid, totaling an estimated $2.7 billion between 1982 and 1988 (including tanks, sophisticated aircraft and training), was provided by the Soviet Union, some Eastern European countries and Cuba.

Contra war . . . The thrust of the Reagan Administration's anti-Sandinista policy centered on the support of

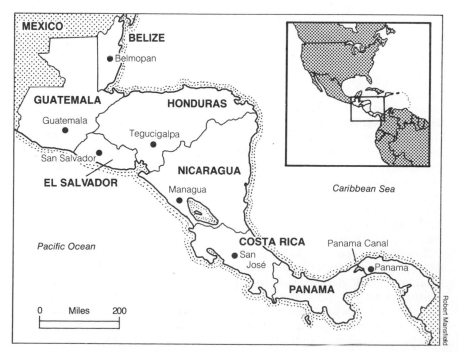

Courtesy Nicaraguan Mission to the UN
Daniel Ortega Saavedra

counterrevolutionary forces, or contras, consisting of ex-members of Somoza's National Guard, peasants from the regions bordering Costa Rica and Honduras, and other Nicaraguans upset by the lack of freedom under Sandinista rule. The original U.S. government explanation for supporting the contras was that they could help prevent the spread of revolution in Central America by intercepting Nicaraguan arms shipments to El Salvador and Guatemala. It soon became apparent, however, that the U.S. would never accept a Communist-led government in Central America and that the primary goal of the contras was to overthrow the Sandinista government.

At their peak, the contra forces included between 12,000 and 15,000 troops. Between 1981 and 1987, they received $265 million in U.S. assistance. Over the nine-year course of the war, nearly 45,000 Nicaraguans, mostly civilians, lost their lives. The war cost Nicaragua $1.8 billion in direct expenses.

In 1984, the Sandinistas finally held the long-promised national elections. Their candidate, Daniel Ortega Saavedra, won 68% of the vote, and opposition parties received about 30%, entitling them to representation in the legislature. A key U.S.-supported opposition coalition—claiming that government control of the media and restrictions on campaigning guaranteed a Sandinista victory—chose not to field a presidential candidate.

Trade embargo . . . In 1985, the Reagan Administration imposed on Nicaragua a trade embargo designed to crush the economy. Since then, President Ortega has twice announced austerity programs aimed at stopping Nicaragua's economic slide. Because the austerity measures involved deep cuts in government spending, most of the social and economic gains from the early days of the revolution have slowly eroded. The infant mortality rate, for example, has shown a steep increase, and illiteracy is again on the rise. Says Sandinista official Omar Cabezas, "To tell the truth, President Reagan was partially successful. He didn't throw us out of power. But he slowed us down about 50 years."

The contra war and the U.S. trade embargo are not the only factors contributing to Nicaragua's economic woes. Sandinista policies favoring the nationalization of some industries and government regulation of others by huge bureaucracies have led to over 50% of the labor force being employed in the nonproductive public sector and have stopped private investment.

The Sandinistas are anxious to bring an end to the trade embargo. Over the

AP/Wide World Photos
José Napoleón Duarte

past two years press restrictions have been relaxed, large numbers of political prisoners have been released and opposition parties are now able to hold political rallies. New elections are scheduled for February 1990, and the government claims it will honor the results. Insists Foreign Minister Miguel D'Escoto: "What we guarantee is that there are going to be elections, free elections…and that whoever the people choose will be the new president of Nicaragua, regardless of the party."

For opposition leaders it is deeds, not words, that continue to cast doubt on the Sandinistas' intentions. Since 1981, at least 7,000 farmers have been jailed on suspicion of being contras. Despite government assurances that there would be no further expropriation of private land, last June three prominent farmers who support the political opposition had their coffee plantations seized.

"The Sandinistas are good fighters," says Alfredo César Aguirre, a former Sandinista, then contra director who returned to Managua in 1989 to participate in the elections, "but they never made the transition from being guerrillas with guns to a government with laws."

El Salvador: endless war

Even as the revolutionaries were entering Managua in 1979, events in El Salvador were hurtling that nation toward armed rebellion. For 50 years the military, with the blessing of the country's powerful "14 families," had ruled El Salvador with little tolerance for political opposition.

During the 1970s, political tensions smoldered. Despite a highly successful industrialization program that generated considerable investment from abroad, 80% of the population continued to live in extreme poverty. After the 1972 presidential elections, the Christian Democratic party candidate, José Napoleón Duarte, widely considered the legal winner, was forced to flee the country.

Death squads . . . By the late 1970s, El Salvador had become increasingly polarized between left and right elements. Marxist guerrilla squads began operating in the countryside, attacking civilian and military targets in an attempt to disrupt the government. In retaliation, right-wing paramilitary groups, representing the landed elite and the wealthy business community, soon emerged. These "death squads" spread their own brand of terror, kidnapping and murdering suspected members of the political opposition. By 1980, politically motivated violence in El Salvador was claiming up to 1,000 lives every month.

In January 1980, following the collapse of one junta after its civilian members withdrew, a second civilian-military junta was formed with Duarte as president. The junta set in motion an extensive land-reform program as well as the nationalization of the country's banks and the coffee-export trade. These measures proved unpopular with the military and many political groups, especially the far-right, and the violence continued to escalate.

During the 1970s, as in much of Latin America, the Catholic Church in El Salvador—in a break from its traditional role—had increasingly become involved in politics as a voice for the poor. In March 1980, Catholic Archbishop Oscar Romero, an outspoken proponent of political reform, was shot and killed while saying mass in San Salvador, the capital city. Though the killing was clearly linked to members of the military, no one has ever been brought to trial for his murder.

The FMLN . . . In October 1980, at the urging of Cuban President Fidel Castro, four separate guerrilla groups came together to form the Farabundo Martí National Liberation Front, or FMLN, named for a Communist leader of the 1932 revolt. In 1981, the FMLN launched a "final offensive" consisting of a military operation combined with a call for a popular uprising. The uprising failed to take place, and the rebels sustained heavy losses. Nonetheless, an estimated 7,000 guerrillas still control considerable portions of the countryside.

Following elections judged to be honest in March 1984, Duarte became president of El Salvador. Under pressure from the U.S., the government succeeded in reducing death-squad activity with the help of the military leaders, who adopted the unprecedented role of defenders of the democratic process. They protected the government against attack from both the right and the left, and, with nearly $1 billion in U.S. military aid, improved its capacity to fight against the FMLN.

The war in El Salvador has devastated the country's economy. The guerrillas have destroyed bridges, trains, electrical facilities and factories, costing the government an estimated $2 billion in damages. Almost 50% of the working population is currently unemployed, and real wages are just half what they were in 1978. Malnutrition and infant-mortality rates have sharply increased while access to basic necessities, such as drinking water and medical supplies, is severely limited, especially in rural areas.

Recent elections . . . In March 1989, Salvadorans again went to the polls to elect a president. This time, disenchanted by official corruption, inefficiency and ineffective reform, voters

T.R. Lansner
Leftist demonstrators seize suspected police agent in San Salvador in March 1989.

rejected the Christian Democratic candidate and instead swung to the right with their selection of Alfredo Cristiani, a member of the National Republican Alliance, or Arena party, whose founder, Roberto D'Aubuisson, has been closely linked to the death squads and the murder of Archbishop Romero. Cristiani has pledged "to continue and improve on the efforts of the Duarte government to respect human rights." However, human-rights monitoring organizations claim there has been an increase in death-squad activity over the past year.

During his inaugural address, Cristiani offered to open peace talks with the rebels, setting no preconditions. In September, the rebels accepted and negotiations, which the U.S. supports, have since begun. Still, it is difficult to predict an end to the bloodshed in El Salvador. As *New York Times* correspondent James LeMoyne has written, "...El Salvador may already have become the Northern Ireland of Central America: a permanent running sore, congenitally incapable of fully healing or being cured, short of the most radical measures."

Guatemala: ailing democracy

In October 1990, Guatemalans will go to the polls to elect a president to replace Christian Democrat Vinicio Cerezo Arévalo, who in January 1986 became the country's first civilian president in 16 years. If the elections go as scheduled and Cerezo is permitted

by the military to pass the presidential sash to a democratically elected successor, it will only be the second time that such an event has occurred in Guatemala's 150-year history.

Guatemalans began to experiment with democracy in 1945, with the election of President Juan José Arévalo, an idealistic university professor who initiated a series of economic and social reforms. In 1951, Arévalo was followed as president by Jacobo Arbenz, a left-of-center ex-military officer whose land-reform program and ties to the Communist party quickly antagonized both the powerful United Fruit Company and the U.S. government. In a 1954 coup engineered by the Central Intelligence Agency (CIA), Arbenz was deposed by Col. Carlos Castillo Armas, who returned the country to military control.

The 1954 coup began an era of political upheaval and violence that continues to plague Guatemala. In 1960 a group of young officers favoring political reform went into the mountains to form a guerrilla movement, beginning one of the world's longest-unbroken armed insurgencies. The guerrillas claimed to be fighting for economic and social equality, a position that gained support among the 50% of Guatemalans who are of Mayan Indian descent.

To combat the rebels, the military developed a counterinsurgency campaign that included destroying villages and burning the countryside in order to eliminate their civilian support. The

T.R. Lansner

Mayan Indians are members of the civil guard. The Guatemalan government claims participation is voluntary, but Indians complain of being forced to join.

army also helped organize right-wing death squads that carried on a murderous "dirty war" against political dissenters, and is believed to have been responsible for some 30,000 deaths during the 1960s and 1970s.

Reign of terror. . . In the early 1980s, spurred by the success of Nicaragua's Sandinistas, the rebels, who reached a peak of 12,000 combatants at that time, redoubled their efforts to topple the Guatemalan government. The military responded with a new reign of terror, including burning crops, killing livestock and massacring entire Indian communities. Between 1978 and 1983, 440 Indian villages were destroyed and from 50,000 to 75,000 Indians were murdered. In 1983, the government began the forced resettlement of Indians living in areas of high rebel activity into so-called model villages, giving the army control over their day-

to-day lives. Civil-defense patrols were also formed, requiring the participation of all Indian men above the age of 18. By 1989, these patrols included over 800,000 men, and were being used primarily to discourage grass-roots political organization.

Because of the army's abuse of human rights, the U.S. halted all military aid to Guatemala in 1977. The military began a series of constitutional reforms in 1984 that led to the election of President Cerezo in December 1985.

Cerezo's election brought a sense of hope for democracy that Guatemalans had not felt since the early 1950s. During the president's first year in office, unions were again allowed to organize, opposition groups could demonstrate openly and the incidence of political violence dropped dramatically.

Over the past four years, however, the optimism has gradually dissolved.

President Cerezo, who has weathered a number of coup attempts, is under constant threat of assassination and openly defers to the military on most matters of national importance.

Honduras: contra worries

Like Guatemala, Honduras has a tradition of military intervention in politics, having suffered repeated coups throughout its history. The least developed country in Central America, it is widely considered the quintessential banana republic.

In 1981, after 18 years of military rule, President Roberto Suazo Córdova was elected to head a civilian government. In 1986, Suazo passed the presidency to José Azcona Hoyo, in Honduras's first transfer of power between elected presidents in half a century.

Honduras has largely managed to avoid the wholesale violence that characterizes politics in Nicaragua, El Salvador and Guatemala. Though the existence of a small leftist rebel group gave rise to a fierce counterinsurgency campaign during the early 1980s, the resulting deaths numbered in the hundreds, not in the tens of thousands. Recent attacks by rebels against Honduran and U.S. military personnel stationed there and retaliatory threats from right-wing groups have led many to fear that political violence may be on the rise.

More troublesome to most Hondurans than domestic political violence is the potential threat to the nation's security caused by the presence of the Nicaraguan contra forces and their families, an estimated 40,000 people, who so far have refused to disband. Hosting the contras was always a mixed blessing for Honduras. For allowing them to stay, the U.S. increased its economic and military aid from virtually nothing in 1980 to over $200 million a year by 1988. But economic activity in the southern region of Honduras was severely disrupted by the contra presence, which sparked political protests, especially by small coffee growers. The contras also provoked numerous border incidents with Nicaragua, many involving skirmishes between Honduran troops and the Sandinista army. Now that the contra war has largely come to an end, the major fear is that the well-armed rebels will turn to banditry and other illegal activities to survive.

Quest for peace

In January 1983, the foreign ministers of four Latin American countries—Colombia, Mexico, Panama and Venezuela—met on Panama's Contadora Island to discuss the possibility of bringing peace to Central America. The Contadora plan, as their draft proposal came to be known, was soon endorsed by four other Latin American nations—Argentina, Brazil, Peru and Uruguay. Together with the original four, these countries came to be called the Group of 8. (Due to political turmoil brought on by dictator Gen. Manuel Noriega's refusal to honor the results of the May 1989 national election, Panama has since been suspended from the group.)

The Contadora plan, which strongly affirmed the principles of self-determination and nonintervention, contained four basic elements: first, it called for an immediate end to all hostilities in Central America; second, it placed limits on the size and weaponry of each country's military; third, it called for the exclusion of all foreign military advisers from the region; and finally, it advocated a halt to support of rebel forces throughout the isthmus. Partly because of resistance from the Reagan Administration, which considered it inadequate, the Contadora plan was never implemented.

In recent years, the Central American governments have themselves taken a more active role in the quest for peace. In August 1987, the presidents of the five republics met in the Guatemalan resort town of Esquipulas and signed a detailed plan for peace in Central America.

The agreement incorporated the four elements of the Contadora plan and listed 10 specific steps to peace. These included an immediate end to all hostilities, amnesty for political prisoners, freedom of the press, free elections, a commitment to democracy and the establishment of a Central American parliament.

At a follow-up meeting in August 1989, the five Central American presidents agreed on a timetable for disbanding the contras. Under the August accords, the contras were given until December 1989 to lay down their arms voluntarily in exchange for peaceful reintegration into Nicaraguan society. The agreement also called on the UN to establish a peacekeeping force of 2,000 men along the Honduras-Nicaragua border.

The Guatemalan agreement grew out of a plan by Oscar Arias Sánchez, Costa Rica's energetic president who received the Nobel Peace Prize in 1987 for his efforts toward regional peace. Because Costa Rica was the only Central American country not torn by bitter internal strife, Arias was in a unique position to push for a meaningful accord.

Due to its neutrality and commitment to the fair treatment of all its citizens, Costa Rica is often referred to as the Switzerland of Central America. Democracy was established there in 1899 and prospered in a land of small farmers and an egalitarian society; in 1949, under a new constitution, the country abolished its army, choosing instead to rely on an 8,000-man Civil Guard, whose primary responsibilities are keeping the peace and border surveillance.

Not that Costa Rica is trouble free. As with the region at large, the country has suffered a severe economic downturn during the past decade. Inflation has been running at 15% for several years, and the country's foreign debt of $4 billion is one of the highest per capita debts in the world. Even though the unemployment rate of 5.5% is the third lowest in the Western Hemisphere, good jobs are scarce, with many families struggling on incomes of $120 to $180 per month, barely enough to meet their basic needs.

U.S. policy: sticks and carrots

IN 1823, President James Monroe declared that "the American continents ...are henceforth not to be considered subjects for future colonization by any European powers." The Monroe Doctrine, as the policy came to be known, was originally meant to counter any possible efforts by Britain, France, Spain and czarist Russia to recolonize parts of the Americas, and it was seen throughout Latin America as a commitment to mutual security and cooperation.

In 1904, the Monroe Doctrine was given a new twist by President Theodore Roosevelt. In what came to be called the Roosevelt Corollary to the Monroe Doctrine, Roosevelt proclaimed that the U.S. had the right to assume the role of an "international police power" in order to prevent European governments from exploiting the region's instability. Under this corollary, the U.S. began its long history of "gunboat diplomacy" and "dollar diplomacy" in Central America and the Caribbean, often sending troops to occupy uncooperative nations, as was the case with Nicaragua from 1912 to 1933. Much of today's anti-U.S. sentiment in Latin America is a legacy of those years.

In the 1930s, the U.S. made a dramatic shift in its policy toward intervention in Latin American affairs by adopting President Franklin D. Roosevelt's Good Neighbor Policy, which stressed the importance of good will between hemispheric neighbors and placed special importance on economic development. The foundation for the policy was laid in 1933 at Montevideo, Uruguay, when the U.S. signed the Convention on the Rights and Duties of States, affirming that "no state has the right to intervene in the internal or external affairs of another."

The Good Neighbor Policy reached

a peak under President John F. Kennedy. In 1961 Kennedy unveiled the Alliance for Progress, an initiative supported by the Organixation of American States, that incorporated political, economic and social reforms and is still considered the most ambitious approach to Latin American development ever designed. Under the alliance, the U.S. promised to provide a major part of the $20 billion that would be needed over a 10-year period and greatly expanded its presence in the hemisphere.

To be sure, neither the Good Neighbor Policy nor the Alliance for Progress brought an end to U.S. military intervention in the region. During the postwar period, the U.S. extended its covert and overt military operations in Latin America. The most notable cases include the 1961 aborted Bay of Pigs invasion of Cuba and the 1965 invasion of the Dominican Republic by 25,000 U.S. Marines.

During the Carter Administration, an attempt was made to introduce a fundamental change in U.S.-Central American relations by downplaying East-West ideological themes in favor of North-South development issues. Carter showed a greater tolerance for socialist governments while loosening ties with right-wing authoritarian governments. Under Carter, human rights became a primary concern, leading to such actions as the aid cut-off to Guatemala in 1977.

Critics claim that Carter's policies were seriously flawed, arguing that he undermined rulers friendly to the U.S., such as Somoza, by his preoccupation with human rights instead of shoring up the status quo. Also, Carter failed to provide adequate economic aid to stimulate the region's flagging economies.

Toward the end of his Administration, Carter suspended economic aid to the Nicaraguan Sandinistas because of their military support of the FMLN in El Salvador and—a few weeks before leaving office—restored military aid to El Salvador after Duarte demonstrated he could control the army.

The Reagan Doctrine

The Reagan Administration saw the conflict in Central America in classic East-West confrontational terms, and the region was made a top policy prior-

ity. It also became a test case for the so-called Reagan Doctrine, which advocated the containment of Communist expansion by any available means.

"The national security of all the Americas is at stake in Central America," President Reagan stated in a speech to Congress in 1983. "If we cannot defend ourselves there, we cannot expect to prevail elsewhere. Our credibility would collapse, our alliance would crumble, and the safety of our homeland would be put in jeopardy."

Reagan's two main concerns in Central America were the consolidation of power by the Sandinistas and the increasing strength of El Salvador's Marxist rebels, which he viewed as part of a "well-orchestrated international Communist campaign." To combat the guerrillas, the Administration increased its military assistance to El Salvador, which went from $6 million in 1980 to $81 million in 1983. During the same period, Reagan authorized the CIA to support and train the Nicaraguan contras and began holding U.S. military maneuvers in the region.

By 1984, total U.S. military assistance to Central America had peaked at $300 million a year. Though El Salvador received nearly two thirds of the aid, Honduras and Costa Rica also got their share. In 1985, the Administration reinstated modest amounts of aid to the Guatemalan army. Total military assistance to the region has fallen since 1985 to a little over $200 million a year.

Economic aid

In 1982, President Reagan announced his Caribbean Basin Initiative (CBI), a comprehensive program to integrate trade, aid and investment in Central America and the Caribbean nations. The CBI centered on the removal of all U.S. trade restrictions on imports from the region as a means for promoting market-oriented growth. Though it has had a positive effect in Central America, the region's high foreign debts and continued political unrest have prevented the program from reaching its full potential.

In 1983, the National Bipartisan Commission on Central America was established to study U.S. interests in the region. In its 1984 report to the President, the commission, chaired by former Secretary of State Henry A. Kissin-

ger, recommended that the U.S. play a pivotal role in promoting economic growth and social change in Central America. In response to the report, the President asked Congress to provide $8 billion in economic support for the region over a five-year period. Annual economic aid to Central America reached $1 billion in 1985, and has since fallen to approximately $600 million.

Contra support

Support for the Nicaraguan contras had become the backbone of Reagan's Central American policy by 1982. By 1984 it was apparent that the contras could not defeat the much stronger Sandinista army. Instead, they were encouraged by the U.S. to carry on a low-intensity war aimed at disrupting the Nicaraguan economy. As part of this plan, the CIA mined Nicaragua's main harbors, temporarily disrupting trade, and distributed a controversial manual on guerrilla warfare to the contras, detailing such techniques as political assassination. Both actions were greatly criticized in the international press.

Obtaining congressional support for the contras was a constant problem for the Administration. From 1982 to 1983, the contras received approximately $50 million in covert funds. Congress openly supported the contras for the first time in 1984, when $25 million in military aid was approved. Due to strong public opposition, funding for weapons was suspended in May 1984; in June 1985, $27 million per year in "humanitarian" aid was granted for such things as food, clothing and medicine. In 1986, full funding of $100 million was approved, but the military portion was again suspended in 1988.

To counter the lack of public support, the Administration sought other means of providing military aid to the contras. One method was to solicit funds from wealthy conservatives; another was through the illegal sale of arms to Iran, and the secret diversion of the profits from those sales to the contra leadership. The discovery of the Iran arms deal in 1986 quickly mushroomed into the Iran-contra scandal, leading to the indictment (and, in at least one case, conviction) of several top Administration officials.

Failed policy?

Critics claim that the Reagan Administration failed to accomplish even the most modest of its goals in Central America. They point out that after eight years of high-level U.S. involvement and billions of dollars in economic and military aid, the Sandinistas are still in power in Nicaragua, the fighting continues in El Salvador and the standard of living in the region has plummeted.

"The Reagan Administration," notes Robert A. Pastor, National Security Council director of Latin American affairs under President Carter, "[was] so preoccupied with Central America and the Nicaraguan contra rebels that it lost sight of the country's purpose and the hemisphere's policy landscape."

Reagan's supporters disagree; they point out that the Reagan Doctrine was successful in keeping the Sandinista revolution from spilling into neighboring countries and in strengthening the foundation for democracy in El Salvador, Guatemala and Honduras. Says Robert Kagan, deputy for policy in the State Department's Bureau of Inter-American Affairs from 1985 to 1988: "Not even the heyday of democracy in the first two years of the Kennedy Administration can compare either in breadth or longevity with the democratic trend of the 1980s."

In March 1989, the Bush Administration and leaders of Congress jointly announced a new U.S. policy plan for Central America, pledging bipartisan support for democracy, peace and security in the region as embodied in the 1987 Guatemalan peace initiative. In exchange for humanitarian funding for the contras through the scheduled elections in Nicaragua in February 1990, the White House agreed to consult regularly with Congress on progress in meeting the goals of peace and democratization in the region.

U.S. policy options

Developing a workable policy toward Central America has not been easy. Often U.S. initiatives have failed to produce their desired results and even contributed to regional instability. What role should the U.S. play in Central America? The following are some of the choices.

❏ **1. Multilateralism—hold the middle ground.** This strategy entails pursuing a course of quiet diplomacy and avoiding bold or dramatic policy initiatives, much as the Carter Administration did. The aim would be to encourage political and social reforms through multilateral cooperation rather than U.S. unilateral actions. This would enable the U.S. to lower its profile in Central America while still maintaining indirect influence. However, such a policy—at least in the short run—would do little to dislodge the Sandinistas in Nicaragua or defeat the rebels in El Salvador.

❏ **2. Interventionism—focus on security issues.** Under this policy, halting the spread of Marxism and even reversing its influence in Nicaragua would take precedence over other policy concerns. The objective would be to maintain pressure on the Sandinistas by having a highly visible U.S. military presence in the region and by renewing aid to the contra forces should the 1990 Nicaraguan elections not produce the desired results.

Proponents claim that this policy is necessary to protect U.S. security interests in the hemisphere and to counter moves by the Soviet Union and Cuba. Critics point to the lack of progress in achieving these goals during the Reagan years as evidence that a different policy is called for.

❏ **3. Stress economic and political development.** Under this option, the U.S. would focus on providing economic rather than military aid to Central America. Support would be given to CACM and other initiatives designed to increase trade. At the same time, the U.S. would encourage democratic reforms and respect for human rights.

This approach would promote political stability by raising the quality of life for all Central Americans. However, it also fails to address the existing political problems in Nicaragua and the rebel war in El Salvador, and would require an increase in U.S. aid at a time when this country is facing its own budgetary concerns.

❏ **4. Benign neglect.** A fourth possible policy choice entails a deliberate U.S. hands-off attitude toward Central America aimed at letting the region solve its own problems. This would save taxpayer dollars and reduce the possibility of U.S. troops being sent to fight in Nicaragua or El Salvador. On the other hand, a policy of benign neglect fails to take into account what many consider the strategic importance of the region to the U.S. and the need for economic and political development there.

★ ★ ★

Despite the large role the U.S. has traditionally played in Central America, policymakers here continue to debate the significance of the isthmus to this country. Some argue that because of its small size and minor influence in the international economic order, the region should not be a major focus of U.S. foreign policy. Others believe, as did President Reagan, that its proximity to North America and inherent political instability should afford Central America a prominent place in U.S. foreign policy discussions.

Boileau, Rothco Cartoons   Kemchs (Mexico City), Rothco Cartoons

Two views of the democratic process in Nicaragua.

Opinion Ballot
||||➡ **on page 93** ||||➡

FOR DISCUSSION

1. President Reagan said, "The national security of all the Americas is at stake in Central America. If we cannot defend ourselves there, we cannot expect to prevail elsewhere." Do you agree or disagree with the President's reading of the situation in Central America?

2. Despite concern over regional stability, the U.S. government has been extremely reluctant to commit U.S. troops to fight in Central America. Do you agree with this policy? Can you think of any circumstance in which you would favor American soldiers being sent to fight in the region?

3. President Carter was criticized for placing too much emphasis on human rights. How important a role should human rights play in U.S. policy?

4. The Reagan Administration based a great deal of its policy toward Central America on support for the Nicaraguan contra forces. Was this an effective policy? Was U.S. support for the contras responsible for the Sandinistas agreeing to hold elections? Or were there other more-effective pressures at work?

5. The U.S. halted economic aid to Nicaragua in 1980 and imposed a trade embargo in 1985–measures that contributed to the country's economic collapse but also helped to strengthen anti-U.S. sentiments. Do you believe these were wise policy choices? Would a more conciliatory approach have helped to moderate the Sandinistas?

6. Should the U.S. pursue a multilateral approach to problem solving in Central America, or is it better to take unilateral action?

7. In all the Central American countries, social indicators, such as health, education and employment, have registered steep declines since 1979. What do you believe is responsible for the worsening economic situation in the region? What, if anything, would you recommend that the U.S. government do to help stimulate Central American economies?

8. U.S. journalist Clifford Krauss believes that "at the end of the day Central Americans have to solve their own problems." Do you think this is true? Should the U.S. have a "hands-on" or "hands-off" policy toward Central America?

SUGGESTED READINGS

Abrams, Elliott, "The Deal in Central America." **Commentary,** May 1989, pp. 29–32. Former assistant secretary of state for inter-American affairs during the Reagan Administration explains the basis for U.S. policy toward Central America in 1987–88.

Anderson, Thomas P., "Politics and the Military in Honduras." **Current History,** December 1988, pp. 425–28+. An essay on the current political situation in Honduras, including a section on U.S.-Honduran relations.

Barry, Tom, and Preusch, Deb, **The Central America Fact Book.** New York, Grove Press, 1986. 357 pp. $10.95 (paper). Provides detailed information on U.S. involvement in Central America, including chapters on each individual country.

Domínguez, Jorge I., and Lindenberg, Marc, "Central America: Current Crisis and Future Prospects." **Headline Series** No. 271. New York, Foreign Policy Association, November/December 1984. 80 pp. $4.00. Two distinguished scholars examine the current conflicts in Central America and the impact on U.S. foreign policy.

LeMoyne, James, "Salvador." **The New York Times Magazine,** February 5, 1989, pp. 19–20+. Ex-bureau chief for **The Times** in San Salvador surveys the destruction caused by a decade of war and political turmoil in El Salvador.

Millett, Richard L., "The United States and Central America: A Policy Adrift." **Current History,** December 1988, pp. 401–4+. Leading Latin Americanist discusses U.S. policy toward Central America.

Pastor, Robert A., "Securing a Democratic Hemisphere." **Foreign Policy,** Winter 1988–89, pp. 41–59. Former National Security Council director of Latin American affairs provides an in-depth overview of current events in Central America.

The Report of the President's National Bipartisan Commission on Central America. New York, Macmillan, 1984. 158 pp. $7.95 (paper). Report to President Reagan on Central America, including historical background, the economy, human rights and security issues.

"U.S. Support for Democracy and Peace in Central America." **Department of State Bulletin,** June 1989, pp. 55–65. Includes statement by President Bush on U.S. policy in Central America and texts of Central American regional accords, as well as fiscal year 1990 assistance requests.

For further in-depth reading, write for the Great Decisions 1990 Bibliography (see page 4).

4.

VIETNAM, CAMBODIA AND THE U.S.

RETURN ENGAGEMENT?

VIETNAMESE TROOPS withdrew from Cambodia last September, ending a decade of occupation. Although the invasion had imposed foreign rule on Cambodians, it brought them relief from the murderous regime of the Communist Khmer Rouge. Vietnam had invaded Cambodia in retaliation for a Khmer Rouge attack and stayed on to assure that the government it placed in power would survive. During the occupation, the Khmer Rouge and two non-Communist opposition forces took refuge in bases near the Thai border. With the departure of the Vietnamese troops, they had a choice: negotiate a political settlement or try to overthrow the Vietnamese-backed government. The choice was not entirely theirs to make. Other nations have a vested interest in their country.

Cambodia, and for that matter all of Indochina, the region comprising Vietnam, Cambodia and Laos, was occupied by France for close to a century, except for the World War II years when Japan took control. In August 1945 Japan surrendered to the allies and its forces withdrew from Indochina. The French colony of Vietnam then became embroiled in the first of three wars, a war for independence from France (1946–54).

In the second war (1960–75), South Vietnam, with U.S. political and military backing, fought and ultimately lost power to a Communist insurgency supported by North Vietnam, the Soviet Union and China. In the aftermath of war, an estimated one million Vietnamese fled their country by boat or on foot rather than endure political repression and economic deprivation.

Cambodia's rash attacks on Vietnam starting in 1977 led to the Vietnamese invasion of Cambodia in December 1978, inaugurating a third Indochina war. Vietnam's withdrawal last Sep-

AP/Wide World Photos

September 25, 1989: Vietnamese troops leave Phnom Penh on their way home.

tember may have closed this chapter, although civil war now appears likely.

Since World War II, the great powers have held four major conferences to end wars in Indochina but peace has not yet taken hold. The most recent conference convened in Paris last August to

work out the details of a political settlement for Cambodia, but the participants could not reach agreement.

Today, the Soviet Union and the People's Republic of China exert a major influence on regional affairs; the U.S. plays a less visible role. In Cambo-

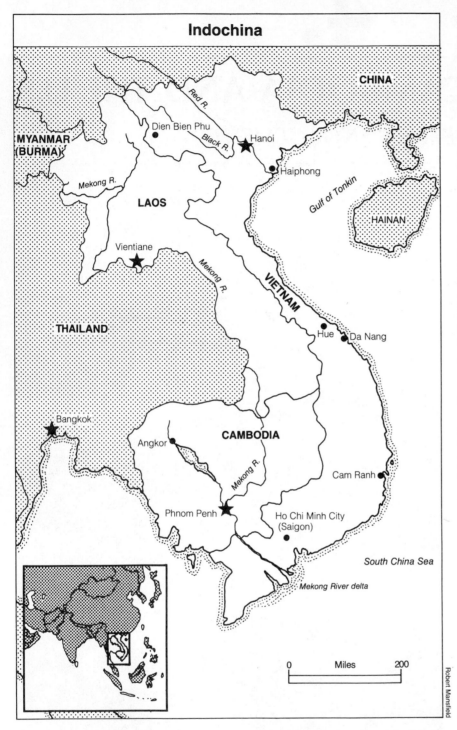

Indochina

CHINA

MYANMAR (BURMA)

Red R.

Dien Bien Phu

Black R.

Hanoi

Haiphong

Mekong R.

LAOS

Gulf of Tonkin

HAINAN

Vientiane

Mekong R.

VIETNAM

THAILAND

Hue   Da Nang

Bangkok

Angkor   CAMBODIA

Mekong R.

Cam Ranh

Phnom Penh

Ho Chi Minh City (Saigon)

South China Sea

Mekong River delta

0   Miles   200

Robert Mansfield

dia the Soviets support the Vietnamese-backed government while China supports the Khmer Rouge. The U.S. and most of the pro-Western countries in Asean, the Association of Southeast Asian Nations (see box), back two non-Communist groups headed by the former Cambodian head of state, Prince Norodom Sihanouk.

What are the options for Cambodia's future? One is continued rule by the present government of Prime Minister Hun Sen. With the Vietnamese army no longer there to protect it, however, its staying power is uncertain. A second option is a coalition government that would include some or all of the three opposition factions. This solution has foundered on the question of whether the Khmer Rouge, whom most Cambodians loathe, should be included. If they are, they may try to subvert the govern-

ment from within. If excluded, the likelihood is that the Khmer Rouge, militarily the strongest of the three, will fight to regain power. If no political solution can be reached, the prospect is for more war, more economic hardship, more refugees and more outside intervention.

The Soviet Union and China are now seeking to remove Indochina as a source of tension between them. They favor a negotiated settlement in Cambodia, but disagree on the specifics.

The non-Communist neighbors of Cambodia and Vietnam, especially Thailand, are wary of Vietnam's past attempts to exert hegemony over the region. They support a coalition government under Prince Sihanouk in Cambodia, but they are divided on their policy toward Vietnam. Thailand is promoting accommodation; Singapore so far has favored continued exclusion of Vietnam from regional affairs.

The U.S. tie

The U.S. severed diplomatic relations with Vietnam and Cambodia in 1975, when both fell under Communist rule. Since then, Washington has sought to isolate Vietnam diplomatically and prevent it from receiving Western aid and trade.

The U.S. denounced Vietnam's invasion of Cambodia and made the withdrawal of its troops a condition for normalizing relations. Although the troops appear to be out, the U.S. has imposed a new condition for normalization—Vietnamese acceptance of a comprehensive political settlement in Cambodia. Vietnam's cooperation in accounting for American servicemen missing in the Vietnam War will also affect the pace and scope of relations.

U.S. involvement in negotiating a peaceful end to the strife in Cambodia evokes for many Americans something they would rather forget—the prior U.S. involvement in the Vietnam War. That conflict cost 58,000 American lives, divided the nation, and tarnished U.S. prestige around the world. The flood of visitors to the Vietnam War Memorial in Washington, D.C., which was dedicated in 1982 in belated recognition of the sacrifices of the veterans of that war, and the brisk sales of books and movies dealing with Vietnam suggest that Americans are at last trying to come to terms with that era.

Have Americans finally put the "Vietnam syndrome," characterized by a U.S. reluctance to get involved abroad, behind them? Is the "Vietnam generation" prepared to put relations with Vietnam on a normal footing? What policy should the U.S. adopt toward Cambodia? In seeking to answer those questions, it is necessary to review the region's history, the roots of U.S. military engagement in Indochina and the lessons of the Vietnam War.

Legacy of colonialism

OUTSIDE INTERVENTION is an old story in Indochina: Vietnam was a Chinese province before it became independent in A.D. 939, and Cambodia and Laos were Buddhist kingdoms influenced by India. Despite foreign conquest and occupation, Vietnam and Cambodia retained their distinctive national identities. They also retained an ancient rivalry. From the 9th to the 15th century A.D., Cambodian kings, enriched by rice cultivation, governed the Indochinese peninsula from the temple city of Angkor. Until the 18th century much of present-day southern Vietnam was ruled by Khmers, who make up 90% of Cambodia's population. Since that time the regional powerhouse has been Vietnam, which has historically considered control of all of Indochina essential to its security. With 67 million people, Vietnam greatly outnumbers Cambodia (with 7 million) and Laos (4 million).

European colonialism in the 19th century changed the political alignments of the region by creating an entity that had not existed before—French Indochina. France invaded Vietnam in the 1850s in the mistaken belief that this would facilitate trade with China, and by 1885 extended its rule over the entire region. Cambodia, which had sought French protection since the 1850s, was made a French protectorate in 1863. After 1887 the five parts of Indochina (northern, central and southern Vietnam, Cambodia and Laos) were placed under the control of a French governor-general in Hanoi. French Indochina, however, was an artificial creation which inspired in the various

Association of Southeast Asian Nations

Asean, or the Association of Southeast Asian Nations, was founded in 1967 to strengthen regional cohesion and self-reliance and includes the states of Brunei, Indonesia, Malaysia, the Philippines, Singapore and Thailand.

Economic cooperation, another reason for Asean's founding, still has far to go. Most members produce and export primary commodities such as rubber, rice and palm oil that compete with rather than complement one another. Brunei's economy is based on oil exports and Singapore, a major regional business center, has important export industries such as electronics.

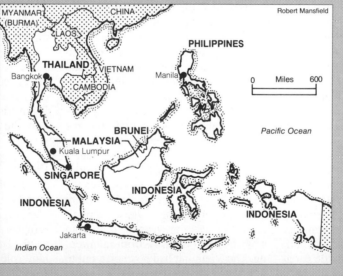

The U.S. and Japan together account for 70% of foreign investment in Asean countries. Collectively, Asean is the seventh-largest U.S. trade partner, with two-way trade in 1987 amounting to $27 billion.

Pro-Western Asean is not a security or defense alliance, although two members, Thailand and the Philippines, are U.S. military allies. Many of its governments have contended with Communist insurgencies and, with the departure of Vietnamese troops from Cambodia, are wary of Chinese intentions. Soviet access to bases in Vietnam is also a cause for concern.

Asean's greatest success has been diplomatic. It took the lead in condemning the Vietnamese invasion of Cambodia, especially at the UN, and was the main backer, along with China, of the Coalition Government of Democratic Kampuchea (Cambodia), headed by Sihanouk.

The prospect of peace in Indochina has ironically put Asean's unity under new strain. Some members, such as Thailand and to a lesser degree Indonesia and Malaysia, have broken ranks with Asean policy and are eager to resume trading with Vietnam. Singapore, ethnically Chinese, so far has opposed dealing with Hun Sen.

If the superpowers agree on a settlement in Cambodia, Asean may once again be relegated to watching outsiders, rather than insiders, determine the shape of the region's politics.

subject peoples no allegiance or loyalty.

During the colonial period, the French developed the Mekong River delta into a major rice-growing region, and planted large parts of Vietnam and Cambodia with rubber trees. Both commodities were exported to France, and by World War II Indochina was the third-largest rice exporter in the world.

Independence movement

The Vietnamese elite helped the French administer Indochina, and French culture flourished in the cities. But for most people, colonial rule was harsh and oppressive and gave rise between the two world wars to a clandestine nationalist movement. Its leader was Ho Chi Minh (1890–1969), who studied and worked abroad before returning to Vietnam in 1941. Ho was a man of action and a master strategist who cooperated briefly with U.S. forces during World War II. In September 1945, after the withdrawal of Japanese troops, Ho, quoting from the U.S. Declaration of Independence, proclaimed Vietnam's independence.

First Indochina war

The French, determined to hold onto their overseas colonies, were not about to grant independence. Negotiations between France and the Vietminh, a nationalist front dominated by Communists, ended in deadlock and war broke out in December 1946.

For the Vietminh, war was not only a matter of military engagements but a political struggle involving every citizen. Ho warned the French, "You can kill ten of my men for every one I kill of yours. But even at those odds, you will lose and I will win." The Vietminh correctly reckoned that time was on their side and the French public would tire of supporting a faraway battle for a lost cause. They adopted guerrilla tactics, which emphasized surprise, continuous attacks, and the use of modest resources against a superior foe. Following the Communist victory in China in 1949, the Vietminh could count on a safe haven across the border and vital Chinese military supplies.

In contrast to Vietnam, there was no significant Communist activity in Cambodia or Laos until the 1950s. Following a well-publicized campaign by Sihanouk, France granted full independence to Cambodia as well as to Laos in 1953.

After eight years of fighting the Vietminh, the French decided to risk all on a major battle at Dien Bien Phu, in a remote valley on the Laotian border. They badly misread enemy capabilities and were defeated in May 1954 in a battle that has since become a byword for military disaster.

Geneva conference

Because the conflict in Indochina affected the interests of all the great powers, an international conference was convened in Geneva, Switzerland, in May 1954 to work out the terms of a peace settlement. The U.S., Britain, France and the Soviet Union were joined by the People's Republic of China, Cambodia, Laos and the opposing Vietnamese factions—the pro-West government of Emperor Bao Dai and Ho Chi Minh's Vietminh, who called themselves the Democratic Republic of Vietnam.

Neither the U.S. nor Britain was prepared to see Bao Dai replaced by a Communist government. Although Vietnam was seen primarily as France's responsibility, the U.S. had underwritten a major part of France's war costs in an effort to keep the Chinese Communists from expanding their domain, and Britain was fighting a Communist insurgency in its nearby colony of Malaya.

Although allies of the Vietminh, the Soviet Union and China readily sacrificed Vietnamese interests to advance their own. As far as China was concerned, a divided Vietnam was a weaker Vietnam and therefore more easily controlled. The Soviets saw partition as a way to prevent the war from expanding and the U.S. from intervening. The Vietminh had no choice but to go along.

The Geneva conference resulted in a cease-fire and the withdrawal of French troops—but not a final political settlement. Vietnam was temporarily divided at the 17th parallel between a Communist north, based in Hanoi, and a non-Communist south, based in Saigon. Nationwide elections leading to unification were to be held in 1956.

The conference in Geneva also gave Sihanouk the international recognition he wanted for Cambodia's neutrality

and independence. However, he was obliged to hold elections to legitimize his rule. In a political masterstroke, he renounced the throne to run for office and was elected prime minister in 1955. Sihanouk was genuinely popular at the time, but his steamroller tactics, which ensured that all the seats in the Assembly went to his handpicked candidates, cost him support. By the early 1960s, opposition to his autocratic rule began to build.

South Vietnam

From 1954 to 1963, South Vietnam was governed by Ngo Dinh Diem, with strong U.S. support. Diem had been raised in France in the lap of luxury and ruled like a mandarin, expecting obedience and refusing to share power. He cracked down hard on Vietminh cells remaining in the south, and alienated peasants by herding them against their will into armed stockades to isolate them from the Communists. Diem also helped landlords regain land that the Vietminh had redistributed to poor peasants during the war against France.

The intensity of the opposition to Diem caught the world's attention when a Buddhist priest set himself on fire to protest his rule in June 1963. That November Diem was ousted and executed in a coup with the knowledge (if not the complicity) of the U.S. A series of successors even less capable than Diem tried, with U.S. support, to contain the growing Communist insurgency.

North Vietnam

In anticipation of Communist rule in northern Vietnam as sanctioned in the Geneva agreements, nearly a million refugees, mostly Catholics, fled to the south. The U.S. Navy played an important role in their evacuation. Hanoi spent the first five years after the war of independence recovering from the widespread damage it had suffered. Then in 1959, after southern revolutionaries had begun attacking the Diem regime, Hanoi resumed the battle for the south. In December 1960 it formed the National Liberation Front (NLF), an umbrella organization of southerners opposed to the Diem government. In less than two years the Communist guerrillas (or Vietcong, meaning Vietnamese Communists) controlled or influenced two thirds of the villages in the south. By late 1964 Hanoi was sending regular forces to South Vietnam.

Second Indochina war

As the struggle between the Vietcong and the Saigon government escalated, so did the size of the U.S. commitment. The number of U.S. military advisers grew from a few hundred in 1961 to 16,700 at the time of President John F. Kennedy's assassination in November 1963. In March 1965 the first U.S. Marines landed at Da Nang to protect an American airfield there. Before long they were dispatched on search and destroy missions and engaged in "pacifying" villages.

U.S. forces were joined by allied troops from South Korea, the Philippines and elsewhere.

The U.S. carried out a massive bombing campaign of North Vietnam, "Operation Rolling Thunder," from March 1965 until November 1968. The U.S. also repeatedly bombed the Ho Chi Minh trail, an intricate and elusive supply network stretching from North Vietnam south through Laos and Cambodia. The bombing did not stop the flow of war matériel nor did it demoralize Hanoi's leadership or affect its ability to wage war. No sooner were roads or bridges destroyed than they were rebuilt. The north's simple agrarian economy was barely disrupted.

The GI experience

For many of the 3 million American soldiers who served there, Vietnam was a nightmare. Many were confused as to U.S. war aims. Their idea of a war was the one in which their fathers had fought, World War II. In that conflict there was no confusion about the enemy; progress on the ground could easily be measured; and U.S. troops were welcomed as liberators.

In Vietnam, everything was different. U.S. soldiers could not distinguish friend from foe—a pro-American Vietnamese from a Vietcong. Also, there were no front lines. Once "liberated," a village would be retaken as soon as the Americans left.

The war exerted great stress, both psychological and physical, on soldiers whose average age was 19—seven years younger than that of servicemen in World War II. On combat patrols, many had to put up for months on end with tropical heat, never-ending rain and relentless insects.

In the latter stages of the war, the troops' morale plummeted and the main preoccupation—especially of the draftees who only had to serve one year—was survival. Drug use became widespread. Thousands were exposed to the chemical herbicide Agent Orange, used to defoliate the countryside and expose the enemy.

Tet offensive

Despite its massive effort, the U.S. was not winning. The Vietcong offensive in February 1968 during Tet, the lunar New Year, marked the turning point of the war. The enemy simultaneously attacked more than 100 cities, including Saigon, where they breached the walls of the American embassy. Although the Tet offensive was a military defeat for the Vietcong, they had now brought the war into urban areas and demonstrated U.S. vulnerability.

The Tet offensive had a powerful effect on public opinion in the U.S., reinforcing opposition to the war and convincing many that the South Vietnamese could not win. Although the U.S. continued to send more men—the number peaked at 543,000 in April 1969—it was the beginning of the end of U.S. involvement.

Many in South Vietnam feared the Communists and hoped that the country, despite the odds, could achieve real democracy, as called for in its 1967 constitution. But the Communists proved to be astute political leaders, both ruthless and effective.

As the war began winding down in Vietnam, hostilities expanded into Cambodia, where U.S. troops operated in "hot pursuit" of the Vietcong in uninhabited areas and for 14 months conducted a secret bombing campaign. In March 1970, the increasingly unpopular Sihanouk, abroad at the time, was deposed by his pro-American, anti-Communist prime minister, Lon Nol. President Richard M. Nixon, in a show of support for the new government, launched a major attack on Communist bases in Cambodia the following month.

Despite continued U.S. military assistance and bombing of Communist targets, the Cambodian government could not hold out. The capital, Phnom Penh, fell to the Communist Khmer Rouge, led by the French-educated Pol Pot, on April 17, 1975. Sihanouk returned to Cambodia from China, where he had taken refuge, in time to anoint the Khmer Rouge as his country's new rulers. Sihanouk's support gave the Khmer Rouge the credibility they would not otherwise have had. Although Pol Pot had Sihanouk placed under house arrest and murdered several family members, Sihanouk continued to support him, possibly out of fear.

Negotiations

As early as the spring of 1965, the U.S. called for talks to end the war. Hanoi refused to participate until April 1968, after President Lyndon B. Johnson agreed to end the bombing of North Vietnam. The negotiations dragged on for six years. The main stumbling blocks were the U.S. demand that all North Vietnamese troops be withdrawn from the south and the North Vietnamese demand that the U.S. set a specific date to withdraw its troops.

In October 1972, shortly before the U.S. presidential election, Washington and Hanoi announced agreement. The Saigon government, however, refused to accept the terms, which permitted northern troops to remain in the south. When the North Vietnamese walked out of the peace talks in December, Nixon ordered a massive bombing campaign against the north. Hanoi returned to the negotiating table, and a final peace agreement was signed in Paris on January 27, 1973. Major provisions were a cease-fire, a withdrawal of U.S. troops, the release of prisoners of war and U.S. aid for postwar reconstruction in North Vietnam.

The U.S. pullout left the Saigon government with only a small, demoralized army to defend the country. Both sides ignored the cease-fire. In March 1975 Hanoi launched a major offensive that caught the U.S. and South Vietnam by surprise. As Communist troops advanced, the Saigon government abandoned the northern provinces and concentrated its troops in the capital. They could not hold it, and on April 30, Saigon fell to Vietcong guerrillas and North Vietnamese troops.

Communist Indochina

NORTH VIETNAM'S long-standing goal of reunification was achieved in 1976, but at huge cost: more than 4 million Vietnamese on both sides, soldiers and civilians, were killed or wounded. Saigon was renamed Ho Chi Minh City, with Hanoi the capital of the Socialist Republic of Vietnam. Upward of 100,000 southerners who had collaborated with the U.S. were banished to harsh "reeducation camps." The government forced others to relocate to "new economic zones."

Relations between Vietnam and China, its erstwhile ally, quickly deteriorated. Vietnam made life intolerable for many merchants of Chinese origin, accusing them of impeding economic progress. Tens of thousands of ethnic Chinese were expelled or fled the country, many by boat.

The killing fields

Once in control of Cambodia, the Khmer Rouge completely restructured the country, which they called by its Cambodian name, Kampuchea. They hoped to expand agricultural production and use the proceeds from exports to industrialize. To accomplish this they emptied entire cities of their inhabitants and forced them to move to the countryside. Phnom Penh became a ghost town.

By 1979 upward of one million people, a quarter of Cambodia's population, had been executed or had died from disease or starvation. The educated, in particular, suffered. The Khmer Rouge's chilling slogan was, "To preserve you is no gain, to lose you is no loss." In the words of Dith Pran, a photographer for *The New York Times* whose escape from Cambodia was portrayed in the film "The Killing Fields," "They seemed like from a different planet and tried to destroy all of us. They were completely crazy."

Third Indochina war

Although Vietnam and Cambodia were both under Communist control by the end of 1975, old antagonisms persisted. Cambodia attacked Vietnamese border areas in 1977 in an attempt to regain territory inhabited by ethnic Khmers but long administered by Vietnam. In retaliation, Vietnam invaded Cambodia in December 1978, drove out the Khmer Rouge, and installed a government headed by Heng Samrin and made up of Khmer Rouge defectors who had been living in Vietnam.

China, outraged by the assault on its Cambodian protégés, attacked Vietnam in February 1979 in a month-long campaign intended, in its words, to "teach it a lesson." But this did not end the Vietnamese occupation. If anything, it taught China a lesson.

China continued its support for the Khmer Rouge, whose forces (30,000–40,000) retreated to the western part of the country. They drew on the refugee camps in Thailand for their manpower to fight against the new Phnom Penh government. The Khmer Rouge leadership remains a mystery to outsiders: Pol Pot, whose name is synonymous with genocide in most of the world, supposedly retired in 1985, but many believe he still issues directives from his base in the Thai border area.

Two non-Communist resistance groups also kept up the pressure to rid the country of Vietnamese forces. One was led by Prince Sihanouk (with about 18,000 troops); the other by Son Sann, a former prime minister (with about 12,000). The three groups operated separately until June 1982, when they entered into a marriage of convenience known as the Coalition Government of Democratic Kampuchea.

Perestroika, Indochina-style

Vietnam's economy was shattered during the second Indochina war and has not yet recovered. Today Vietnam is one of the poorest countries in the world, with per capita income estimated at $130 to $150 a year. The population has to contend with acute food shortages, a scarcity of jobs and high inflation. Production is hampered by the poor state of the country's infrastructure. Only about 10% of Vietnam's roads are paved; the railroad linking north and south is in poor condition (it takes longer to go from Hanoi to Ho Chi Minh City today than it did before 1945); and its ports can only handle half of the country's shipping needs.

In 1986 a Communist party congress reshuffled the top leadership and named an economic pragmatist, Nguyen Van Linh, to the party's highest post. Central economic planning was scrapped in favor of a more market-oriented economy, and investment in agriculture and light industry was increased. Military expenditures, which accounted for as much as a third of the budget, were reduced.

At present, three quarters of Vietnam's exports (agricultural and handicraft products, seafood, rubber and coal) go to the Soviet Union and Eastern Europe. Businessmen from Thailand and Japan, as well as other Southeast Asian countries, have shown an interest in developing Vietnam's offshore oil and gas deposits, light industry, fish and seafood production and tourism.

One of Vietnam's top priorities is getting economic assistance from the International Monetary Fund, the World Bank and the Asian Development Bank; it is also counting on Japanese aid and investment.

By late 1989 the pace of economic reform had slowed. Party leaders were apparently frightened that demands for political freedoms that had affected China and Eastern Europe could spread to Vietnam.

In **Cambodia** (as it is once again known), the Hun Sen government has provided a measure of stability and appears to have won a degree of acceptance from Cambodians. Hun Sen is prime minister and number three in a government headed by Communist party General Secretary Heng Samrin. To his critics Hun Sen is a Vietnamese puppet, but many Cambodians prefer him to rule by the Khmer Rouge.

The Hun Sen government reintroduced free-market principles in the early 1980s and encouraged foreign investment. In 1989 it adopted a new constitution, strengthened safeguards on private property, reinstated Buddhism as the state religion and sponsored a Khmer renaissance. In Phnom Penh, privately owned shops, restaurants and even discos opened.

After the collapse of the Paris conference in August and the withdrawal of Vietnamese forces in September, Cambodians awaited the future with foreboding. Although the Khmer Rouge claim to have changed their ways, no one doubts that they want to rule Cambodia again. In late October Khmer Rouge forces captured the strategically located town of Pailin in western Cambodia. In anticipation of a showdown, the Soviets doubled military aid to Hun Sen in the first half of 1989 over 1988 levels.

The Khmer Rouge and others charge that Vietnam, while ostensibly withdrawing, has actually infiltrated settlers to "colonize" Cambodia. The issue is muddied since ethnic Vietnamese, originally brought by the French to work on Cambodian rubber plantations, have always lived in Cambodia, especially in border areas. At the Paris conference Prince Sihanouk claimed that there were 1.25 million Vietnamese living on Cambodian soil. The Phnom Penh government uses the number of 80,000, and Western diplomats in Bangkok, 200,000 to 400,000. Hun Sen has invited the UN to send in observers to determine the truth.

Refugee issues

For manpower the Khmer Rouge and the non-Communists alike have forced into service some of the 300,000 Cambodians now living in refugee camps along the Thai-Cambodian border. The refugees are part of a human tide displaced by war and its aftermath. There are also about 75,000 Laotian refugees living in Thailand.

A conference held in Geneva in 1979 assured the "boat people" fleeing Vietnam and other Indochinese refugees asylum in nearby countries such as Hong Kong, Malaysia, Thailand, Indonesia and the Philippines, provided that other countries later accepted them for permanent resettlement. Since 1975, over 1.5 million Vietnamese, Cambodians and Laotians have left their homes; 1.2 million have resettled in the West. The U.S. took in about 60%, with the rest going to Canada, Australia, France and Britain.

Until 1985, the number of Vietnamese boat people resettled in the West exceeded the number of new refugees arriving in temporary safe havens. But in the late 1980s the exodus greatly increased due to worsening economic conditions in northern Vietnam. Today, some 90,000 Vietnamese languish in camps throughout Southeast Asia awaiting permanent relocation.

The countries of final asylum like the U.S. are no longer ready to accept as many refugees from Southeast Asia as before and some are drawing the line between political and economic refugees. Whereas 10 years ago virtually all leaving the region were considered political refugees who faced persecution for their beliefs if they returned home, now many are escaping economic hardship. In March 1989 the Asean countries began screening all arrivals, and Hong Kong, the major destination for boat people, announced it had run out of room and would forcibly repatriate any immigrants it believed had come for economic reasons.

A refugee conference held in Geneva in June 1989 reflected the changed attitude toward the boat people. Britain and most Southeast Asian nations favored returning the refugees; the U.S., the Soviet Union and Vietnam opposed forced repatriation. In the end the delegates asked Vietnam to prevent its people from leaving and urged those who had left to return voluntarily. But

AP/Wide World Photos
Prince Norodom Sihanouk

few want to go back. In the first six months of 1989, over 20,000 boat people arrived in Hong Kong; only 143 returned to Vietnam voluntarily.

Other actors

During the Vietnam War, the Soviet Union and the People's Republic of China both backed North Vietnam. Afterward, historical animosity between China and Vietnam resurfaced and the U.S.S.R. became Vietnam's main benefactor. In return, the Soviets received the use of military facilities at Cam Ranh Bay and Da Nang.

AP/Wide World Photos
Prime Minister Hun Sen, Vietnam's man in Cambodia.

Each of the Communist giants is now confronted with internal demands for economic and political modernization and appears less interested in subsidizing and competing for the allegiance of Third World countries. The historic visit of Soviet leader Mikhail S. Gorbachev to Beijing, China, in May 1989 officially ended 30 years of estrangement between the two nations, but the meeting did not lead to an agreement on Cambodia.

China is hostile to Vietnam and will not improve relations until there is a settlement in Cambodia. It is happy to see the Khmer Rouge harass the Hun Sen government. In the words of a Western diplomat in Beijing, "they don't love the Khmer Rouge for itself. They love the fact that each dollar they put in Khmer Rouge hands produces a dead Vietnamese."

China's goal appears to be to pressure Hun Sen militarily so at a future conference he will be more accommodating to Khmer Rouge demands.

Thailand opposed the Vietnamese occupation of Cambodia and provided the Khmer Rouge with sanctuaries and supply lines. Thai traders are eager to see peace return so that battlefields can be turned into marketplaces. Thailand's Prime Minister Chatichai Choonhavan has developed informal ties with the Phnom Penh government and has tried to promote a cease-fire in Cambodia.

The 'Vietnam syndrome'

THE VIETNAM WAR may ultimately be judged to have had greater impact on the U.S. than on Vietnam. It was the longest war the U.S. has fought and the first war it "lost," in spite of a heavy expenditure of American lives and money, a total of $141 billion. The war was brought into every American's living room by the nightly television broadcasts. It strained the trust between government and people, sharply divided U.S. society and indelibly marked a generation that came of age during its course.

Americans had backed their government's objective of keeping South Vietnam out of Communist hands and sending U.S. troops to combat the Communist insurgency. But as the casualties mounted and the prospect of victory receded, a massive antiwar movement polarized the country, forcing one President to abort his bid for a second term and severely damaging another.

Five Presidents, one goal

The basic U.S. objective, endorsed by every President since Harry S. Truman, was to prevent Communists from taking power in South Vietnam. Fear of Communist expansionism in Asia stemmed from the victory of Mao Zedong in China in 1949 and the North Korean attack on South Korea in 1950. President Dwight D. Eisenhower shared the view that communism had to be stopped in Indochina: otherwise, he warned, the Southeast Asian countries would fall to communism like a row of dominoes. However, he overruled his top advisers and refused to intervene at Dien Bien Phu to prevent the French defeat.

In the fall of 1954 the U.S. helped form the Southeast Asia Treaty Organization (Seato), made up of the U.S., Britain, France, Australia, New Zealand, Thailand, Pakistan and the Philippines. Seato's mission, like that of its counterparts, the North Atlantic Treaty Organization (NATO) and the Central Treaty Organization (Cento), was to contain Communist expansion.

President Kennedy's aims were the same as his predecessors': "We want the war to be won, the Communists to be contained, and our men to come home. We are not there to see a war lost." Kennedy greatly increased the number of U.S. military advisers and sought to strengthen the South Vietnamese economy by creating the largest economic aid mission in U.S. history and funding it to the tune of hundreds of millions of dollars.

Kennedy's successor, Lyndon Johnson, introduced U.S. ground troops in the south and carried out an air war against the north. For this he needed legislative authority. In response to an alleged North Vietnamese attack on two U.S. destroyers, Congress passed the Tonkin Gulf Resolution on August 7, 1964. It authorized the President "to take all necessary steps, including the use of armed force," to prevent a Communist takeover of South Vietnam. The resolution was used to justify a major escalation of U.S. involvement between 1965 and 1968.

President Nixon took office in January 1969 and promised to deliver "peace with honor." Nixon sought to "Vietnamize" the conflict by gradually scaling down U.S. force levels and having Saigon's troops do more of the fighting. But these tactics did not work; the Saigon government was too corrupt and its army was reluctant to fight.

Nixon simultaneously sought to negotiate, first in secret and later in public. Determined not to be the first President to lose a war, he did succeed in concluding a peace agreement—but its terms meant the end of the South Vietnamese government.

Lessons of the war

There is no consensus on the "lessons" of the Vietnam War, except that perhaps, as journalist Stanley Karnow observed, it was "the war nobody won." President Ronald Reagan, among others, believed that the U.S. could have prevailed if it had had the will and had committed more men and matériel. U.S. Presidents, indeed, always insisted Vietnam was a *limited* war.

The news media were accused of stirring up U.S. popular opposition to the war, especially after Tet, thus giving solace to Hanoi and restraining U.S. Administrations from implementing a winning strategy. Some policymakers blamed Congress for cutting off support.

Others pointed out that the U.S. effort was doomed to fail because it was based on support for a corrupt, unpopular government in Saigon. Vietnam, many maintained, was simply not worth fighting for.

Some American strategists regarded the war, like the Korean War or World War II, as mainly a contest for territory. But in Vietnam there were no front lines, and guerrilla warfare required unconventional tactics. There were no set-piece battles by which to measure victories and defeats. On one point there appears to be consensus: the U.S. never really understood the enemy. The U.S. continued to believe that if it applied enough firepower, the Hanoi government would crack; it never did.

In seeing the Vietnam conflict as part of the Communist drive for world power orchestrated by Moscow and Beijing, the U.S. disregarded the long history of antagonism between Vietnam and China and failed to recognize what was essentially an anticolonial, nationalist struggle.

After the war, most Americans wanted to hear nothing more about Vietnam. But Vietnam would not go away. As former Secretary of State Henry A. Kissinger later wrote, "Vietnam is still with us. It has created doubts about American judgment, about American credibility, about American power—not only at home, but throughout the world. It has poisoned our domestic debate. So we paid an exorbitant price for the decisions that were made in good faith and for good purpose."

'No more Vietnams'

Whatever the lessons of Vietnam, the war was a major turning point in U.S. foreign policy and left many Americans disillusioned about foreign adventures. The postwar consensus that had given the government the benefit of the doubt in foreign-policy making fell apart, and was replaced by a new reluctance to intervene abroad. Congress, which had repealed the Tonkin Gulf Resolution in 1970, sought a more assertive role in foreign policy. The 1973 War Powers Resolution, landmark legislation that curbs the President's ability to take military action abroad, reflected the new attitude of Congress.

As for the Pentagon, a new generation of military officers became more cautious about employing military force, especially without the clear support of the American people. Many in the military believed that policymakers had put them in an untenable position in

AP/Wide World Photos
Cambodian refugees trek to Thai camp.

Vietnam, leaving them to take the blame when U.S. policy failed.

Indochina policy

The Carter Administration (1977–81) attempted to normalize relations with Vietnam. Negotiations broke down, however, when Vietnam demanded the aid promised in the peace agreement and the U.S. insisted that Vietnam first had to give a complete accounting of missing servicemen. Another factor working against improved ties to Vietnam was the priority given to good relations with China. Former national security adviser Zbigniew Brzezinski reportedly encouraged the efforts of China and Thailand to revitalize the Khmer Rouge in order to harass Vietnam.

The Reagan Administration ruled out normalizing relations with Hanoi until it withdrew its troops from Cambodia and accounted for all U.S. prisoners of war (POWs) and soldiers missing in action (MIAs). The Bush Administration has now imposed a new condition, that of reaching a satisfactory settlement in Cambodia. Both Administrations voted in favor of the Khmer Rouge continuing to represent Cambodia in the UN. The U.S. believes it would set a bad precedent to recognize a government imposed by force.

The issues currently of principal importance to the U.S. include:

❐ **Cambodia's future.** The Bush Administration believes that a comprehensive settlement must be reached by all the parties to the conflict; that it must provide for free elections; and that an interim coalition government must be formed under Prince Sihanouk's leadership. Secretary of State James A. Baker 3d told the Paris conference last July, "the U.S. strongly believes that the Khmer Rouge should play no role in Cambodia's future." However, if Sihanouk deems it necessary, the U.S. would support the inclusion of the Khmer Rouge in a coalition government. The chief obstacle to a settlement, according to the U.S., is Hun Sen and his Vietnamese backers.

Opposing viewpoints

The most controversial aspect of U.S. policy is over including the Khmer Rouge in an interim government. Critics believe it is morally repugnant to help restore to power a regime responsible for the deaths of upward of a million of its citizens. "The U.S. does not have the luxury of recusing itself from moral judgments. In this regard there is a view of many, including this member, that Pol Pot should be brought before an international tribunal for war crimes," Rep. Jim Leach (R-Iowa) told a congressional hearing last September.

Critics believe the U.S. could put more pressure on China to stop backing the Khmer Rouge. They say Washington should also reconsider its hostility to Hun Sen.

U.S. support for Sihanouk also is questioned. "The time has come for Washington to rethink its confused and confusing strategy," *The New York Times* commented after the collapse of the Paris conference. "...Tying U.S. policy to the Prince's gyrations no longer makes sense."

The Administration maintains that Sihanouk is the only national figure with enough credibility in Cambodia to form an effective government and one that would attract international support. The U.S., therefore, is willing to follow the prince's lead on how to deal with the Khmer Rouge. It believes that, if allowed into the government, the Khmer Rouge will be easier to control.

Critics fear that if they are included in a coalition government, the Khmer Rouge will subvert it from within and their forces will be able to break out of their isolated camps and spread throughout the country. They note that Sihanouk is notoriously unpredictable and has changed sides repeatedly all his life.

Observers felt that by his obstinacy in refusing to come to terms with Hun Sen in Paris, Sihanouk squandered a chance for a peaceful settlement. According to one delegate, "this was his conference to prove he could be the father of his country and a bridge between factions. He failed." But the U.S. maintains it was the obduracy of Hun Sen and Vietnam that torpedoed the conference.

What is the main U.S. interest—removing Hun Sen from power or preventing the return of the Khmer Rouge? What should the U.S. do if the Khmer Rouge try to fight their way back to power?

❏ **Relations with Vietnam.** Before normalizing diplomatic relations and lifting its trade embargo, the U.S. wants Vietnam's troop withdrawal verified and a comprehensive solution reached in Cambodia. U.S. economic pressure on Hanoi, it is argued, was instrumental in Vietnam's withdrawal from Cambodia. The U.S., therefore, should keep up the pressure until Hun Sen agrees to a political settlement in Cambodia acceptable to Washington.

Opponents of present policy say that by withdrawing its troops, Vietnam fulfilled the primary U.S. condition for recognition. Therefore the U.S. should lift the economic embargo and normalize relations. By continuing to isolate Vietnam the U.S. only strengthens the hardliners in the government and makes them more dependent on Moscow. In

addition, lifting the U.S. economic boycott would lead to an improvement in economic conditions in Vietnam, which would help stem the flow of boat people.

❏ **MIAs/POWs.** The fate of the 2,377 U.S. soldiers unaccounted for in Indochina is still a potent issue for many Americans. Of this number 1,253 are presumed dead, 1,123 are listed as killed in action, and one is symbolically listed as a prisoner of war. Most POWs and MIAs were Air Force and Navy aircrews; others were Army and Marine Corps personnel captured on the ground.

The Vietnamese government denies that it holds any POWs. Since 1985, Hanoi has permitted U.S. teams to excavate sites believed to contain the bodies of American servicemen. In return for help in locating MIAs, Vietnam requested humanitarian aid from the U.S. for its war victims, including orphans, the disabled and those harmed by chemical warfare. The U.S. government indicated it was sympathetic to these requests and has quietly assisted private aid efforts.

The U.S. government refuses to rule out the possibility that Vietnam and Laos are holding American prisoners, although it has no firm evidence. There were some 9,200 reports of live sightings between April 1975 and March 1989, the vast majority of which turned out to be spurious. Some Americans may have remained in Indochina voluntarily.

Some individuals and organizations believe that the U.S. government has information that Americans are being detained, and they have demanded the release of raw intelligence data to allow independent evaluation. Both Congress and the Department of Defense, however, refuted these reports, and private "rescue missions" have come back empty-handed.

❏ **Indochina refugees.** The U.S. wants Southeast Asian countries to continue to give asylum to refugees, pending their safe and orderly emigration. The U.S. has taken in 857,000 Indochinese refugees since 1975 and financed their resettlement. Many have come to the U.S. under the Orderly Departure Program, set up in 1979 to facilitate the legal emigration of Vietnamese who helped the U.S. during the war. Under

this program 6,000 Amerasians, children fathered by American servicemen who are regarded as outcasts by other Vietnamese, have come to the U.S., along with 10,000 relatives. An estimated 40,000 remain; the U.S. expects to admit 10,000 more Amerasians and their families in 1989.

The U.S. has also contributed over $500 million since 1979 to support the refugee camps in Southeast Asia. Whereas the U.S. insists that only political refugees are eligible for resettlement, it opposes forced repatriation.

Should the U.S. increase the number of refugees it accepts from Indochina? The Bush Administration plans to let in a total of 125,000 refugees from all countries in 1989; of these 51,500 would be from Indochina. About half would come directly from Vietnam and half from the refugee camps. If the U.S. increases the quota, countries would be more willing to give temporary asylum to the boat people rather than turn them away.

On the other hand, raising the quota for Indochinese refugees would mean smaller quotas for others facing political persecution. Moreover, there are economic constraints on the number of refugees the U.S. can accept.

★ ★ ★

According to a well-informed observer of Indochina, the Indian journalist Nayan Chanda, "the story of the last decade should serve as an object lesson: history and nationalism—not ideology—shape the future of this volatile region."

If this is the case, why should the U.S. want to get involved again in Indochina? As one prominent member of the Vietnam generation, Rep. Chester G. Atkins (D-Mass.), put it, "the U.S. and Vietnam are inextricably linked by the wounds of war. We have economic links, security interests and humanitarian concerns that permanently bind us to Southeast Asia, and Vietnam in particular." These multiple interests will influence the role the U.S. plays in this region's recovery from its third war in 45 years.

Opinion Ballot
⫸ **on page 93** ⫸

FOR DISCUSSION

1. According to former diplomat George W. Ball, the Vietnam War was "probably the greatest single error made by America in its history." What did he mean? Do you agree or disagree?

2. Are Americans still affected by the "Vietnam syndrome"? What was the most important lesson of the war, in your opinion? How has it affected U.S. foreign policy in recent years?

3. Has the time come for the U.S. to stop trying to isolate Vietnam and extend diplomatic recognition? Should the U.S. continue to attach conditions?

4. President Eisenhower feared the "domino effect" in Southeast Asia: if one country fell to communism, the rest would fall. Ultimately only Vietnam, Cambodia and Laos ended up with Communist governments. Is communism still a threat to Southeast Asia? If so, which country poses the greatest threat—China, the Soviet Union or Vietnam?

5. The question of whether to deal with the Khmer Rouge poses a moral dilemma for Americans. Should the U.S. insist they be excluded from power at all costs? Are they more dangerous outside the government or as part of a coalition with Prince Sihanouk?

6. A generation of Americans born since the late 1960s is searching for explanations of the meaning of the Vietnam War. How would you explain that period? Did you or anyone in your family serve in the war? participate in the antiwar movement?

7. There have been three Indochina wars since World War II. Do you think the conflicts stemmed from communism or nationalism? How do you account for the Communists' success in taking over movements of national liberation?

8. What interests do the U.S., the Soviet Union and China share in Indochina? How do their interests differ?

9. The countries in Asean have taken different positions on a settlement in Cambodia, although U.S. Administrations claim they follow Asean policy. Should the U.S. play a stronger leadership role in getting the Asean countries to agree on excluding the Khmer Rouge from power?

10. At congressional hearings on Indochina, Rep. Stephen J. Solarz (D-N.Y.) said he had never dealt with a more politically and morally complex problem. Does the U.S. understand what is happening in Indochina any better now than two or three decades ago?

SUGGESTED READINGS

Baker, James A., 3d, "International Efforts for a Peaceful Cambodia." **Department of State Bulletin,** October 1989, pp. 25–27. U.S. policy statement at the opening of the Paris conference, July 30, 1989.

Chanda, Nayan, "Civil War in Cambodia?" **Foreign Policy,** Fall 1989, pp.26–43. Journalist who has followed Indochina for two decades examines roots of the present conflict and predicts "the road to national reconciliation may be long and tortuous."

Clifford, Geoffrey, and Balaban, John, **Vietnam: The Land We Never Knew.** San Francisco, Calif., Chronicle Books, 1989. 144 pp. $18.95 (paper). Superb photos and evocative text attempt to separate the country from the war.

"Indochina Issues." Newsletter published by an independent research and public education organization. The Indochina Project, 1755 Massachusetts Ave., N.W., Washington, D.C. 20036. Annual subscription (10 issues) $20.00.

Karnow, Stanley, "Vietnam: The War Nobody Won." **Headline Series** No. 263. New York, Foreign Policy Association, March/April 1983. 64 pp. $4.00. Excellent overview of the Vietnam War and postwar Vietnam by award-winning journalist, excerpted from his book, **Vietnam: A History.**

Osborne, Milton, **Southeast Asia: An Introductory History,** 4th ed. Boston, Mass., Allen & Unwin, 1989. 264 pp. $15.95 (paper). A brief but illuminating introduction to the history of the region. Highly recommended.

Steinberg, David Joel, ed., **In Search of Southeast Asia,** rev. ed. Honolulu, University of Hawaii Press, 1987. 590 pp. $18.50 (paper). Comprehensive history of Southeast Asia with extensive up-to-date bibliography.

"Vietnam: Hard Road to Peace." **National Geographic,** November 1989, pp. 561–621. Beautifully illustrated articles profile Hanoi, Hue and Saigon today.

★   ★   ★

Vietnam: A Television History. Award-winning seven-volume video set produced in 1983 for public television analyzes the causes, costs and consequences of the Vietnam War. Available from Signals, P.O. Box 64428, St. Paul, Minn. 55164-0428. $195.00.

For further in-depth reading, write for the Great Decisions 1990 Bibliography (see page 4).

5.

THIRD WORLD ARMS BAZAAR
DISASTER FOR SALE?

T.R. Lansner

U.S.-supplied mujahideen in Afghanistan prepare to attack a government outpost during the Soviet occupation, 1983.

IF YOU HAVE KEPT your eyes mainly on the U.S. and the Soviet Union this past year and a half," said *The Economist* (London) magazine in September 1989, "you probably think the world is becoming a safer place to live in. Well, look elsewhere."

As the superpowers began reducing their missile arsenals, Third World countries were adding to theirs. (In this article, "Third World" refers to all the countries of Africa, Latin America, the Middle East and Asia, except for Japan.) In the Iran-Iraq War, both sides fired over 1,000 long-range missiles at one another, killing civilians miles from the front lines. Both used chemical weapons; Iraq also used them against its own Kurdish minority. The fighting, which finally ended in 1988 after eight years, absorbed some $60 billion worth of arms—over 20% of Third World arms imports—according to Congressional Research Service expert Richard

F. Grimmett. It was the most destructive conflict ever fought between two Third World countries, killing as many as a million and a half people, wounding 2 million more and leaving a million and a half refugees, by some estimates. Losses to Iran's oil industry alone could amount to $250 billion; rebuilding could cost both countries $500 billion.

While it may have been the deadliest war, the Iran-Iraq conflict was only one of more than 30 fought in the Third World during the 1980s. Countries in volatile areas are increasingly well-armed: Muammar Qaddafi's Libya was reportedly able to make nerve gas by early 1989, with the help of a West German firm. Pakistan moved closer than ever to a nuclear-weapons capability. Sixteen countries, according to the U.S. Arms Control and Disarmament Agency (ACDA), had or were trying to build ballistic missiles by 1988, giving them the ability to hit distant targets within minutes with any kind of weapon, conventional, chemical or nuclear.

Over half of all arms deals with and deliveries to the Third World between 1981 and 1988 involved the U.S. or the U.S.S.R. The superpowers agree on the need to block the further spread of ballistic missiles as well as nuclear- and chemical-weapons capabilities, but they are far from agreement on limiting the trade in conventional arms.

Even if the superpowers refuse to sell them arms, Third World countries can turn to the small but growing number of other suppliers who attach fewer strings to sales. More are doing the buying as well as the selling: although the value of Third World arms-sales agreements in 1988 reached only about half the 1982 peak of nearly $60 billion, according to Grimmett, the total was considerably higher than 20 years ago.

Arms purchases represent only a fraction of the Third World's total military spending, which exceeded combined expenditures on health and education in the mid-1980s. Third World military spending, like arms sales, is down, but even in 1987 when it hit a 10-year low, the total came to a whopping $176 billion, according to ACDA. Despite a rising debt burden and declining prices for many of their major export commodities, low-income countries as a whole "currently allocate around 20% of central government budgets to defense," according to Barber Conable, president of the International Bank for Reconstruction and Development, or World Bank.

What can be done to control the further spread of weapons and military technology to the Third World? What will be the consequences for developing nations—and for the U.S.—if the arms trade continues unabated?

Sellers and buyers

IN 1987, THIRD WORLD nations bought three quarters of the arms that changed hands internationally. Most of these weapons are conventional (as opposed to nuclear or chemical)—items like guns, tanks and aircraft—but increasingly they are highly sophisticated and destined for areas like the Middle East, where tensions run high and wars are frequent.

At the same time, chemical, nuclear and ballistic-missile technology is proliferating. India, Pakistan and South Africa are all now believed to have the ability to build nuclear weapons on short notice; Israel may have 60 to 100 on hand already, according to Jane's *Defense Weekly*. Chemical-weapons technology has spread even further; Central Intelligence Agency director William Webster thinks 20 nations may already be producing them. At least 9 Middle Eastern countries now have ballistic missiles; Webster believes 15 countries will be building their own by the year 2000.

Why sell?

Except for the superpowers, most arms producers export weapons for profit. The French and British, who were the third- and fourth-largest arms exporters to the Third World between 1983 and 1987, need the export business to help keep their defense industries running at capacity in peacetime. The same is true for newer arms producers like China and Israel. Israel spends considerable sums on military research and development—a costly proposition for such a small country— to retain its technological edge over its Arab adversaries. Arms accounted for just over 4% of total Israeli export revenue in 1987, but they have earned twice that in other years.

Although they are not uninterested in the money, the superpowers have tended to sell weapons largely for political and strategic reasons—to make friends and influence allies in the Third World.

Moscow remains the largest supplier of weapons in terms of quantity, although many experts believe that when military services, technology transfer and quality are factored in, the U.S. is ahead. The U.S.S.R. has provided large quantities of weapons to allies such as Cuba and Nicaragua, either free of charge or at low cost; and it has traded arms for the use of military facilities, as in Ethiopia, Vietnam and Syria. Since the 1970s, the Soviets have also looked for cash customers like India and Iraq. Moscow's sales have dropped in recent years, as demand has slackened and buyers like India and Iraq have sought to diversify their sources. The Soviet bloc also reduced military aid to long-time ally Nicaragua by 20% in 1989, according to U.S. intelligence sources.

U.S. arms sales

In addition to bolstering allies in the East-West competition, the U.S. has used military aid and arms sales to line up support for other U.S. foreign policy objectives. Israel and Egypt have acquired large amounts of U.S. weapons since 1979, when the Carter Administration (1977–81) promised them to both countries as an incentive to negotiate a peace treaty. Saudi Arabia, a vital oil supplier, a moderate Arab state and a U.S. ally, buys more U.S. arms than any other country.

Most early post-World War II U.S. weapons transfers came from surplus war stockpiles and were made free of charge under the Military Assistance Program to U.S. allies in the North Atlantic Treaty Organization. U.S. military aid spread to Asia, the Middle East and later Latin America during the 1950s and 1960s, as the focus of the effort to contain communism shifted. Not until the Kennedy Administration (1961–63), when war surplus stocks began to run out and the U.S. faced a balance-of-payments deficit, did the U.S. make a conscious effort to increase arms sales.

Military assistance grants have been largely phased out; most aid now is in the form of foreign military sales credits, which reduce the amount of cash a poorer buyer needs to make a deal, or in loans guaranteed by the U.S. government.

The Nixon Doctrine

In 1969, President Richard M. Nixon (1969–74) decided that the U.S., in light of its long, costly and unpopular involvement in the Vietnam War, could no longer afford to pick up so much of the tab for defending its allies. In the future, he announced, the U.S. would provide military and economic assistance, but would "look to the nation directly threatened to assume the responsibility of providing the manpower for defense" and for paying for more of its own weapons.

The Nixon Doctrine was put to the test in a strategically vital region. At the end of 1971, when the British pulled the last of their troops out of the Persian Gulf region, Washington felt it needed a local ally to help keep Moscow from extending its influence in the area. Shah Mohammad Reza Pahlavi of Iran, with whom the U.S. had had a close relationship since helping to restore him to power in 1953, was willing to step in, on condition that the U.S. sell him sophisticated weapons. In 1972, the U.S. reversed its policy of not selling high-technology weapons to Third World allies and secretly agreed to sell Iran "any conventional weapons systems that it wanted," without subjecting such sales to State or Defense Department review.

In 1973–74, Iran and the other members of the Organization of Petroleum Exporting Countries (OPEC) quintupled the price of oil. The Federal deficit soared as a result, and the U.S. looked for a way to get OPEC countries to spend some of their petrodollars in the U.S. What Iran and Saudi Arabia most wanted was advanced U.S. military technology, and between 1973 and 1977, the value of Iranian arms imports more than tripled—and over three quarters came from the U.S. This huge new market also provided American arms

firms with new customers at a time when the U.S. was ending its involvement in Vietnam and the Pentagon had cut back arms purchases.

The debate heats up

As the level of U.S. weapons sales rose during the 1970s, the congressional debate over U.S. arms-transfer policy grew more heated. The debate had begun in the late 1960s, fueled by the war in Vietnam and weapons sales to military governments in Latin America. These prompted Congress to adopt the 1968 Foreign Military Sales Act, which placed restrictions on sophisticated U.S. military hardware that could be sold to developing countries.

In 1974, Congress passed the Nelson Amendment, requiring the President to report any military sale of $25 million or more and giving Congress 20 days to veto such a sale. A year later, the amendment was incorporated into the 1976 International Security Assistance and Arms Export Control Act, which, in a slightly modified form, was passed over President Gerald R. Ford's veto. The legislation was intended to shift the focus of U.S. policy toward "restricting, not expanding, the world arms trade," according to the Senate Foreign Relations Committee. It required additional reporting of transactions by the executive branch to Congress, extended the congressional veto period for proposed transactions and forbade the extension of military aid to military dictatorships.

The Carter theory

Jimmy Carter shared the concerns that had led to the new legislation. In May 1977, he announced that in the future, arms sales would be viewed "as an exceptional foreign policy implement, to be used only in instances where it can be clearly demonstrated that the transfer contributes to our vital national security interests." He laid out guidelines that set a dollar ceiling on new deals, strictly limited high-technology military sales and coproduction arrangements with Third World countries, and placed the "burden of persuasion" on proponents of a sale rather than on its opponents.

In practice, however, little changed in U.S. arms-sales policy over the next several years. The Administration discovered how useful an instrument selling weapons could be in securing the cooperation of other governments, especially in the case of the 1979 Israeli-Egyptian peace treaty: Israel was promised $2.2 billion in arms credits and Egypt $1.5 billion, and both received additional grants as well. In 1977 and 1978, the Carter Administration also concluded deals to sell AWACS (airborne warning and control system) radar planes to Iran, and advanced F-15 jet fighters to Saudi Arabia as part of a package that included substantial sales to Egypt and Israel.

Where the Administration was most successful in trimming arms sales was in Latin America. But Washington's refusal to sell Latin American governments significant quantities of arms simply spurred them to build their own or buy weapons elsewhere: the value of European weapons deliveries to Latin America soared during the Carter years.

In addition to complaining that it cost U.S. arms makers valuable business, critics also objected that Carter's policy hurt U.S. influence in Latin America, leaving a gap which was filled by the Soviets. As Jeane Kirkpatrick, later President Ronald Reagan's permanent representative to the United Nations, wrote in *Commentary* in 1979, Carter's policies had "not only proved incapable of dealing with the problems of Soviet/Cuban expansion in the area, they have positively contributed to them and to the alienation of major nations, the growth of neutralism, the destabilization of friendly governments, the spread of Cuban influence and the decline of U.S. power in the region."

The Reagan Doctrine

President Reagan's official arms-sales statement announced that the U.S. would "deal with the world as it is, rather than as we would like it to be." The U.S. would sell weapons where such sales would help the U.S. and its allies "to project power in response to threats posed by mutual adversaries" and prevent friends from being "at a military disadvantage." The U.S. would also sell arms to enhance "U.S. defense production capabilities and efficiency."

In an effort to repair the weakened U.S. position in the Persian Gulf after the overthrow of the shah in 1979, Reagan increased arms sales to friendly Persian Gulf states. In the largest deal to date with Saudi Arabia, he removed restrictions on equipment that would increase the range and offensive capabilities of the F-15s already sold to Saudi Arabia by the Carter Administration, and sold the Saudi government five AWACS planes in addition. The deal created a furor, in large part because of concerns for Israel's security, and Congress forced the Administration to postpone the sale for a year. When the Iran-Iraq War threatened the Persian Gulf oil-shipping lanes, the Reagan Administration also sold Kuwait a $2 billion package of F-18 aircraft and an assortment of missiles.

Under what became known as the Reagan Doctrine, Washington also increased levels of military assistance, both to governments like El Salvador, which faced a leftist insurgency, and to anti-Communist resistance groups. The U.S. provided shoulder-held Stinger antiaircraft missiles to the Afghan *mujahideen* (insurgents) fighting the Soviet occupation of their country and to the rebels under the command of Jonas Savimbi fighting the Cuban-backed government of Angola. It also provided large quantities of weapons to the Nicaraguan counterrevolutionaries (the contras) fighting the leftist Sandinista government, and provided aid to neighboring Honduras in order to provide a refuge and backup support for the contras.

In the wake of the Iran-contra scandal, in which it was revealed that the U.S. government had secretly sold weapons to Iran and funneled some of the profits to the contras, the Administration was forced to delay additional aircraft sales to Saudi Arabia on several occasions. This infuriated the Saudis and prompted them to conclude a $29 billion arms deal with the British in 1988.

The provision of Stingers to the Afghan resistance movement also provoked opposition because of fears, which later proved well founded, that they would wind up in the hands of U.S. enemies such as Iran.

Why buy?

In 1985, the U.S. spent more than 6.5% of its gross national product (GNP) on defense and had about ten soldiers for every 1,000 citizens. By contrast, Nicaragua spent over 17% of

Mike Keefe, *The Denver Post*

its GNP on its military that year and had 23 soldiers per 1,000 citizens. Iraq spent 30–50% of its GNP on the military for most of the years of the Persian Gulf war, with some 50 out of every 1,000 people fighting.

Nicaragua and Iraq were at war. Saudi Arabia and Oman were not, and yet Saudi Arabia spent 25% of its GNP on its military in 1985 and 13% in 1987; and Oman spent 23% in 1987. Why do some Third World countries spend so much on their military establishments in peacetime?

Security is one obvious answer. Decolonization led to the creation of some 100 new nations between 1945 and 1980, whose defense needs were no longer provided for by their former colonial rulers. In sub-Saharan Africa, for example, imports of major weapons increased dramatically during the 1950s and 1960s as 27 new nations began equipping their fledgling armed forces.

Each country's idea of its defense needs is different. Regional rivalries and frequent wars have led neighbors to arm themselves against one another in the Middle East, South Asia and South America.

In Africa, many of the conflicts have been fought not between but within individual countries as a result of colonial boundaries and social structures retained after independence that have little relationship to ethnic, religious and tribal divisions. Ethnic groups that

were artificially separated have fought to redraw borders, while national governments have resisted the damage that would do to their hard-won sovereignty. Africa's arms purchases more than doubled in the late 1970s, outstripping all other Third World regions in growth, albeit from a smaller base.

Having one's own armed forces is an important symbol of sovereignty; for countries aspiring to regional power status, having the best weapons in the region helps establish their leadership. A strong and well-supplied army is also critical for governments facing an armed insurgency. In the Third World, a large number of governments are either led by military officers or have very close ties with them.

Arms and security

While building a bigger and better military establishment would appear to strengthen a developing nation's security, many believe that it does the exact opposite. They argue that increasing the numbers and kinds of weapons—especially if those weapons are perceived as offensive, like long-range bombers—in areas of political instability makes wars more, not less, likely and permits them to drag on longer with more-destructive results. The counterargument is that wars are not caused by weapons, but are the product of economic, political and social tensions.

The goods: a glossary

Ballistic missiles: Propelled by booster rockets, ballistic missiles are guided for part of their flight path, then pulled by gravity and wind toward their targets. The high speed and ability of the most advanced ballistic missiles to carry large and destructive warheads—including chemical or nuclear weapons—make them both dangerous and hard to defend against. Many countries have ballistic missiles that can travel over 100 miles, some over 1,000.

Seven countries that have the technology to produce ballistic missiles or related parts—Britain, Canada, France, Italy, Japan, the U.S. and West Germany—banded together voluntarily in 1987 in the **Missile Technology Control Regime (MTCR).** The regime does not call for a total embargo on the transfer of technology and it only restricts sales of complete rocket systems that can carry an 1,100-pound bomb (thought to be the minimum weight needed to carry a nuclear weapon 190 miles). Rocket engines, warheads, warhead parts and guidance systems are also restricted. A second, broader category of items (including equipment needed to produce rocket propellant and computer software, for example) may be restricted in certain cases, if there is reason to believe they could enable the buyer to build missiles.

Chemical and biological weapons: Chemical weapons contain toxic liquid or gas that kills or maims. Biological weapons contain living organisms, such as viruses or bacteria, that cause disease or death. The 1925 **Geneva Protocol** bans the use of both chemical and biological weapons, though not their production and stockpiling. Moreover, most signatories reserved the right to use chemical weapons if attacked with them. A 1972 **Biological and Toxin Weapons Convention** forbids their production, development and stockpiling, but does not cover chemical weapons. (The U.S. ratified both the 1925 and 1972 conventions in 1975.)

Conventional weapons: Nonnuclear, nonchemical weapons. This is a broad term, covering the most primitive guns to the most sophisticated modern jet fighters. "Major" conventional weapons systems refer to aircraft, ships, armored vehicles (like tanks) and missiles.

Nuclear weapons: A general term referring to two types of arms: atomic weapons, whose power comes from splitting the nucleus of an atom (fission); and thermonuclear weapons, in which two nuclei are combined (fusion) to produce vastly more power. Most of today's nuclear weapons have the power of thousands or millions of tons of a conventional explosive like TNT.

To produce a nuclear weapon, a country has to know how to separate a fissionable form of uranium or plutonium from the far more common nonfissionable kind to make "enriched" material that is over 90% fissionable. (Natural uranium is only 0.7% fissionable.)

The major treaty for controlling the spread of nuclear weapons is the **Nuclear Nonproliferation Treaty (NPT),** signed in 1968 and in force since 1970. Signatories to the treaty who have nuclear weapons—the U.S., Britain and the U.S.S.R.—pledge not to transfer nuclear weapons technology to nonnuclear weapons countries but to share with other countries technology with civilian applications (nuclear power, for example). Nonnuclear signatories pledge not to seek to acquire a weapons-making capability and to accept International Atomic Energy Agency (IAEA) safeguards on their nuclear activities. The purpose of the safeguards is to determine that all nuclear materials are being used for civilian purposes and to sound the alarm if evidence of diversion to a weapons program appears. The nuclear weapons powers also pledge to "pursue negotiations in good faith on effective measures relating to cessation of the nuclear arms race at an early date and to nuclear disarmament...."

Either way, many believe that large military budgets are unhealthy. In the words of the 1980 Report of the Independent Commission on International Development Issues, under the chairmanship of former West German Chancellor Willy Brandt, the "buildup of arms in large parts of the Third World itself causes growing instability and undermines development." Diverting scarce resources to the military leaves too little money and too few trained people to do an adequate job of alleviating poverty, hunger, disease and illiteracy—all of which Third World countries share to a greater or lesser degree. Third World countries as a whole spend almost four times as much on their military establishments as they do on health care, and 50% more than they do on education, according to Ruth Leger Sivard, who has been compiling an annual report on world military and social expenditures for over a decade. And when wars do occur, the consequences for development are devastating.

Although early students of the development process viewed military rule as helpful, many now believe that it distorts the process and makes transition to democratic rule unlikely. Some think that to protect their power and privileges, military or authoritarian regimes are likely to rely on "the weapons and loyalty of security forces...against internal disaffection," in the words of Jagat S. Mehta of the Lyndon Baines Johnson School of Public Affairs at the University of Texas. Some believe they are also more inclined to adventurism abroad. One example cited is Argentina's unsuccessful 1982 invasion of the British-held Falkland Islands. At the time, the military junta was rapidly losing support because of a deepening economic crisis.

A changing market

By the end of the 1980s, sales of weapons to the Third World countries had fallen off. One explanation for the drop is the countries' need to absorb the large quantities of arms bought in the late 1970s. Another is the interest payments on their burdensome debt, which have left many countries with less cash to spend.

In addition, countries that previously imported most of their weapons now have or are acquiring the technology to build their own, and sales of technology are rising. Israel, India and Brazil are producing major conventional weapon systems. Many Third World producers are also selling their wares, mostly to other Third World countries. Their weapons are less sophisticated; they are therefore less expensive, which makes them attractive to many Third World purchasers, who are often more interested in low-technology, combat-proven equipment anyway. Developing nations are also spending more on spare parts, refurbished secondhand weapons and "upgrade kits" to modernize weapons already in their arsenals, rather than buying new ones.

Why produce?

Over 90% of the major weapons built in the Third World are made in just nine countries: Argentina, Brazil, China, India, Israel, the two Koreas, South Africa and Taiwan. Largely as a result of sales to Iran and Iraq during the war, China has recently joined the ranks of the world's major arms exporters, dwarfing other Third World producers.

In its 1986 study on Third World arms production, the Stockholm International Peace Research Institute concluded that a developing country's main reason for establishing its own arms industry was to free itself from dependence on imports from unpredictable suppliers. Israel and South Africa, for example, are both internationally isolated "pariah" states that have faced arms embargoes and other restrictions; both have developed significant, advanced-weapons industries of their own.

Regional ambitions may play a role, as they do in motivating countries to buy arms. Developing nations are also interested in creating high-technology "spin-off" industries, such as electronics and aircraft. Third World countries maintain, too, that they need their own weapons to protect themselves from

T.R. Lansner

Pakistani arms dealer displays his wares.

superpower intervention in their affairs.

The spread of technology

The proliferation of sellers combined with the drop in demand has changed the arms trade significantly: buyers now have more leverage than sellers to cut a good deal. Whereas in the past the U.S. could attach political or economic strings to a sale, buyers can now go elsewhere for many items if they do not like the terms.

In fact, buyers have been able to insist on "sweeteners" that lower their costs. In many cases today, a seller will actually subsidize a sale to a recipient country through an "offset" agreement, in which the seller agrees to accept something the buyer produces as part of the payment.

"Coproduction" agreements have increasingly been incorporated in arms deals: a seller sells not only a weapon system, but also supplies the parts and helps the buyer build it in his own country, or licenses the buyer to produce it. That way a buyer gains the know-how to service the weapons and to build the next generation itself—which is how most Third World arms industries got started. Third World countries also help each other with financing arms projects: Egypt and Iraq are both helping to fund Argentina's Condor missile project.

The black market

The result of such licensing and coproduction agreements is that the technology for producing weapons continues to spread. If political motives get countries started in arms production, economic necessity soon turns them into arms exporters in order to fund their weapons industry. Not all producers feel bound by restrictions on the use of the technology they buy or by internationally agreed-upon embargoes: Israel, for example, is suspected of having violated a mandatory 1977 UN embargo by selling large quantities of weapons to South Africa. Although the Israeli government has denied it, Israeli officials have admitted privately that they need to make sales even in violation of existing agreements in order to fund Israel's defense effort.

The black market for illegal weapons is believed to have grown significantly during the 1980s, although it is impossible to know by how much. Among the principal customers were pariah states like Iran and South Africa that cannot purchase weapons through legitimate channels, as well as terrorist organizations, drug runners and other underground groups. These groups are interested largely in such items as rifles and ammunition, which are easily concealed while in transit.

Coproduction and licensing agreements have contributed to the illegal arms trade because they bring more people into the act. As the number of

private dealers involved in the trade has grown, governments' control over the arms traffic—especially in older, less-advanced equipment—has diminished.

Iran during the war was a prime example: under Operation Staunch, the U.S. boycotted the sale of weapons to Iran and pressured American allies to follow suit. The U.S. and Soviet Union also cooperated to block the flow of weapons to Iran. But Iran was able to procure large amounts of ammunition and other supplies, some of it illegally. In fact, Iran was able to obtain arms from suppliers in at least 33 nations; sellers in 28 countries supplied both sides of the conflict.

Spreading disaster

SIPA

The effects of chemical weapons: Halabjah, Iraq, 1988.

THE SPREAD of conventional weapons throughout the Third World has been accompanied by a growth in the number of nuclear powers and a rise in the spread—and use—of chemical weapons.

Israel, South Africa, Pakistan and India are the so-called threshold countries that could become full-fledged nuclear powers in the near future. None has signed the Nuclear Nonproliferation Treaty (NPT) or joined the International Atomic Energy Agency (IAEA) and submitted to the safeguards process; all are believed to have the capability to produce nuclear weapons. Pakistan and India officially deny the intent to build them; Israel has maintained a policy of deliberate ambiguity on the subject,

saying only that it "will not be the first to introduce nuclear weapons into the Middle East." More recently, however, it has implied that it would use nuclear weapons in response to a chemical attack. Israel is reported to be working on a thermonuclear weapon.

India conducted a nuclear explosion in 1974, which technically makes it a nuclear power according to the terms of the NPT, even though it says the explosion was a peaceful one. It is also reported to be working on a thermonuclear weapon. Although neither India nor Pakistan is believed to be stockpiling nuclear weapons, both are assumed to have enough materials and know-how to construct and test several dozen on short notice.

Brazil, Argentina, Iraq and North Korea have unsafeguarded nuclear reactors which could be used for weapons research programs; Brazil and Argentina can already produce nuclear weapons material. Iran and Libya are also believed to have ambitions.

All of these countries, along with another dozen or more, are working on acquiring or even learning to build sophisticated bombers and ballistic missiles with which to deliver nuclear weapons over long distances. India tested a ballistic missile with a 1,500-mile range in May 1989. Even without nuclear warheads, ballistic missiles are dangerous: their use by Iraq in the Persian Gulf war caused civilian casualties 300 miles from the front. Saudi Arabia's 1988 purchase of huge Chinese missiles gives it the ability to hit Israel or even the Soviet Union with a heavy dose of explosive power.

Third World countries that now have the technology to produce ballistic missiles probably also know how to make chemical weapons. Egypt, Syria, both Koreas, Israel and Libya are all suspected of having chemical weapons; both Iran and Iraq used them during the Persian Gulf war. Iraq's use of chemical weapons against Kurds living in the northern Iraqi city of Halabjah in March 1988 killed an estimated 3,000-5,000 people. Libya allegedly now has the largest chemical weapons factory in the Third World, which by January 1989 was reportedly capable of producing 40 tons of nerve gas a month, according to U.S. intelligence sources.

Controlling the spread

Efforts to restrict the proliferation of weapons and the technology for producing them, if they are to succeed, depend on a considerable level of agreement among a large number of actors. That kind of agreement has proved elusive even within the U.S. government and between the U.S. and its allies, let alone between the U.S. and the Soviet Union or between sellers and potential Third World buyers.

Nonproliferation efforts have been most successful with nuclear weapons, on which the largest number of players seem to agree, and least successful for conventional weapons, on which there is a huge divergence of views. Chemical weapons fall in between.

Safeguards

The U.S. has been interested in controlling the spread of nuclear weapons since 1945, but U.S.-Soviet differences over how to do so stalled progress for over a decade. The logjam was broken with the founding of IAEA, which went into operation in 1957. Although IAEA safeguards have generally worked well in monitoring what is done with nuclear material imported for civilian use, countries that have developed their own nuclear facilities with an eye toward building a weapons program—like India, Pakistan and Argentina—have by and large not assented to IAEA inspections.

The 1968 NPT expanded the safeguards process and added provisions for sanctions against signatories who are found to have violated the treaty's provisions. Again, the problem is that those states that have refused to sign the agreement are the same ones that are known to have or suspected of having or being close to possessing nuclear weapons: Israel, Pakistan, South Africa, Argentina, Brazil and India.

As of mid-1989, 141 countries had signed the treaty. While most Western countries believe that the treaty should be extended for an indefinite time period when it comes up for renewal in 1995, many Third World voices object that the treaty discriminates against the

©1989 Mike Luckovich, *Times-Picayune*

nuclear have-nots. They also argue that the nuclear weapon countries have not held up their end of the bargain, which requires them to make serious efforts to disarm. Many point to the lack of a comprehensive test ban (underground testing is still legal) as a symbol of the superpowers' unwillingness to divest themselves of their nuclear weapons.

Chemical-weapons control

Chemical-weapon-control efforts began before World War I. The use of gas in that war led to the 1925 Geneva Protocol. Although it was widely observed for several decades, violations have increased over the past 20 years. Chemical weapons—the "poor man's atomic bomb"—are not that difficult to make; violations are hard to police since many of the same chemicals that make weapons can also make legitimate products; chemical sales are highly profitable; and the Geneva Protocol contains no enforcement mechanism.

Multilateral negotiations on a convention that would outlaw chemical weapons completely have been in progress at the 40-nation United Nations Conference on Disarmament in Geneva off and on for 20 years. In 1985, 19 chemical-producing nations banded together to form the Australia Group and agreed to restrict the export of materials critical to chemical-weapons production. But the signatories dis-

agreed over what materials should be covered, and not all were equally committed to reaching a consensus.

In January 1989, 149 nations met in Paris and adopted a document reaffirming their commitment to the Geneva Protocol and calling for redoubled efforts toward a comprehensive ban on "development, production, stockpiling and use of all chemical weapons," and for their destruction.

But problems remain. The most serious is verifying compliance with a ban because it is so hard to tell the difference between a chemical plant and a chemical-weapons factory. It would be relatively quick and simple to remove all evidence of weapons production before an inspection, say experts.

Political obstacles are likely to prove even more intractable. At the 1989 Paris conference, Arab countries demanded the right to keep their chemical weapons until Israel gets rid of its nuclear arms (the conference rejected the demand). Other Third World nations objected to Western efforts to stop the proliferation of chemical weapons while some among them, including the U.S., are continuing to produce them.

CATT and the MTCR

Talks on conventional arms transfers and ballistic missiles have made the least progress of all.

Although there is a ballistic Missile Technology Control Regime (see box), it is a voluntary agreement lacking collective enforcement and verification means. Neither the U.S.S.R. nor China is a party to the agreement, nor are any Third World producers, many of whom find the regime discriminatory.

The Carter Administration initiated the Conventional Arms Transfer Talks (CATT) with the Soviet Union in 1977 in the hope that if the two biggest conventional arms sellers could agree to adopt restraints, they could convince other arms exporters to do so as well. By July 1978, the superpowers had agreed that a transfer-limits arrangement should contain provisions for deciding what types of governments should and should not be eligible to receive arms, what sorts and quantities of arms should be transferred, and procedures for implementing such an agreement. Quarreling within the Carter Administration and deteriorating relations with Moscow led the U.S. to abandon the talks by 1979, and they have never been resumed. An early

Reagan statement indicated that the U.S. would "not jeopardize its own security needs through a program of unilateral restraint."

Third World put-down?

Within the Third World, conventional arms control has by and large been viewed with suspicion and hostility. Third World countries have condemned efforts to control supplies as discriminatory, designed to keep the have-nots from joining the elite club of haves. Krishnaswami Subrahmanyam, director of India's Institute for Defense Studies, argues that the industrialized world sees the growing military capabilities of developing nations "as a potential challenge to the world order dominated by the present set of developed countries; hence the excessive and somewhat distorted focus on military spending by the developing countries in the strategic literature of the industrialized world." Third World countries resent the suggestion that they buy arms

for prestige instead of genuine security reasons. They point out that, among other things, the developing world needs to protect itself against the tendency of the superpowers to extend their own quarrels to the Third World and to intervene in other countries' affairs.

South Americans have demonstrated some interest in a regional agreement to limit arms transfers ever since an arms race got under way there in the late 1960s. When the rising price of oil triggered an economic crisis in 1973–74, countries were eager to lower military spending. At a conference held in Ayacucho, Peru, in 1974, Argentina, Bolivia, Chile, Colombia, Ecuador, Panama, Peru and Venezuela agreed on the general need for limiting the acquisition of offensive weapons and lowering arms spending. But efforts to build on the declaration with concrete agreements failed because of differences among signatories and Brazil's refusal to participate.

U.S. arms-transfer policy

THE U.S. HAS STRONGLY supported nuclear nonproliferation efforts over the years. It has used its influence to press nonsignatories to join the NPT and IAEA, and it convinced Taiwan in 1988 to abandon a nuclear program of potential military significance. Washington has also successfully pushed for tightening restrictions on the export of nuclear technology and expanding the safeguards process.

A question of priorities

Critics charge, however, that the U.S. has weakened the nonproliferation regime by not pressing two of its allies, Israel and Pakistan, hard enough on the issue of proliferation. Israel, which is believed to have had a nuclear weapons capability since 1968, has never faced sanctions from the U.S. because of its nuclear program because Washington considers its alliance with and support for Israel crucial to the preservation of U.S. interests in the Middle East. Pakistan, which probably crossed the nuclear threshold in 1986, lost U.S. mili-

tary assistance only temporarily in 1979 and 1987 because of its nuclear program.

Despite the Symington Amendment to the 1985 Foreign Assistance Act, requiring annual certification that Pakistan does not possess any nuclear weapons in order to receive U.S. aid, the Bush Administration is going ahead with plans to provide Pakistan with a six-year $4 billion aid package, and is considering the sale of 60 F-16 jet fighters to the government of Pakistani Prime Minister Benazir Bhutto as well. In this case, withdrawing American aid would have conflicted with the U.S. goal of supporting the Afghan mujahideen against the Soviet occupation, an effort in which Pakistan was playing a key role. Since the Soviet withdrawal from Afghanistan in February 1989, Bush and Bhutto have continued to cooperate on seeking a political settlement in Afghanistan that will permit some 3.5 million Afghan refugees in Pakistan to go home.

On chemical weapons, President

Bush has made achieving a comprehensive ban on production, stockpiling and use a priority of his Administration, although he continues to have doubts about how verifiable a total ban would be. The Administration said in May 1989 that "in principle" it would approve legislation imposing sanctions on countries that use chemical weapons or help other countries to build them. In the meantime, the U.S. is now making "binary" weapons, which do not become lethal until their two chemical components are combined. The components are stored separately, unlike older stocks, and are therefore safer. The U.S. is now in the process of destroying the older weapons.

The Bush Administration has been actively talking about chemical-weapons control with the Soviet Union, which first admitted it had chemical weapons in 1987, but far fewer than Western estimates suggested. Since then, the two sides have reached agreement on the need for on-site inspections as part of any treaty. At the UN in September 1989, Bush suggested that both superpowers cut their stockpiles to one fifth of present U.S. levels as a spur to the multilateral negotiations going on in Geneva. The U.S. has stated that within eight years of a Geneva treaty, it would destroy most of its remaining stockpile, leaving only 2% to deter use by any nonsignatory country. The Soviet Union countered with an offer to stop producing chemical weapons immediately and to begin destroying all stockpiles if the U.S. would halt production of its binary weapons.

Washington and Moscow have also agreed to work toward limiting the spread of ballistic missiles. Where much remains to be done is in the area of conventional weapons sales; although the Soviet Union has said it is willing to restart the CATT talks, the U.S. has not expressed interest in resuming them.

Options

The volume of arms bought and produced by the Third World has dropped in recent years. What, if anything, can the U.S do to ensure that this trend continues?

❏ **1. Restrict sales of weapons and the technology to build them.** The U.S. should encourage the resumption of talks on conventional-arms transfers and on tightening the MTCR, and should work toward involving a larger number of countries—both buyers and sellers—in both sets of talks. In the meantime, the U.S. must take unilateral steps to restrict sales of weapons, components and related technology to the Third World, especially to volatile regions and to repressive regimes which could use them against their own citizens, urges Michael T. Klare, director of the Five College Program in Peace and World Security Studies in Amherst, Mass. Even if increasing numbers of weapons are not the cause of wars, they do seem to prolong conflicts and to increase their destructiveness. Wars not only hurt the countries involved, but they are dangerous to U.S. political and economic interests. The leverage the U.S. once had through the sale of weapons was never long-lasting, according to Klare, and structural changes in the arms trade have weakened that leverage considerably.

Political scientist Stephanie G. Neu-

man of Columbia University disagrees and believes that arms sales give the U.S. significant leverage. Because the superpowers continue to dominate arms sales—particularly in sophisticated equipment—joint U.S. and Soviet restraint can limit the supplies of weapons combatants obtain. Neuman notes that security assistance programs have served the U.S. well: they have provided the U.S. with influence in distant spots without the direct involvement of U.S. military forces.

❏ **2. Stop producing binary chemical weapons.** If the U.S is serious about stopping the spread of chemical weapons, it should begin at home; its failure to cancel production of its own new chemical weapons will feed the widespread Third World conviction that nonproliferation attempts are discriminatory. Now that the U.S. and U.S.S.R. agree on the need for on-site inspection, they should take the lead and sign a bilateral chemical-weapons agreement.

The Administration has insisted on keeping its options open because of the difficulties in verifying a total chemical-weapons ban. If the U.S. is to have a reliable and safe deterrent against other countries' chemical weapons, it needs to replace its current stockpile with safer binary weapons.

❏ **3. Work toward a comprehensive test ban (CTB) on nuclear weapons.** The major objection of Third World countries, both those that have and those that have not signed the NPT, is that the U.S. and the other nuclear powers have not dismantled their own nuclear arsenals. Even strategic-arms agreements between the superpowers

do not preclude the testing and development of new and more dangerous weapons. A CTB would be a first and significant sign to the nonnuclear states that it is safe to give up their own aspirations to nuclear weapons.

The U.S. government, however, has consistently argued that as long as nuclear weapons exist, testing is needed to ensure the safety and reliability of the American nuclear deterrent. Government sources have also expressed doubt that they could adequately monitor whether other countries were refraining completely from nuclear testing.

★ ★ ★

The U.S. cannot stop the spread of weapons to the Third World without the help of other industrialized nations—and of Third World countries themselves. What can it do to encourage others' restraint?

Opinion Ballot
⏩ **on page 94** ⏩

FOR DISCUSSION

1. There are two conflicting views of the relationship between arms sales and war: (a) arms sales to the Third World increase the likelihood of and destructiveness of wars, and (b) weapons do not create wars; wars create a demand for weapons. Which do you agree with? Can you cite examples to support your conviction?

2. Do you think that U.S. arms sales are more often useful or more often counterproductive in the pursuit of U.S. foreign policy goals? Can you give examples?

3. Third World countries have resisted most efforts by developed nations to restrict their access to military technology or weapons on the grounds that they are discriminatory. Do you think that they are right to do so?

4. What steps, if any, could the U.S. and other industrialized countries take to persuade Third World nations to spend less on their military establishments?

5. Do you think the U.S. should be more consistent in applying sanctions against the spread of nuclear capabilities, even if it means angering close allies like Israel? Why or why not?

6. What guidelines would you suggest to determine what governments should be allowed to buy U.S. arms? Anyone who can afford to pay? Only those who need weapons for self-defense? Only democratically elected governments? Others?

7. U.S. arms manufacturers complain that, in the absence of a multilateral agreement to limit arms transfers, American refusal to sell arms to a country usually means more business for another seller with fewer scruples. Should there be a free market in arms? Why or why not?

8. Selling weapons to other countries is often cited as a way to keep weapons costs down: producing more and selling some means a lower price per unit. What do you think of this rationale?

9. Do you agree or disagree with the Bush Administration's decision to go ahead with production of new binary chemical weapons? Why or why not?

10. Do you believe the U.S. should negotiate and sign a comprehensive test ban on nuclear weapons? Why or why not?

SUGGESTED READINGS

Bartholomew, Reginald, "U.S. Efforts Against the Spread of Chemical Weapons." **Department of State Bulletin,** September 1989, pp. 74–77. Statement of the undersecretary of state for security assistance, science and technology before a congressional committee, June 1989.

Klare, Michael T., **American Arms Supermarket.** Austin, University of Texas Press, 1984. 312 pp. $12.95 (paper). History of U.S. arms-sales policy and recommendations for change.

_____,"Deadly Convergence: The Perils of the Arms Trade." **World Policy Journal,** Winter 1988–89, pp. 141–68. Argues for multilateral action, led by the superpowers, to negotiate limits to transfers of conventional arms and technology.

Laurance, Edward J., "The New Gunrunning." **Orbis,** Spring 1989, pp. 225–37. Background on the black market in weapons, by political scientist, formerly with ACDA.

"Look What I Found in My Backyard." **The Economist** (London), May 27, 1989, pp. 44–45. Spread of ballistic missiles in the Third World and implications.

Neuman, Stephanie G., "Arms, Aid and the Superpowers." **Foreign Affairs,** Summer 1988, pp. 1044–66. Columbia University professor argues that the superpowers retain considerable control over the arms trade.

_____, "The Arms Market: Who's On Top?" **Orbis,** Fall 1989, pp. 509–29. Review of recent trends in the arms trade.

"The New Face of War," **World Press Review,** March 1989, pp. 11–21. Articles from around the world about chemical weapons.

Pierre, Andrew J., **The Global Politics of Arms Sales.** Princeton, N.J., Princeton University Press for the Council on Foreign Relations, 1982. 352 pp. $11.95 (paper). Background on the international arms market.

Smith, Gerard C., and Cobban, Helena, "A Blind Eye to Nuclear Proliferation." **Foreign Affairs,** Summer 1989, pp. 53–70. Background on U.S. proliferation policy, with special attention to Pakistan and Israel.

Spector, Leonard S., "New Players in the Nuclear Game." **Bulletin of the Atomic Scientists,** January/February 1989, pp. 29–32. Update on nuclear proliferation by expert at the Carnegie Endowment for International Peace.

For further in-depth reading, write for the Great Decisions 1990 Bibliography (see page 4).

6.

UNITED NATIONS

NEW LIFE FOR AN AGING INSTITUTION?

AFTER DECADES of declining influence and growing skepticism among its member countries, the United Nations has once again been thrust into the center stage of international relations. A string of conflict-resolution and peacekeeping successes, as well as the sustained efforts and accomplishments of some of its specialized agencies, has given the UN new respectability and recognition. As Secretary General Javier Pérez de Cuéllar has noted, there seems to have been "a return to the earlier hope that greeted the birth of the world organization."

The UN's list of achievements over the past two years is indeed impressive. The UN in 1988 alone:

❖ helped to expedite the withdrawal of Soviet troops from Afghanistan;

❖ brokered a cease-fire in the 10-year war between Iran and Iraq;

❖ oversaw agreements between South Africa, Cuba and Angola that provided for the independence of Namibia and the removal of Cuban troops from the region;

❖ launched a peace initiative to end the war for control of the Western Sahara fought by Morocco and the Algerian-backed Polisario guerrilla movement;

❖ brought Greece and Turkey to the bargaining table on the question of unifying the island of Cyprus; and,

❖ received the Nobel Peace Prize in recognition of its peacekeeping efforts in some of the world's most troubled areas.

For longtime UN-watchers, the organization's recent successes come as no surprise. To them, these accomplishments represent the culmination of years of quiet but determined diplomacy. As Edward C. Luck, president of the United Nations Association of the United States of America (UNA-USA), points out, the opening of peace negotiations or the final signing of an armistice are not the organization's major achievements. "People say that the UN is working better and therefore it's doing good things," says Luck. "But we should not overrate the changes by pretending that it was a bad UN before and now all of a sudden it's good. The secretary-general has been doing the same kind of work through all those lean years when everyone said the UN wasn't doing anything."

New York City: UN member flags with General Assembly and glass façade of Secretariat in background.

United Nations

Renewed superpower interest

At the beginning of the 44th General Assembly in September 1989, President George Bush—himself a former U.S. permanent representative to the UN—noted that the organization is an international forum with the potential to do great things. "The UN," said the President, "is moving closer to that ideal."

Bush's remarks echoed similar sentiments expressed earlier by both former U.S. President Ronald Reagan and Soviet President Mikhail S. Gorbachev. In 1988, Reagan said the U.S. was "determined that the UN should succeed and serve the cause of peace for humankind." At the 1988 Communist party conference in Moscow, Gorbachev predicted that "a universal system of international security will take shape, primarily through enhancing the role and effectiveness of the UN."

The renewed superpower interest in the UN reflects a growing realization that finding solutions for today's problems will require greater international cooperation. According to Richard N. Gardner, a professor of international law at Columbia University, a former deputy assistant secretary of state for international organization affairs under the Kennedy and Johnson Administrations and ambassador to Italy, the superpower leaders are moving toward a policy of multilateral cooperation because of a common realization that it is the best means for resolving certain regional conflicts and such "transborder" problems as global warming and weapons proliferation.

"There is a new spirit in Moscow and Washington," claims Gardner. "Multilateralism is now *realpolitik*."

"You need multilateral solutions for today's problems," agrees the UNA's Luck. "It's a pragmatic, not an ideological point of view."

It is widely accepted that without the support of the superpowers none of the UN's recent successes would have been possible. The new cooperative spirit now evident in both the U.S. and the Soviet Union is truly a dramatic reversal from a trend toward unilateral action that had been growing since the early 1970s.

In the 1950s and early 1960s, the UN was primarily a Western-led organization. As the decolonization process, which began in the early 1950s

United Nations

Javier Pérez de Cuéllar

and was strongly supported by the U.S., gathered momentum, newly independent Third World nations soon constituted a majority in the General Assembly. These countries tended to use the UN as a forum for airing grievances against the industrialized West, especially the U.S., making it increasingly difficult for Americans to view the institution in a favorable light. By the early 1980s, most American policymakers had come to see the UN as an impediment to U.S. policy goals.

The Soviet Union, on the other hand, long played the role of a "spoiler" at the UN, taking frequent advantage of its veto power to block U.S. and Western initiatives and disrupting orderly procedure in a variety of ways. Many Americans can vividly recall the 1960 address to the General Assembly of then Soviet Premier Nikita S. Khrushchev, during which he hammered on a table with his shoe. Though the Soviet Union has never dominated the General Assembly in the way the U.S. once did, by aligning with the more-radical Third World nations it was often able to use their anti-U.S. sentiments to its advantage.

Most analysts agree that the shift in superpower policies toward the UN dates from Gorbachev's "new thinking" in foreign policy. In a 1987 article in the official Communist party newspaper, *Pravda,* Gorbachev called for the UN to become more active on a wide range of issues, including regional-conflict resolution and other areas in which the Soviet Union had traditionally opposed UN involvement.

Limitations

Of course, the success or failure of the UN does not rest solely on the attitudes of the U.S. and the Soviet Union. The organization now includes 159 countries, over 80% of them developing nations that consider themselves to be nonaligned. All are represented in the General Assembly, where each nation has one vote.

The Security Council, which has primary responsibility within the UN for maintaining international peace and security, is comprised of five permanent members (Britain, China, France, the Soviet Union and the U.S.), each of which has veto power over all substantive decisions, and 10 nonpermanent members elected by the General Assembly for two-year terms.

Because of its structure, the UN's ability to achieve the goals of international peace and security, respect for human rights and economic and social progress as expressed in its Charter has met with limited success. No permanent member of the Security Council, for example, would hesitate to veto a resolution that it believed was contrary to its own policy goals. At the same time, the resolutions passed by the General Assembly may be approved by a large majority but they are nonbinding. Without the approval of the five permanent members they are unlikely to be translated into action. Thus, because the UN works best when there is a consensus, the organization sometimes has difficulty responding effectively, especially in crisis situations.

Even when a consensus for action is reached, the UN is hobbled by the lack of an enforcement mechanism. For example, if a country refuses to allow peacekeeping forces on its territory or persists in human-rights violations, there is little the secretary-general or any other UN official can do to force compliance. As Seymour M. Finger, a senior fellow at the Ralph Bunche Institute and a former ambassador with the U.S. permanent mission to the UN, points out, the secretary-general has no troops and a budget that is only about one thousandth the size of that of the U.S. government, about $885 million a year.

"So," says Finger, "the success of the UN depends on the attitudes of governments. When governments are willing to cooperate, the UN can be very successful."

Despite its limitations, the UN has managed to function for 45 years. Not only has it brokered peace agreements and stationed peacekeeping forces around the globe, but it has also adopted declarations on a wide variety of issues, ranging from *apartheid* to decolonization, disarmament and human rights, and held conferences on such diverse subjects as the law of the sea, the human environment, food, population and the status of women.

From the ashes of war

During the 20th century, fear of the destructiveness of modern warfare and the desire for peace through collective security have tempered international relations. Following World War I, in which 11 million people died and 21 million were wounded, the League of Nations was established at the initiative of President Woodrow Wilson.

The League represented a multilateral attempt to create a mechanism to promote the peaceful settlement of disputes between nations. Headquartered in Geneva, Switzerland, the League's structure was similar to that of the UN, with an assembly, composed of representatives of all member states; a council of representatives from the leading Allied powers; a secretariat or executive body presided over by a secretary-general; and the Permanent Court of International Justice. One of the League's main purposes was to enforce the terms of the Treaty of Versailles (1919).

The U.S. Senate—bowing to isolationist sentiments of the day—refused to ratify U.S. membership, seriously weakening the League. Though it continued to function throughout the 1920s and most of the 1930s, the outbreak of World War II in 1939 brought an end to the League's activities. The war, which took 60 million lives, proved to be the most expensive and destructive conflict in human history. In 1944, as the war began to wind down, President Franklin D. Roosevelt hosted a meeting of the Big Four powers (Britain, China, the Soviet Union, and the U.S.) at Dumbarton Oaks, an estate in Washington, D.C., to lay the foundation for a postwar international order.

Despite differences that existed even then between the Soviet Union and the other three countries, the Dumbarton Oaks proposals formed the basis of the UN Charter, adopted at the San Francisco Conference on June 26, 1945. The Charter was signed by 50 nations. Poland was not present at the conference but was allowed to join as the 51st founding member.

Unlike the League of Nations, the UN, headquartered in New York City, enjoyed wide support in the U.S. and its Charter was quickly ratified by the Senate. The preamble to the UN Charter encompassed many of the ideals that Americans believe in and for which they had fought. Reflecting the postwar division of power, the Charter gave a power of veto to the Big Four nations plus France.

Shattered hopes

The expectations raised in San Francisco were soon disappointed. Almost from the onset, East-West conflicts dominated and divided the UN, beginning with the presence of Soviet troops in northern Iran in 1946. During the next few years tensions between the U.S. and the Soviet Union erupted elsewhere—Greece, Eastern Europe, Berlin, Korea and China, where in 1949 Soviet-backed Communists defeated U.S.-backed Nationalists, who fled to Taiwan.

By 1950, the cold war—as the East-West ideological confrontation came to be called—was raging. When Communist North Korea attacked South Korea, the UN was able to take collective action only because the Soviet Union was boycotting the Security Council because of its failure to seat the Chinese Communists. The UN's expeditionary force of troops from 16 nations, led by the U.S., was soon engulfed in a full-scale war that lasted three years.

The cold war, with varying intensity, went on for decades. The hopes for a forceful and independent world body that could resolve conflicts and defuse tensions were shattered by the recriminations and superpower maneuvering of the 1950s and 1960s. In many instances, such as the Soviet invasion of Hungary in 1956 and the U.S. involvement in Vietnam from 1964 to 1975, the UN played little or no part in shaping events.

The Third World

Prior to World War II, much of what is now called the Third World (a designation for poor, developing countries, mostly located in the southern hemisphere) remained in the hands of a few major European powers, principally Britain and France. Both countries controlled colonies in Asia, the Middle East, northern and sub-Saharan Africa and the Caribbean. The war and the cost of rebuilding their economies after the war made it difficult for the Europeans to continue administering their colonies. This, coupled with growing nationalist sentiments throughout the world, sparked a broad-based movement toward decolonization. It reached its peak in the early 1960s, when many countries, especially in Africa, achieved independence.

Refugees in Ethiopia, a founding member of the UN, receive assistance from Unicef and other international agencies.

The decolonization process had a profound effect on UN membership. From 1946 through 1950, the UN added only nine new members. In 1955, however, an additional 16 members were added. In 1960, 17 new countries, 16 of them African, became members. By 1964, total membership had reached 115.

The burgeoning Third World membership altered the agenda and the voting patterns of the General Assembly. In 1960, the General Assembly adopted the Declaration on the Granting of Independence to Colonial Countries and Peoples, over the stiff opposition of the main colonial powers. After 1960, it concentrated heavily on issues such as black-majority rule in southern Africa, the Arab-Israeli conflict and economic disparities between the developing South and the industrial North.

In the Middle East, the secretary-general and the Security Council took an early lead in the search for a peaceful solution to regional conflict by proposing terms for the partition of Palestine in 1947. In 1949 the General Assembly established the UN Relief and Works Agency for Palestine Refugees in the Near East.

Since the 1967 Arab-Israeli war, the majority in the General Assembly has tended to be stridently anti-Israel. In 1975, for example, the General Assembly passed a resolution equating Zionism with racism, a move which deeply offended the U.S. and most of the other Western powers. Every year since 1982 the General Assembly has voted on a procedural motion to include on the agenda the lifting of Israel's credentials for participating in the General Assembly. (In 1989, only 37 countries voted in favor—down from 41 in 1988—while 95 voted against.)

New economic order

Since 1960, economic discussions at the UN have centered on strategies and programs to promote Third World development. In the early years, North-South economic debates concentrated on economic and technical aid. The focus shifted in 1964 to trade with the convening of the first UN Conference on Trade and Development (Unctad). At the meeting a group of developing countries formed the so-called Group of 77 (which now has 127 members).

Their purpose was to present a unified bargaining position in the face of the richer countries of the North.

With the prodding of the Group of 77, the General Assembly attempted to address the disparity in wealth between the rich and poor nations. In 1974, the General Assembly adopted the Declaration on the Establishment of a New International Economic Order (NIEO), based on "equity, sovereign equality, interdependence, common interest and

Karsh, Ottawa
Dag Hammarskjöld

cooperation among all states…," and a program of action with which the developing countries hoped to achieve greater control over their natural resources and, ultimately, a greater share of the economic pie.

Many analysts thought that faster Third World economic growth would help create new markets and thus lead to greater economic activity on a global scale. It was also believed that improving living standards in developing countries would ease such problems as population growth and political unrest. Nonetheless, the U.S. and several European nations opposed the NIEO's call for expropriation of foreign investment without compensation in accordance with international law, the approval of commodity cartels, price indexing and

other measures viewed as restricting international economic activity.

By 1975, both the U.S. and the European Economic Community had, at least in principle, accepted some of the declaration's concepts. However, attempts to implement the new economic order were frustrated by global events, such as the sharp increase in the price of oil in 1979–80, the second in six years, and the deep worldwide recession of the early 1980s, which greatly reduced the demand for Third World commodities. In the past few years, the NIEO has been shelved as developing nations searched for more pragmatic ways to solve their economic problems.

Structural problems

Apart from the larger, global tensions, UN headquarters has been beset by a number of internal difficulties. One criticism that has frequently been leveled at the UN staff is that its leadership has been weak and often ineffective. When Pérez de Cuéllar became secretary-general in 1981, he inherited from his predecessor, the Austrian Kurt Waldheim, a UN headquarters with over 13,500 staff members. Since 1986, as the result of a budgetary and administrative-reform package pushed by the U.S. and other major donors and approved by the General Assembly, the secretary-general has managed to trim the staff by 13% and strengthened his personal control over UN peacemaking diplomacy and other critical areas.

The Secretariat (as the headquarters staff is known) was meant to be an international civil service. According to Article 100 of the UN Charter, neither the secretary-general nor his staff should "seek or receive instructions from any government or from any other authority external to the organization." In practice, however, the Secretariat soon became politicized at all levels and in nearly every aspect of its work, with member countries openly lobbying for specific jobs and attempting to influence their nationals in the Secretariat in the conduct of their work.

This "politicization" of the Secretariat severely hampered the secretary-general's ability to develop a staff capable of operating independently of member governments. In addition, member countries have often been accused of recommending people to the Secretariat who lack the necessary credentials and training to perform their duties. As Finger wrote in 1975, the UN has "never hired the cream of the crop," but instead "has settled perhaps too easily for average quality personnel," an assessment which many analysts argue is still true today.

Weak leadership

Criticism has been leveled not only at the staff, but also at the selection of the secretary-general. According to Shirley Hazzard, an American journalist who has written extensively about the UN, even from its earliest days the major powers seemed content with appointing to the position individuals who could be easily influenced, rather than those who would take seriously the Charter's mandate for establishing an independent civil service.

The first secretary-general, Norwegian Trygve Lie (1946–53), was forced to resign by the Soviet Union because of his support of UN intervention in the Korean War. As Lie's successor, Dag Hammarskjöld (1953–61) managed to bring a measure of both prestige and independence to the job, though in the process he so alienated the Soviet Union that, shortly before his death, it called for replacing the position with a three-person directorate. Hammarskjöld, a Swede, was succeeded by U Thant (1961–71), a Burmese, whose tenure coincided with the Vietnam War. U.S. opposition to UN involvement in resolving the war tied U Thant's hands and underscored one of the UN's weaknesses.

Under Austrian Kurt Waldheim (1972–81) the Secretariat became a larger and even more unwieldy bureaucracy than it had been previously. In 1981, Waldheim's bid for an unprecedented third term—for which he lobbied heavily—was blocked only by a veto from the People's Republic of China. Both the U.S. and the Soviet Union, seeing Waldheim as a "pliable" secretary-general, had favored his reelection.

Pérez de Cuéllar, who first came to the UN in 1971 as Peru's permanent representative, has brought back to the office of secretary-general much of the prestige and prominence it enjoyed in Hammarskjöld's time.

The UN's long agenda

DESPITE ITS MANY shortcomings, the UN as well as its agencies has managed to pursue a broad and fairly successful agenda during its 45 years. Key among its many activities have been peacekeeping, development, disarmament, promotion of human rights and the welfare of children.

Peacemaking and peacekeeping. Of the long list of UN objectives, peacemaking and peacekeeping remain preeminent. Peacemaking refers to the providing of a forum for debate and negotiation and a channel for quiet diplomacy to help resolve international conflicts. Peacekeeping refers to the use of observers or military forces to prevent a return to armed hostilities once a cease-fire has been achieved. Article 1 of Chapter I of the UN Charter states that the primary purpose of the UN is:

To maintain international peace and security, and to that end: to take effective collective measures for the prevention and removal of threats to the peace, and for the suppression of acts of aggression or other breaches of the peace, and to bring about by peaceful means, and in conformity with the principles of justice and international law, adjustment or settlement of international disputes or situations which might lead to a breach of the peace.

The concept of peacekeeping developed as a means to circumvent the cold-war confrontation among the permanent members of the Security Council, who were reluctant to see one another's troops used for coercive actions. Peacekeeping forces are established either by the Security Council or the General Assembly, usually at the recommendation of the secretary-general. They can only be dispatched with the consent of the warring parties, and must not interfere with the internal affairs of the host country or in any way favor one side in a conflict.

Unlike normal military forces, UN troops are only lightly armed and are prohibited from using force except in self-defense. Their role is limited to keeping warring parties separated in order to reduce tensions and create the climate for the peaceful resolution of conflicts.

Keeping the peace has proven to be no easy chore. According to a report by World Priorities, a nonprofit research organization based in Washington, D.C., during the past 30 years, 81 major wars have been fought and nearly 13 million people have died in them.

The UN's first involvement in peacekeeping came in 1948, when an international team of observers was sent to monitor events in Palestine. Since then, the UN has organized 15 peacekeeping operations, including six observer missions (which operate unarmed) and eight expeditionary forces. Most recently, in 1989, peacekeeping forces were dispatched to Namibia and Nicaragua.

Notwithstanding the recent successes, peacekeeping can often be a frustrating assignment. During the 1960–64 peacekeeping operation in the Congo (now Zaire), for example, UN forces (though they were ultimately credited with preventing the country's breakup) became embroiled in a civil war. Notes Sir Brian Urquhart, former UN under secretary for special political affairs who was known as Mr. Peacekeeper during his time at the Secretariat, "There have been times when the peacekeeping function was more like that of an attendant in a lunatic asylum, and the soldiers had to accept abuse and harassment without getting into physical conflict or emotional involvement with the inmates."

Some notable peacekeeping accomplishments include the UN Emergency Force (UNEF II), that was dispatched to the Suez Canal area during the Egyptian-Israeli conflict of 1973, and the UN Disengagement   Observer   Force

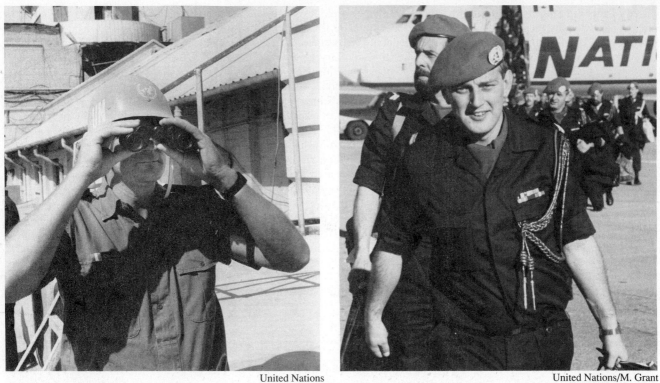

United Nations   United Nations/M. Grant

A member of the UN Iran-Iraq Military Observer Group supervising the cease-fire (l.). UN police monitors from the Netherlands arriving in Namibia to oversee the transition to independence.

(UNDOF), that was sent to monitor a disengagement agreement between Israel and Syria in 1974.

As with most military expeditions, peacekeeping operations are also expensive. Maintaining UN forces in Namibia until the country is granted full independence (scheduled for April 1, 1990), for example, is expected to cost from $500 million to $700 million.

Disarmament. The first resolution adopted by the General Assembly, just months after the U.S. dropped nuclear bombs on the Japanese cities of Hiroshima and Nagasaki, was on disarmament. Over the past four decades, the subject has received continuous attention at the UN, and the original resolution was followed by numerous multilateral treaties limiting the testing and deployment of nuclear weapons. In 1959, for example, the Antarctic Treaty declared the South Pole region a nuclear-weapon-free zone, and in 1967, the treaty on outer space prohibited nuclear and other weapons of mass destruction from being placed in orbit around the earth, on the moon or any of the planets. Between 1967 and 1980, an additional six treaties were signed, ranging from the prohibition of nuclear weapons in Latin America to restric-

tions on certain conventional weapons.

Despite its concern over disarmament, the General Assembly has often adopted resolutions too sweeping for practical application, such as the 1961 call for "general and complete disarmament." What is more, the superpowers have tended to follow their own agenda regarding arms limitations, test bans and disarmament, making multilateral action difficult to achieve. The recent improvement in relations between the U.S. and the Soviet Union, especially in the field of arms negotiations, has been warmly applauded at the UN. In the words of Secretary General Pérez de Cuéllar, "Every person on this earth has a stake in disarmament."

Human rights. As with disarmament, the promotion of human rights has been a major concern for the UN since its earliest years. In 1947, under the chairmanship of Eleanor Roosevelt, the Commission on Human Rights drafted the Universal Declaration of Human Rights. It was approved by the General Assembly on December 10, 1948, a date that has since been annually observed as Human Rights Day. The declaration sets forth the basic rights and freedoms to which all men and women are entitled, including the

right to life, liberty and security of person. It has served as a model for many of the constitutions drafted by new nations.

In nearly every year since 1948, the General Assembly has adopted resolutions, declarations and conventions concerning specific human-rights issues.

The UN's record in dealing with human-rights issues has also been mixed. The UN Commission on Human Rights, comprised of representatives from 43 governments, has in the past shown a high degree of political selectivity, focusing much of its attention on Israel and South Africa, while complaints against other governments were often not discussed. In recent years, however, the Human Rights Commission has shown a greater willingness to address all complaints. In 1989, for example, in its first action against a permanent member of the Security Council, the commission condemned China for suppressing the pro-democracy rally in Beijing's Tiananmen Square.

Development. The UN Charter recognized the importance of promoting social progress and better living standards when it established the UN Economic and Social Council (Ecosoc).

Ecosoc, composed of representatives of 54 member states, meets twice a year and is the principal organ to coordinate the economic and social work of the UN with the specialized agencies and other institutions, including the semiautonomous UN Development Program (UNDP), founded in 1965.

With 5,000 projects worth some $7.5 billion currently being carried out in more than 150 countries, the UNDP is the largest multilateral channel for technical and preinvestment aid. Working with some two dozen UN specialized agencies, the program covers virtually the entire spectrum of economic and social development—from agriculture, industry, power production and transport, to health, housing and education. The UNDP has sent teachers to Botswana, engineers to Nepal, trade specialists to Poland and air-traffic control consultants to Ecuador. Funding for UNDP is provided by voluntary contributions from UN member governments.

Another UN agency that has played an important role in development is the International Bank for Reconstruction and Development (IBRD or World Bank). The World Bank was established in 1944 to promote international investment for the development of productive resources. The bank, which picks up where the UNDP leaves off, offers long-term loans for such major development projects as hydroelectric dams and deep-water ports.

For all the attention devoted to development by the UN and its agencies, progress has been uneven, with the poorest countries in particular lagging far behind. Within the next 40 to 50 years, world population is expected to increase from the present 5 billion to between 8 billion and 14 billion. Most of this increase will be concentrated in already crowded Third World urban areas, which suffer from high levels of disease brought on by contaminated drinking water as well as sewage and waste disposal problems.

Welfare of children. Another area in which the UN early accepted responsibility was that of child welfare. The UN International Children's Emergency Fund (Unicef) was created in 1946 by unanimous vote in the General Assembly. Its original function was to provide emergency assistance to the

destitute young victims of World War II. In 1953, the General Assembly made Unicef's mandate permanent, changing its name to simply the UN Children's Fund (although the acronym Unicef was retained). In 1965, Unicef was awarded the Nobel Peace Prize for "the promotion of brotherhood among the nations."

Since the early 1950s, Unicef has concentrated on finding ways to eliminate the widespread malnutrition, disease and illiteracy afflicting millions of children in the developing world. It prides itself on taking a nonpolitical approach to child welfare and has thus managed to gain access to countries where other UN organizations are not allowed to operate. Unicef provides aid in three major ways: through assistance in the planning and design of services for children; delivery of supplies and equipment for these services; and provision of funds for the training of personnel needed to work with and for children (including teachers, nutritionists, health and sanitation workers, social workers and community leaders). As with the UNDP, funding for Unicef is largely provided by voluntary contributions from governments.

According to UN statistics, 40,000 children worldwide die every day, 95% of preventable causes, and another 40,000 are crippled for life through illness. As grim as these figures are, notes Unicef's executive director James P. Grant, there has been significant improvement in child welfare over the past four decades.

"In the 1950s," says Grant, "70,000 children were dying every day, the vast majority of preventable causes. Forty thousand may still be an unacceptable number, but it is clear that we are making progress."

The specialized agencies. Much of the UN's work is carried on by specialized agencies that are independent of the UN, with their own governing bodies, bylaws, budgets, staffs and memberships. These organizations work with the UN and each other through Ecosoc. Some of the agencies, such as the Universal Postal Union (UPU), predate the founding of the UN by a half-century or more.

Other specialized agencies deal with financial development and monetary issues (IBRD, IDA, IFC, IMF): agriculture (FAO); education, science and culture (Unesco), and many other transborder problems. As with the UN in general, they are sometimes subject to political turmoil. During the 1970s and early 1980s, for example, Unesco took actions that were viewed as hostile by many Western powers, causing the U.S. and other countries to withdraw from the organization.

Milk is distributed to refugee children in Somalia; Ecosoc strongly endorsed the secretary-general's appeal for urgent assistance.

UN Photo/Peter Magubane

Where does the U.S. stand?

DURING ITS EARLY, formative years, the U.S. was the undisputed leader at the UN. U.S. taxpayers picked up 40% of the organization's total costs, and the U.S. and its allies formed a powerful majority. Despite cold-war confrontations and the increasing challenge from newly independent states, support for the UN generally ran high among Americans until the late 1960s. The U.S. position at the UN changed during the Nixon and Ford Administrations, when America—reeling from its defeat in Vietnam—often found itself outvoted and outmaneuvered by an increasingly hostile Third World voting bloc. It was in 1974, for example, that the Palestine Liberation Organization's (PLO) chairman, Yasir Arafat—an avowed enemy of Israel, a U.S. ally—received a warm welcome at the UN. It was also during this period that the nonaligned countries began aggressively promoting the NIEO.

In opposition

In its defense, the U.S. adopted a sharper tone. In a speech before the General Assembly, John A. Scali, the U.S. permanent representative to the UN from 1973 to 1975, criticized the organization for passing "one-sided, unrealistic resolutions that cannot be implemented." Under Scali's successor, Daniel P. Moynihan, who served as permanent representative for only eight months (1975–76), the U.S. adopted a policy of confronting the nonaligned bloc. Incensed by the 1975 Zionism-is-racism resolution, Moynihan responded with a U.S. resolution calling for the release of political prisoners throughout the world—a move calculated to show the hypocrisy of the majority in its selective approach to human rights.

Though much of the drama of those tumultuous years took place in the General Assembly, it is in the Security Council records that the shift in sentiments at the UN can be most accurately measured. Between 1945 and 1970, the Soviet Union cast 105 vetoes in the Security Council, while the U.S. only cast 1. Over the next six years, from 1971 to 1976, the Soviet Union cast 5 vetoes and the U.S., 20. In Moynihan's

words, the U.S. was now "in opposition" at the UN.

During Jimmy Carter's presidency (1977–81), the U.S. struck a conciliatory tone at the UN. Carter appointed Andrew Young as his permanent representative to the UN (1977–79). Young was an outspoken critic of racism who had worked with Dr. Martin Luther King, Jr. in the U.S. civil rights movement of the 1960s. He quickly gained the confidence of many nonaligned countries, especially the Africans, who saw him as a champion of the antiapartheid battle. In the Security Council in 1977, the U.S. voted with the majority for a mandatory arms embargo against South Africa, a move not dreamed of just a few years before.

Young, however, was forced to resign after it was revealed that he had held an unauthorized meeting with a PLO official. He was replaced by Donald McHenry, a young black American who had already distinguished himself as a career diplomat with long UN experience.

The Reagan years

Under President Reagan, the U.S. again went through a period of confrontation at the UN. As his first permanent representative, Reagan chose Jeane J. Kirkpatrick (1981–85), a neoconservative who quickly showed a willingness to confront both the Soviet bloc and the Third World in a manner that was reminiscent of Moynihan.

During the Reagan Administration's first term (1981–85), the U.S. adopted what appeared to many observers to be a more unilateralist approach to foreign policy. Following a Security Council resolution condemning the 1983 U.S. invasion of Grenada, for example, President Reagan is reported to have said that the fact that the U.S. was voted down by eight votes "didn't bother his breakfast one bit." One U.S. official was even quoted as remarking that the UN could "go elsewhere" if it did not like Reagan's policies.

In 1983, the U.S. Congress passed Public Law 98-164, setting several conditions on American participation in the UN. One provision of the law states

that if Israel is illegally denied its credentials at the UN, the U.S. will "suspend its participation in the General Assembly…" Another provision requires that the secretary of state report to Congress each year on the voting record within the General Assembly of each member country, so that Congress can assess a particular country's support of the U.S. when considering requests for military and economic aid.

In 1985, Congress went a step further by passing the Kassebaum amendment, which called for withholding dues to the UN pending cost-cutting and structural reforms within the Secretariat. Since the U.S. is now responsible for 25% of the UN's regular budget (a percentage roughly equal to its share of the combined gross national product of all UN member countries), failure to pay its dues soon put the UN under severe financial constraints. By 1988, the U.S. owed the UN nearly $500 million in back dues and an additional $250 million in arrears for peacekeeping operations (which is also an obligatory payment), prompting Pérez de Cuéllar to warn that the UN would soon have to begin curtailing its activities.

During his second term in office (1985–89), President Reagan's attitude toward the UN changed. In 1985, Ambassador Kirkpatrick, who had softened her tone considerably, was replaced by Vernon Walters, a retired army general and deputy director of the Central Intelligence Agency who was widely admired for his linguistic and diplomatic skills. In September 1988, the President announced that he was releasing $44 million to cover payment of U.S. dues to the UN through the end of that year and pledged to pay off the balance owed.

In 1987, the Soviet Union paid more than $200 million in arrears to the UN, including money promised for past peacekeeping operations. It has an outstanding UN debt of $175 million.

Lost influence

Though many analysts originally viewed the withholding of dues as an effective means of forcing much-needed reforms on the organization, it is generally agreed that the continued failure to make back payments has hurt U.S. prestige and influence. According to Richard Gardner, "A country that owes over half a billion dollars to the world organization is in a weak position to claim its fair share of key Secretariat posts."

John Washburn, a retired U.S. diplomat who now holds a high-level UN post, believes that withholding dues has upset many U.S. allies and could set an unhealthy precedent. "These payments are international legal obligations, not voluntary contributions," says Washburn. "Withholding them is simply not the kind of game that a real leader plays."

So far, President Bush has offered more praise than criticism to the UN. His choice of Thomas R. Pickering—a respected career diplomat with experience in arms negotiations, the Middle East and Central America—as permanent U.S. representative was seen as an indication that the Administration plans to make the organization a high foreign policy priority. The President has adopted the Reagan formula on dues— full payment of the current year's assessment and installment payment of all U.S. dues in arrears. While Congress is expected to fulfill his first request, it may be years before all back debts are paid.

U.S. policy options

In light of the UN's recent achievements and the Soviet Union's changed attitude toward the world body, is a course change in U.S. policy toward the UN in the coming decade called for? The following are just two of the many U.S. policy options.

❏ **1. Make the UN a more important foreign policy priority.** Many analysts believe that the U.S. must focus more official attention on the organization than it has in recent years, since many of the most pressing issues on the U.S. and the global agenda (including drugs, the environment and terrorism) require a multilateral approach. The U.S. should also be more willing to attempt to resolve disputes in the Security Council and the General Assembly. It should also pay its back dues in full, propose only the most qualified candidates to fill staff positions at the Secretariat, and become involved in the ap-

United Nations/J.K. Isaac
Leaders of the UN Interim Force in Lebanon confer on Israeli withdrawal.

pointment of leadership posts of all UN agencies. As one UN-watcher put it, "When was the last time anyone at the White House gave two seconds thought to who should be head of the Food and Agriculture Organization or Unesco?"

Critics argue that despite recent successes, the UN is still a cumbersome vehicle for solving international disputes and the U.S. is often in the minority on issues important to it and its allies. Even if Congress were prepared to come up with funds to pay back dues (given the current U.S. budgetary difficulties, this is unlikely), many—including some members of the Bush Administration—would prefer that the U.S. continue to use its financial leverage to push for further reforms.

❏ **2. Use the UN selectively as one of many avenues for achieving U.S. policy goals.** This option recognizes that some international problems call for a multilateral approach, others are best dealt with in their regional context and still others require unilateral actions. The issue is not whether or not the U.S. should use the UN as a foreign policy tool, but under what circumstances a multilateral approach is in the U.S. best interest. According to Gardner, "neither dogmatic unilateralism nor utopian multilateralism is an appropriate policy for a superpower in a complex and dangerous world."

Proponents of this option argue that the UN is best suited for tackling such transborder issues as controlling the spread of AIDS, environmental pollution and the population explosion, and

that U.S. policy goals can best be served by addressing these issues within the international forum. On the other hand, on some issues—especially sensitive security matters and those where the U.S. has been traditionally at odds with the General Assembly—little would be gained by seeking a UN consensus.

An argument against the selective approach policy is that it could undermine the growing spirit of cooperation within the UN system at a time when the potential for multilateralism has never been greater. Since the Soviet Union has expressed interest in expanding the UN's role in resolving conflicts, the U.S. should be willing to give multilateralism a chance, without placing preconditions on what it will or will not address within the international organization.

★ ★ ★

Just how far the U.S. should go in restoring its support for the UN is a question for debate. Should the organization become a priority for the Bush Administration? If so, what results can be reasonably expected? In what circumstances can the UN be used effectively to promote U.S. foreign policy goals? Should it be used? Or is it better to chart an independent course, relying instead on unilateral actions?

Opinion Ballot
IIII➡ **on page 94** IIII➡

FOR DISCUSSION

1. The UN was founded to promote peace, security and cooperation in solving international problems. In your opinion, has it succeeded in its goals? Has the U.S. benefited from its existence? Or has the UN been an impediment to U.S. policy?

2. Some analysts believe that the U.S. should take a selective approach toward the UN, using the organization to deal with some issues, but reserving the right to take independent action on others. Do you share their view? What arguments can you make in favor of or against such an approach?

3. The U.S. is currently responsible for 25% of the UN budget. In your opinion, does the U.S. pay too much or not enough for what it gets from the UN?

4. During the 1980s the U.S. withheld its UN dues in order to force structural changes on the organization. Do you think this was a good or bad policy? Under what, if any, conditions would you recommend withholding U.S. dues in the future?

5. The UN is increasingly being used to address such transborder issues as global warming and international terrorism. Do you think the organization can deal effectively with such problems? How could the UN enforce its decisions in these matters on uncooperative member nations?

6. In what field do you think the UN is most effective: peacekeeping and peacemaking, economic development and the struggle against poverty, human rights, disarmament, or some other?

7. Mikhail Gorbachev has stressed greater cooperation in the UN at a time when the U.S. has been accused of being the organization's "number one deadbeat." How should the U.S. respond to Gorbachev's "new thinking" toward the UN?

8. Some analysts believe that if the UN did not exist it would have to be invented now. Do you agree? What role do you envisage for the UN in the decade that lies ahead?

SUGGESTED READINGS

Basic Facts about the United Nations. New York, UN Department of Public Information, 1987. 178 pp. $3.00 (paper). Detailed information about the origin, purpose and structure of the UN and its agencies.

Gardner, Richard N., "The Case for Practical Internationalism." **Foreign Affairs,** Spring 1988, pp. 827–45. Former U.S. diplomat argues in favor of a pragmatic approach to greater international cooperation.

Hazzard, Shirley, "Reflections: Breaking Faith." **The New Yorker,** September 25, 1989, pp. 63–99, and October 2, 1989, pp. 74–96. A critical perspective of the five men who have held the post of UN secretary-general.

Luck, Edward C., and Gati, Toby Trister, "Gorbachev, the United Nations, and U.S. Policy." **The Washington Quarterly,** Autumn 1988, pp. 19–35. Excellent discussion on current superpower attitudes toward the UN.

MacLeod, Scott, "A Very Civil Servant." **Time,** December 5, 1988, pp. 50–52. Interview with longtime UN diplomat Sir Brian Urquhart, "Mr. Peacekeeper."

Norton, Augustus Richard, and Weiss, Thomas G., "Burden Sharing: Turning Again to UN Peacekeepers." **The New Leader,** March 20, 1989, pp. 12–14. Discussion of the value of employing UN peacekeeping forces to help resolve regional conflicts.

"Peace on the March." **Time,** September 26, 1988, pp. 34–36. Report on the achievements of UN peacekeeping forces.

"Prospects for a New Era of World Peace." **Department of State Bulletin,** November 1988, pp. 1–8. Includes the text of President Ronald Reagan's final address to the General Assembly, the White House statement on release of U.S. funds for the UN and a joint communiqué by the permanent members of the Security Council.

A Successor Vision: The United Nations of Tomorrow. New York, United Nations Association of the United States of America, 1987. 120 pp. $10.00 (paper). Available through the Publications Department, UNA-USA, 485 Fifth Avenue, New York, NY 10017. Report on the management, governance and role of the UN with recommendations on how to improve its effectiveness.

Tessitore, John, and Woolfson, Susan, eds., **Issues before the 43rd General Assembly of the United Nations.** Lexington, Mass., Lexington Books, 1989. 228 pp. $14.00 (paper). Annual publication presenting background on major topics on UN agenda.

For further in-depth reading, write for the Great Decisions 1990 Bibliography (see page 4).

7.

PALESTINIAN QUESTION

IS THERE A SOLUTION?

THE STRUGGLE to establish an Arab state in Palestine has bedeviled Middle Eastern politics—and international diplomacy—for much of the 20th century and, since the founding of Israel in 1948, has helped fuel five regional wars. The demand by Palestinians—now 5 million strong—for a state of their own has been endorsed by much of the international community. Their fate, however, remains unresolved.

Two decades of occupation of the West Bank and the Gaza Strip, areas which Israel took from Jordan and Egypt, respectively, in the 1967 war, bred an alienated generation that despaired of achieving independence and felt abandoned by their Arab brethren. Since 1985, when Israel began to crack down hard on protesters in the occupied territories, tension has grown. A major uprising, or *intifada,* to use the Arabic term, against Israeli rule broke out in December 1987 and continues to this day.

The Palestine Liberation Organization (PLO), the leading group representing Palestinian interests, buoyed by the international sympathy aroused by the intifada, seized on it to push for statehood. In a major policy reversal, the PLO announced its acceptance of UN Security Council Resolution 242, which calls for trading land for peace. The PLO also recognized Israel's right to exist and renounced terrorism.

The uprising ended the illusion of normalcy on the West Bank and in Gaza, and forced Israelis to rethink their policies. At stake, most Israelis believe, is the very survival of their state. There are, at present, 3.2 million Jews and 750,000 Arabs in Israel, and 1.7 million Palestinians in the territories. Should Israel satisfy Palestinians' longings for "a flag and a passport" in the interests of peace? Or would an

AP/Wide World Photos
Revolt on the West Bank: Palestinian stone-throwers challenge Israeli army.

independent Palestinian state pose an unacceptable danger to Israel and become a hotbed of terrorism? Are there options short of statehood that Palestinians will accept?

By late 1989, both the peace process and the intifada were faltering. Israel could not end the Palestinian uprising, and the Palestinians had been unable to wring any significant concessions out of the Israelis.

The U.S. has long been Israel's most dependable—and occasionally only—supporter in the international community. President Harry S. Truman played a key role in Israel's independence in 1948 by assuring U.S. recognition of the new state. Beginning with Dwight D. Eisenhower and culminating with Jimmy Carter, who brokered the Camp

David accords between Israel and Egypt, American Presidents have attempted to promote peace in the region.

Unlike most U.S. Presidents, George Bush came into office already well-briefed on the issues underlying the Arab-Israeli conflict. Although this Administration's support of Israel appears to be more restrained than Ronald Reagan's, so far the U.S. has not applied pressure on Israel's government to make concessions to the Palestinians.

The Administration's policy is constrained by strong support for Israel in Congress and among the American public. Israel receives $3 billion annually in U.S. military and economic aid. But bilateral relations have come under considerable strain since the intifada began. Television and newspaper accounts of Israeli brutality in the occupied territories have evoked sympathy for the Palestinians, and many American Jews and members of Congress have begun to criticize Israeli policies.

The U.S. faces hard policy choices: whether to press Israel to relinquish the territories or support Israel's claim to the land. U.S. diplomacy helped restore peace to the Middle East after the 1967 and 1973 Arab-Israeli wars. Can it do so again?

Palestinians and Israelis

Palestinians and Israelis both claim the territory between the Mediterranean Sea and the Jordan River as their ancestral home. Each people looks back to a golden age when their culture flourished. Both have known the loss of their homeland and have been sustained by the dream of reclaiming it. Jews and Muslims both revere Jerusalem as one of their holiest sites. During their 2,000 year diaspora (or dispersal), the Jews suffered inquisition, pogroms (organized massacres) and the death of 6 million in the Holocaust. The Palestinians, for their part, recall the exile and hardships suffered at the hands of Israel as well as the Arab states since their diaspora in 1948.

The nature of the struggle by the two sides for a homeland has changed form several times during the 20th century. At first, it pitted Palestinian nationalists against Jewish Zionists. With the birth of Israel in 1948, the conflict changed to one between Israel and the Arab states; since the 1967 war, it has reverted to being primarily a struggle between Israelis and Palestinians.

Painfully aware of their own tragic histories, Israelis and Palestinians have often been indifferent to the other's suffering. Possessed of their own national dreams, each today has great difficulty acknowledging the legitimacy of the other's political claims. The problem is not between a right and a wrong, but between two peoples asserting competing rights to the same land.

A tangled history

During antiquity Palestine was conquered by numerous outsiders, including Egyptians, Assyrians, Babylonians, Persians, Greeks, Seleucids and Romans. According to the Bible, God led the Hebrew tribes out of bondage in Egypt to safety in Palestine, which they called "the land of Israel." Although never the sole occupants of Palestine, the Jews (the word originally meant "one from Judea," the region surrounding Jerusalem) formed lasting ties to the land and were in possession of most of what corresponds to present-day Israel by 1100 B.C. They held power on and off for the next 1,200 years. In A.D. 66 the Jews revolted against Roman rule, and after seven years their rebellion was crushed. Jerusalem was later destroyed and plowed under by the Romans, and most surviving Jews were sold into slavery or otherwise scattered throughout the Roman world.

The Palestinians claim descent from the Canaanites, Philistines and other tribes who were ancient inhabitants of the land known in Arabic as Filastin. Most of the local population, largely Christian at the time, converted to Islam after the Arab conquest in A.D. 637, although an indigenous Christian community has always lived in Palestine. In the Middle Ages, Christian crusaders from Europe fought to regain the Holy Land from the Muslim "infidel." They established short-lived Crusader kingdoms, the last of which succumbed in A.D. 1291. The Ottoman Turks, based in Istanbul, captured Palestine early in the 16th century and held it until World War I.

The contest for Palestine began in earnest in the late 19th century as Jews and Arabs were both affected by the tide of nationalism sweeping Europe. Arabs under Ottoman domination wanted independence from their Turkish overlords. Jews, who throughout their diaspora had yearned to return to Zion (one of the Biblical names for Jerusalem), sought a state of their own.

Theodore Herzl, a Jewish journalist living in Vienna, Austria, was one of the founders of modern Zionism. Herzl made his appeal for a return of the Jews to Palestine at a time of virulent anti-Semitism, manifested by the Dreyfus Affair in France (1894–1906) and the pogroms of czarist Russia.

Many Jews, particularly in the U.S. and Western Europe, were not Zionists but identified with the countries where they lived. Nor were all Zionists Jews; some Christians believed that the return of Jews to Palestine had to precede the second coming of Christ.

The Balfour Declaration

The Zionist dream was summed up by the phrase, "a land without a people for a people without a land." The problem was that the ancestral land of the Jews was by no means uninhabited. The Ottoman Empire opposed Jewish colonization in Palestine, but that did not stop Jews from immigrating there. Some came in the late 1880s, and many more arrived from Russia after the 1905 revolution failed. By 1914, 85,000 Jews lived in Palestine alongside some 600,000 Arabs, both Muslim and Christian.

During World War I, Britain promised to support the creation of independent governments in the Ottoman-controlled portions of Arab lands if the Arabs would revolt against the Turks. This promise conflicted, however, with later commitments the British made. In an effort to attract Jewish support for the allies and to ward off French claims to Palestine, Foreign Secretary Arthur James Balfour promised that Britain would work to establish a Jewish national home in Palestine. He wrote in 1917, "His Majesty's Government view with favor the establishment in Palestine of a national home for the Jewish people,…it being clearly understood that nothing shall be done which may prejudice the civil and religious rights of existing non-Jewish communities in Palestine…."

The Balfour Declaration, a masterpiece of equivocation, did endorse the Zionist desire for a homeland, but it did not promise to transform Palestine into a Jewish state. After all, most of the inhabitants were not Jewish. Satisfying the competing claims of Arab and Jew has proven impossible ever since.

British mandate

After the war, Britain and France carved up the Arab portions of the Ottoman Empire into zones of influence that were known as mandates and technically supervised by the League of Nations. The mandate for Syria (including present-day Lebanon) was awarded to France and that for Iraq and Palestine (including present-day Jordan) to Britain. The mandates for Syria and Iraq were intended to prepare those countries for independence, but the Palestine mandate was designed to bolster Britain's strategic position in the

Middle East as well as accommodate Zionist goals.

Arab nationalists protested bitterly that Britain had gone back on its wartime promises of supporting their right to self-determination. Zionists were also unhappy because, by creating the Emirate of Transjordan in the area east of the Jordan River, Britain reduced the portion of Palestine available for a Jewish homeland.

Jewish-Arab relations worsened in the 1930s, as more Jews immigrated to Palestine to escape Nazi persecution. In 1936 Arabs held a six-month general strike which the British High Commissioner characterized as "a state of incipient revolution." The strike was followed by an Arab rebellion that lasted until 1939.

That year Britain, which wanted to forestall Arab hostility during the anticipated war with Germany, announced the ending of its mandate in 10 years, if conditions permitted. In the meantime Jewish immigration would be strictly limited and restrictions placed on land purchases. The Jews felt betrayed, especially since the 1937 Peel Commission, sent by Britain to examine the causes of the strike, had recommended partition, with a small portion of Palestine allotted for a Jewish state.

Israel's birth

After World War II, the British announced their intention to leave Palestine, and they turned the problem over to the United Nations. In November 1947, the General Assembly passed a resolution partitioning Palestine into independent Arab and Jewish states. The area around Jerusalem was to become an international zone administered by the UN as a permanent trusteeship. The Jewish state would include more than half the territory of Palestine, although Jews only constituted a third of the population. The Arabs rejected the plan and fighting broke out.

Israel declared itself a sovereign state on May 14, 1948. The following day Arab armies from Transjordan, Syria, Lebanon, Iraq and Egypt invaded, along with token forces from Saudi Arabia. Israeli forces prevailed due to their tactical skills and greater numbers, the lack of an effective Arab command and poor morale among the Arab armies. Israel extended its control

to 78% of the territory, more than it would have received under the UN plan.

Dr. Ralph J. Bunche, an American diplomat serving the UN, chaired the negotiations that led to an armistice between Israel and Egypt in February 1949. In July Israel reached similar agreements with Lebanon, Transjordan and Syria.

The war resulted in major population shifts. In 1947, the Arab population in Palestine was estimated at 1.3 million and the Jewish population, 650,000—or 33% of the total. After the war, the Jews constituted about 77% of the population in the part of Palestine that became Israel.

About 133,000 Arabs remained and became Israeli citizens and an estimated 600,000 to 760,000 became refugees. The largest number fled to the West Bank. The rest went to Gaza, occupied by Egypt in 1948, and to other Arab countries, especially Lebanon, Syria and the East Bank. Emir Abdullah annexed the West Bank and joined it with

the East Bank (formerly Transjordan) to form the new state of Jordan.

Why the Palestinians left has been a subject of bitter controversy. The most thorough analysis, published in 1987 by Israeli scholar Benny Morris, concludes that "the Palestinian refugee problem was born of war, not by design, Jewish or Arab. It was largely a by-product of Arab and Jewish fears and of the protracted, bitter fighting…[I]n smaller part, it was the deliberate creation of Jewish and Arab military commanders and politicians." The Palestinian exodus was paralleled by an influx of 500,000 Jews from Arab countries into Israel.

The politics of exile

Among Arabs the events of 1948 are referred to as *al-nakba,* the disaster. Many Palestinians suddenly found themselves homeless refugees, their political aspirations—which in other areas culminated in Arab sovereignty—cut short by the founding of Israel. Arab governments did not want to integrate them into their own countries for politi-

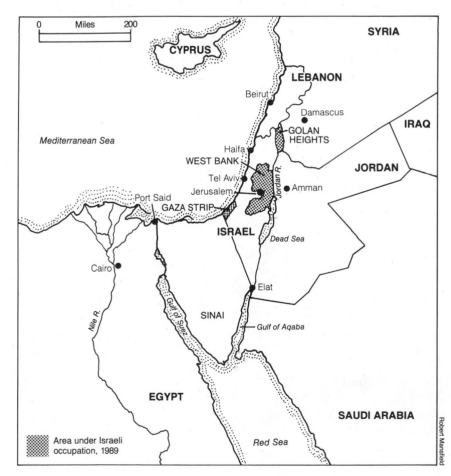

cal and economic reasons, and most Palestinians did not want to be assimilated, lest their demand for a homeland be forgotten.

The reception accorded the Palestinians in exile varied. Only Jordan offered them citizenship. Skilled workers and professionals found employment in the Arab states of the Persian Gulf. In Lebanon, where the refugees threatened to upset the numerical balance between Christians and Muslims, strict curbs were placed on residence and employment. Egypt and Iraq took few Palestinians, whereas Syria assimilated large numbers.

Many Palestinians ended up in refugee camps, where they were cared for by the United Nations Relief and Works Agency for Palestine Refugees in the Near East (UNRWA). But they never forgot the "paradise" they had left. An anthropologist interviewing Palestinians in the camps in Lebanon in the late 1970s found that "there is no detail of village life, from crops to quarrels, that people cannot remember in microscopic detail, in spite of—or perhaps because of—the completeness of the severance of their past."

Starting in the 1950s, and especially in the 1960s, Palestinians formed popular organizations that mobilized groups such as women, teachers, students and

workers and kept alive a sense of national identity that later found expression in political organizations like the PLO.

Rise of the PLO

The six-day war in June 1967 was a political turning point for the Middle East. Israel delivered a humiliating blow to the Egyptian, Jordanian and Syrian armies and tripled the size of its territory. Israel took the West Bank (including East Jerusalem) from Jordan; the Gaza Strip and Sinai (the latter was returned in 1982) from Egypt; and the Golan Heights (incorporated into Israel in December 1981) from Syria. Over 200,000 refugees, including many Palestinians who had taken refuge on the West Bank in 1948, fled to Jordan.

The sense of frustration and despair that was widespread among Arabs was particularly acute among the Palestinians. With their hope that the Arab states could restore their homeland crushed, they became more militant under the leadership of the PLO.

The PLO is an umbrella organization for various Palestinian factions. It was organized by Arab leaders in 1964 as a means of controlling the Palestinians. The predominant group within the PLO is Fatah, which was founded by Yasir Arafat in the late 1950s. Arafat's

ability to mediate between competing factions in the PLO is legendary, as is his reluctance to alienate any of them.

Fatah's main rival is the Popular Front for the Liberation of Palestine (PFLP), a Marxist group. Founded in 1967 by a Greek Orthodox physician, George Habash, the PFLP has appealed to Christians who favor a secular ideology based on Arab unity.

Under Arafat, who was elected chairman in 1969, the PLO carried out terrorist acts to publicize its cause. It drew recruits from a new generation, especially in the refugee camps, that had grown up with a hatred for Israel and a determination to regain their homeland.

The turn to terrorism boosted morale among Palestinians but it did not seriously damage Israel and it outraged international public opinion. The PLO was associated in Western minds with deeds such as the massacre of Israeli athletes at the Munich Olympics in 1972, the assassination of U.S. and European diplomats in the Sudan in March 1973, and the killing of many Israeli civilians in raids on schools, buses and towns, including Ma'alot, Kiryat Shemona and Nahariyya.

By 1970, the increasingly aggressive activities of Palestinian forces in Jordan posed a challenge to the authority of King Hussein. The PFLP's hijacking and destruction of three Western jet planes set the stage for a bloody showdown. In "Black September" 1970 King Hussein's predominantly Bedouin army attacked the Palestinian guerrilla bases and refugee camps in Jordan, killing thousands. The survivors fled into Lebanon and Syria.

Turn to diplomacy

In October 1973 Egypt and Syria launched a surprise attack on Israel. Although Israel, aided by a massive airlift of U.S. arms, prevailed militarily, the Arab armies performed creditably and restored a large measure of Arab pride and confidence. The Arab oil-producing states penalized the U.S. for helping Israel by placing an embargo on oil deliveries and quintupling the price.

In the wake of the war, the PLO attempted to cultivate a more moderate image abroad, and to some degree it succeeded. In October 1974 a majority

Sanitation workers at UN refugee camp in Jordan.

UNRWA photo by M. Nasr

Arafat greeted by Saudi Arabia's ambassador at the UN in 1974.

Prime Minister Shamir, leader of Israel's Likud bloc.

of Arab states designated the PLO as "the sole legitimate representative of the Palestinian people." Arafat addressed the UN General Assembly that November, and the UN gave the PLO observer status—just short of outright recognition.

The PLO developed a "state within a state" in Lebanon, including an extensive network of armed camps. In retaliation against PLO raids, Israel invaded southern Lebanon in March 1978; it withdrew two months later following the installation of a UN peacekeeping force. Southern Lebanon, however, continued to be a PLO stronghold. In June 1982, Israel invaded again, supposedly to remove PLO bases within 40 kilometers of its border. A more important goal of this invasion, many believe, was to remove the PLO as a source of influence in the West Bank. Israeli forces pushed on to Beirut, the capital of Lebanon, and eventually forced the PLO out of the country.

PLO after Lebanon

In driving the PLO out of Lebanon, Israel eliminated the Palestinian military threat across the border. But it did not succeed in destroying the PLO or quashing the demand by Palestinians for a state of their own. "The war reinforced a bitter feeling of isolation and betrayal among Palestinians, a feeling that Camp David had already inflamed," according to historian Rashid Khalidi.

Today the PLO is a coalition of six factions, the most important of which is Fatah, based in Tunis, Tunisia's capital. Of the smaller radical factions, three, including the PFLP, are based in Damascus, Syria, and two in Baghdad, Iraq. A few parties that reject Arafat's leadership are based in Syria and Libya.

The PLO has long been plagued by internal divisions, although since the intifada began it has become more unified. It has been held together by its ability to rally Palestinians, particularly in times of crisis. Arafat himself—the "Old Man" to his followers—is a legendary survivor in the maelstrom of Middle Eastern politics.

One reason behind Arafat's power is that he controls a great deal of cash. *The Economist* (London) magazine reported in 1986 that Arafat is in charge of both the Palestine National Fund and the much larger and more secretive Fatah fund, estimated at $7 billion to $8 billion. The PLO has a 5,000-person bureaucracy that runs its diverse business and charitable interests, which include hospitals in Lebanon, kindergartens in Egypt and plantations in Africa.

Occupied territories

Since the 1967 war, Israel has increasingly integrated the economies of the West Bank and Gaza with its own. By the eve of the uprising in 1987, four out of ten workers in the territories were employed in Israel, mostly as unskilled labor. They accounted for a third of the territories' income, some $700

million. Little industrial development took place in the territories proper, which became dependent on Israeli imports.

To help reduce Israel's vulnerability to attack, after the 1967 war the Labor government encouraged Israelis to establish temporary settlements at strategic points on the **West Bank**. The Likud bloc, a coalition of conservative parties the most important of which is Prime Minister Yitzhak Shamir's Herut party, greatly expanded the number of settlements after it took power in 1977. The Likud's rationale for the settlements was different from that of Labor: it wanted to establish a nucleus of Jewish settlers on the land in order to frustrate any attempt to relinquish the territory at a future date. Some settlers came out of ideological commitment, others because of economic incentives such as cheap housing and tax relief. Today there are over 100 settlements with nearly 70,000 settlers—many of whom are determined never to leave.

To support the settlements, Israel has seized almost one third of the territory on the West Bank, including 90% of the cultivable land and 75% of the water resources, according to Meron Benvenisti, who directed the West Bank Data Project, a nonpartisan research institute in Jerusalem, from 1982 to 1989. Israel has spent $3 billion on infrastructure, including housing, roads and electricity. The lesson that Benvenisti draws is that the process has now become irreversible: it is too late to separate the West Bank from Israel.

The Israeli occupation, although it brought a rise in the standard of living of Palestinians, bred hatred and alienation. Israel obstructed the development of local leadership or effective political organizations on the West Bank: Palestinian officials who opposed Israeli policies were removed (some were deported). Under the Iron Fist policy imposed in 1985, Palestinian protesters were subject to search, arrest, interrogation, deportation, house arrest, curfew, and abridged freedom of expression and travel.

Gaza, about 25 miles long and 4 to 9 miles wide, is a densely populated, poverty-stricken "hellhole made to order for terrorism," according to *The Jerusalem Post.* The local economy, based on citrus production, cannot provide enough jobs, and many Gazans are obliged to seek work in Israel. Three quarters of the population are refugees from the 1948 war who live in camps administered by UNRWA. Unlike West Bank Palestinians, "the residents of Gaza have no historic ties with the Hashemite Kingdom," and few want a union with Jordan, according to Professor Ann Mosely Lesch of Villanova University.

The intifada

Two decades of mounting frustration in the territories, compounded by the Palestinians' sense of abandonment, eventually led to an explosion. At a summit meeting in Amman, Jordan, in November 1987, the Arab states relegated the Palestinian issue to second place on their agenda—after the Iran-Iraq War. Many Palestinians were shocked and felt deserted. It did not take long for an incident to spark the uprising.

On December 8, 1987, an Israeli tank transport crashed into a van carrying Palestinian workers to the Gaza Strip, killing four of them. Spontaneous demonstrations broke out in Gaza and the West Bank and quickly mushroomed into a general revolt against Israeli rule. There had been protests in the occupied territories before, but never of this scale or duration.

The revolutionary "troops," for the most part, were young boys armed with stones and an occasional Molotov cocktail. This ensured sympathetic media coverage and reflected the fact that Palestinians have few arms.

At first, the objective of the uprising was to get Israel to improve the conditions of occupation, release prisoners, withdraw its army from populated areas and cancel restrictions on political activities. Eventually, the major demand was for a Palestinian state.

PLO challenged

By all accounts the intifada took the PLO by surprise and challenged it to come up with new policies. King Hussein's decision to relinquish sovereignty over the West Bank in July 1988 added to the pressure on the PLO to act. In November, the Palestine National Council (PNC)—regarded as the PLO's government-in-exile—in a symbolic act declared the existence of an independent Palestinian state in the West Bank and Gaza, with Jerusalem its capital. This declaration was based on the original UN partition resolution of 1947. The PNC also accepted UN Security Council resolutions 242 and 338, thereby implicitly recognizing Israel.

The PNC's declarations did not go far enough to convince the U.S. that it had changed its policies, so in December 1988 Arafat explicitly recognized Israel's right to exist, accepted UN resolutions 242 and 338 and renounced terrorism. In response, the U.S. dropped its long-standing prohibition on negotiating with the PLO. In addition, in May 1989 Arafat referred to the PLO charter, which says that "armed struggle is the only way to liberate Palestine," as having "lapsed."

The lack of progress toward a solution caused growing divisiveness among Palestinians. Those who ignored strikes and boycotts risked being ostracized or attacked. By November 1989 over 100 Palestinians had been killed by other Palestinians for collaborating with the enemy. Over 550 had been killed by Israeli forces.

The PLO's leadership of the uprising appears to be eroding. Hard-liners in the PLO have brought increasing pressure on Arafat to produce results. At a Fatah congress in August 1989, 90% of the delegates endorsed Arafat's diplomatic approach, but made no reference to his recognition of Israel or his renunciation of terrorism. In fact, Fatah voted to intensify armed struggle until the occupation ended. The Islamic fundamentalist organization Hamas (the Movement of Islamic Opposition), which has some support in the West Bank and Gaza, rejects the idea of peaceful coexistence with Israel and advocates an Islamic state with laws based on the Koran.

Elections ahead?

While casualties mounted, the diplomats placed their hope on a nonviolent solution, namely elections. Prime Minister Shamir suggested that elections in the West Bank and Gaza could lead to local autonomy for Palestinians, with the final status of the territories to be worked out later. But Israel's conditions, including a prohibition on PLO participation in the elections, were unacceptable to Palestinians.

Palestinians believe that if the U.S. pressed hard enough, it could force Israel to grant them a homeland. Their estimation of U.S. influence may be exaggerated; the U.S. has long maintained that it would not force Israel to take action it believed would endanger its security.

The Soviet Union

The Soviet Union, which has helped arm the PLO and given it diplomatic support since 1968, supports the demand for a Palestinian state. Soviet leader Mikhail S. Gorbachev has pressed the PLO to moderate its policies to increase the chances for peace.

The Soviet Union regards the Middle East as within its legitimate sphere of interest and believes a comprehensive solution should be worked out at an international conference. However, at present the Soviet Union has no diplomatic ties with Israel, and this limits its role as a broker.

Can the differences between Israelis and Palestinians be bridged with ballots, not bullets? Thomas L. Friedman, who spent six years in Lebanon and Israel as a *New York Times* correspondent, believes that the legacy of bitterness is such that neither side can ever be fully satisfied. "In the current political environment, focusing on permanent solutions is a prescription for deadlock....Neither side can ever sign away its dreams; a final, comprehensive solution for the Palestine problem is today a contradiction in terms..."

The Palestinians between Arabs and Israelis

FOR TWO DECADES after 1948, Palestinian nationalism was eclipsed by the intense ideological struggles sweeping the Arab world. Many Palestinians placed their faith in the pan-Arab movement led by Egypt's President Gamal Abdel Nasser to regain their homeland. But Arab leaders were not eager to see the formation of a Palestinian state that could become a destabilizing influence.

After the 1967 war, the Palestinians increasingly asserted their independence from the Arab governments. Although they still relied on Arab states for financial, military and diplomatic support, they knew that when the chips were down—such as in Jordan in 1970 and in Lebanon in 1982—they could not count on Arab leaders for help.

Arab politics

The Palestinians have been an important factor in inter-Arab politics for four decades. Each country views them from a different perspective.

Egypt has officially been at peace with Israel since 1979, and peace is essential for its economic prospects as well as the continuation of large-scale U.S. aid. For peace to continue, Egypt believes, the Palestinian problem must be solved. Egyptian President Hosni Mubarak has good relations with Arafat at present, and has tried—so far without success—to act as a middleman in a peace settlement.

Syria has long championed the Palestinian cause, but by backing factions hostile to Arafat it helped to splinter the movement. Syrian President Hafez Assad reportedly is unhappy with the intifada since it has boosted Arafat's stock. Syria keeps its own Palestinian population under strict control.

Although some Palestinian guerrillas have found their way back to **Lebanon,** the continuing civil war there rules Lebanon out as an important factor in Palestinian politics at present.

Jordan, which controlled the West Bank from 1948 to 1967, has been encouraged by the U.S. and Israel to negotiate on behalf of the Palestinians, but King Hussein has always been ambivalent about playing such a role and many Palestinians do not accept his leadership. A short-lived effort to form a common negotiating front with Arafat collapsed in 1986. Jordan clearly must be a party to a peace settlement, but it is unlikely it will take the lead unless there is a consensus to do so.

Saudi Arabia is the leading conservative Arab state and as such fears the instability the Palestinians inject into the Middle East. The Saudis are major financial backers of Fatah because they regard its leaders as the most moderate and because they want to assure peace in their kingdom. Although Saudi Arabia is one of the closest U.S. allies in the Middle East, it has not supported U.S. diplomatic initiatives, such as Camp David, that come at the expense of the Palestinians.

Israeli views

As far as Israel was concerned, Palestine as a name on the map disappeared in 1948, and Israelis hoped that the displaced Arabs would be quietly assimilated into neighboring countries. Israelis feared that acknowledging the right of Palestinians to self-determination would undercut their own claim to the land.

Making peace with Egypt in 1979 provided a major psychological boost to Israelis and demonstrated that their country might eventually be accepted by other Arab states. But none has followed Egypt's example: normalization of relations is only likely to come in the context of a comprehensive settlement.

Continued Israeli occupation of the territories has led to ominous demographic trends in Israel: at the present rate of increase, Arabs may constitute half the population by the year 2000 if the West Bank and Gaza remain under Israeli jurisdiction. Israelis face the agonizing choice of whether they want to live in a Jewish state or as a minority in a nonsectarian state.

The 1982 invasion of Lebanon, which many Israelis came to oppose, undermined confidence in the government and showed the limitations of a military solution to the region's problems. It also polarized Israeli public opinion, which ranges from leftists who do not object to a Palestinian state to rightists who would end the problem by "transferring" the Palestinians to Jordan. But even among most hawks and doves, there is a consensus that Israel should not return to its pre-1967 borders, that Jerusalem should remain united, that the government should not agree to a Palestinian state or allow Palestinian refugees the right to return.

The intifada has increased pressure on Israelis to find a diplomatic solution. The Labor party, led by Shimon Peres, endorses the idea of trading land for peace, and has become more flexible about negotiating with Palestinians. Peres has favored holding an international peace conference, and believes that failure to reach a compromise settlement would be fatal for Israel. Outside of Israel, Peres's ideas have widespread support.

Prime Minister Shamir represents the hard-liners. He emphasizes the historic right of Jews to live in Judea and Samaria, the Biblical names for the West Bank, and fears that relinquishing the territories would gravely endanger Israel's security. Without the West Bank, Israel is only nine miles wide at its narrowest point. Shamir refuses to negotiate with the PLO. He also opposes an international conference on the grounds that the Soviets and Arab states would gang up against Israel and force it to make too many concessions.

Peres (1984–86) and Shamir (1986–present) have alternated in leading coalition governments. Their differences have paralyzed domestic decisionmaking, perplexed foreign observers, and left the public, itself divided, frustrated.

The uprising has had serious consequences for Israel's economy. Palestinians in the territories have stopped buying many Israeli products. The construction industry in Israel, which depends heavily on Arab labor, has been hard hit by strikes. By November 1989, Israel was in the 11th month of a deep recession, with unemployment hovering around 10% and inflation running at 23%. The intifada was not wholly to blame, but it had made things considerably worse.

U.S. policy: the search for solutions

AMERICAN Administrations long regarded the Palestinians as primarily a refugee problem. They have been wary of Palestinian political aspirations and no President has endorsed their demand for a state.

Support for Israel has long been one of the pillars of U.S. policy in the Middle East. Administrations have regarded Israel as a bastion of democracy in the Middle East and a "strategic asset" in fighting terrorism and opposing Soviet inroads. Many Americans believe the U.S. has a moral duty to support it.

An alternative view notes that U.S. support for Israel has angered Arab states whose friendship the U.S. needs to assure a steady flow of oil. Because Israel is assured of U.S. backing, some maintain, it has refused to deal with the Palestinians and this has kept the region in turmoil.

Since the 1967 war, the U.S. has periodically tried to help resolve the Arab-Israeli dispute. The U.S. position is expressed in UN Security Council Resolution 242, which it helped formulate. The resolution emphasizes "the inadmissibility of the acquisition of territory by war" and calls for the "withdrawal of Israeli armed forces from territories occupied in the recent conflict." The resolution did not specify that *all* occupied land was to be relinquished.

The resolution also acknowledges the right of "every state in the area" (that is, Israel) "to live in peace within secure and recognized boundaries."

U.S. diplomacy

The high point of U.S. diplomacy in regard to the Arab-Israeli dispute came during the Carter Administration (1977–81). President Carter persuaded Egyptian President Anwar al-Sadat and Israeli Prime Minister Menachem Begin to sign two trailblazing agreements at Camp David: one provided for Israeli withdrawal from Sinai and an Israeli-Egyptian peace treaty; the other was a framework for Palestinian autonomy in the West Bank and Gaza Strip.

Under this framework, which was never implemented, Egypt and Israel agreed to transitional arrangements for the West Bank and Gaza, which would not exceed five years. Residents would elect representatives who would participate in negotiations to determine the final status of the areas.

In the decade after the Camp David accords, the Arab-Israeli dispute was on the back burner of U.S. diplomacy. The priority of the Reagan Administration (1981–89) was to exclude Soviet influence from the Middle East and build a "strategic consensus" of regional states to oppose Soviet encroachment. Although Reagan himself was considered

the most pro-Israeli of American Presidents, he was not prepared to enter into the kind of personal diplomacy that had been crucial at Camp David. Reagan also questioned the legitimacy of the PLO's leadership of Palestinians.

In the aftermath of Israel's invasion of Lebanon in June 1982, the U.S. sent in troops as part of a multinational peacekeeping force to help evacuate the PLO from Beirut. With Israel's position strengthened in the region, the Administration saw a new opportunity for peace. In September 1982 Reagan proposed giving Palestinians in the West Bank and in Gaza self-government in association with Jordan. Reagan said the U.S. would oppose both Israeli annexation and an independent Palestinian state. The plan was rejected by Israel and received without enthusiasm by the Arab states.

Thereafter, Secretary of State George P. Shultz shied away from Middle East diplomacy until his last year in office, when he proposed holding an international conference in which the Palestinians would be represented in a joint delegation with Jordanians. The plan was accepted by neither the Israelis nor the Palestinians.

Enter Bush

President Bush took office at a time when the Israeli-Palestinian conflict had again become a major international issue. His Administration, however, sees limited opportunities for diplomacy and would prefer that the parties directly involved come up with a peace plan.

In a major policy speech in May 1989, Secretary of State James A. Baker 3d stunned many supporters of Israel by urging Israel to abandon "the unrealistic vision of a greater Israel" and to "forswear annexation," both key policies of Shamir. He also urged Palestinians to amend their charter and "translate the dialogue of violence in the intifada into a dialogue of politics and diplomacy."

By late 1989, the Administration was discouraged by the lack of progress in ending the intifada. Procedural wrangling over how to hold elections in the territories and who would represent the

Tents shelter Palestinians whose houses were demolished by Israeli authorities.

UNRWA photo by M. Nasr

Palestinians in peace talks had consumed much time while the major issues remained unaddressed.

Policy options

One decision facing the Bush Administration is how strong a leadership role to play. Many note that in the Middle East, if the peace process does not go forward, it goes backward. According to Rep. Lee H. Hamilton (D-Ind.), "the status quo is a prescription for trouble. U.S. interests simply do not allow us to drift along waiting for a more favorable environment.... We ought not shirk our responsibilities."

Clearly, the U.S. cannot solve the problem alone. But those who favor the U.S. asserting stronger leadership argue that the U.S. is the only mediator accepted by all sides, and regional leaders have urged its participation. Other observers note that, with Israel refusing to withdraw from the occupied territories and the Palestinians insisting on statehood, there is nothing to negotiate about.

Then there is the question of Palestinian representation. Israelis and Palestinians are deadlocked over the issue, with Israel fearing that even if an accord can be struck with Arafat, it would be repudiated by other, more hard-line, Palestinians.

How can the U.S. help get negotiations started? According to one school, the main obstacle is Israel; Palestinians have already made significant concessions for peace. Therefore the U.S. should put pressure on Israel to be more forthcoming and stop insisting on veto power over Palestinian negotiators. The pressure could consist of putting restrictions on or scaling down U.S. aid to Israel.

Those opposed to this course argue that Palestinian "concessions" are only a façade to gain U.S. sympathy. Although Arafat has recognized Israel, the intifada continues, and so do terrorist attacks, as the Israeli government has charged. A majority of Congress is pro-Israel and cannot realistically be expected to approve a significant cut.

A further issue is what kind of settlement to seek: a comprehensive solution (the approach favored by Carter) or

UNRWA photo by George Nehmeh

Israeli soldiers guard the Dome of the Rock (Islam's third-holiest shrine) in Jerusalem.

limited agreements that lead step-by-step to an overall settlement (the approach favored by former Secretary of State Henry A. Kissinger).

It sometimes seems as if all ideas have been tried and all have failed. But new ideas continue to surface. Gidon Gottlieb, director of the Middle East Peace Project at the Council on Foreign Relations, blames language for impeding a solution. Gottlieb notes, for example, that Israeli governments have always distinguished between the state of Israel and the land of Israel, and that the Palestinians are now coming around to the same concept. Both Israelis and Palestinians might live in their homelands and be accorded special privileges there, he points out, even if they were not within an Israeli or Palestinian state. Given the will to succeed, there might still be a way to finesse the issues diplomatically.

Should the U.S. reconsider its opposition to a Palestinian state? Recent Administrations have accepted the the-

ory that such a state would introduce an element of instability in the Middle East, would pose a security threat to Israel, would be subject to Soviet influence and would not be viable economically. "A new Palestinian state could well become... a solution that brings short-term relief for Western guilt, but only at great long-term cost," according to Steven L. Spiegel, a University of California professor. Some Israelis point out that such a state already exists, namely Jordan, where over half the population is Palestinian, and there is no need for another one.

On the other hand, international support for such a state has grown over the past two years. Arab leaders claim that a Palestinian state would halt the further radicalization of the PLO and deter terrorist acts. Since the destruction of the PLO infrastructure in Lebanon, they assert, the Palestinians have posed no real threat to Israel.

Other possible solutions, such as an exercise of joint sovereignty by Israel and Jordan, have not really been explored. The most difficult problem of all will probably be the status of Jerusalem.

Should the U.S. support Soviet participation in the Middle East peace talks? Some argue that this would give the Soviets leverage in the Middle East at U.S. expense. On the other hand, many argue that until the Soviet Union is allowed a role, there can be no settlement.

★ ★ ★

It seems clear that ultimately both sides must compromise to achieve peace, which may take generations to be accepted. What compromises are worth making, and how soon? What role should the U.S. play? Should it act as a catalyst, risking failure, or should it wait until there is a strong enough mandate for peace within the region to resolve the problem that has kept the Middle East in upheaval for some four decades?

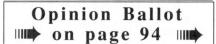

Opinion Ballot
⫸ **on page 94** ⫸

FOR DISCUSSION

1. Palestine has been called the "twice-promised land," an area Britain reserved for both Jewish Zionists and Palestinian nationalists. Can you think of any way to reconcile their competing claims to the land?

2. The U.S. has said it favors self-determination for Palestinians, as long as this does not include statehood. Is there anything inconsistent about such a policy?

3. Since the U.S. and the Soviet Union cosponsored an international conference following the 1973 war, the Soviets have been shut out of the Arab-Israeli peace process. Do you think the U.S. should agree to including them in the search for peace?

4. U.S. Administrations have always considered Israel's security to be non-negotiable. What do you think constitutes security for Israel? A land buffer from its enemies? Military force? Diplomatic recognition? Something else?

5. Israelis and Palestinians will both have to make compromises if a peace settlement is to be reached. What steps do you think Israel could take without endangering its security? What steps could the Palestinians take without forgoing their dream of a homeland?

6. How forceful a role should the U.S. play in ending the intifada? Should it threaten to cut back financial assistance to Israel unless it advances the peace process? Or should the U.S. wait for the parties themselves to formulate a viable settlement plan before stepping in?

7. Is it reasonable for the Israelis to insist that the PLO be excluded from peace negotiations? Who should represent the Palestinians? Should they be entitled to choose their own representatives, even if they have connections with the PLO?

SUGGESTED READINGS

Baker, James A., 3d, "Principles and Pragmatism: American Policy Toward the Arab-Israeli Conflict." **Department of State Bulletin,** July 1989, pp. 24–27. Major policy statement of May 22, 1989, notable for blunt tone toward Israel.

Cobban, Helena, **The Palestinian Liberation Organization: People, Power and Politics.** New York, Cambridge University Press, 1984. 305 pp. $10.95 (paper). History of the PLO, especially its predominant group, Fatah, by journalist based in Lebanon in the late 1970s.

Hart, Alan, **Arafat: A Political Biography.** Bloomington, Indiana University Press, 1989. 560 pp. $18.95 (paper). Favorable biography by British foreign correspondent based on interviews with top PLO leaders.

Journal of Palestine Studies. The leading scholarly journal devoted to Palestinian affairs, published jointly by The Institute for Palestine Studies and Kuwait University. Available to individuals for $18 annually (4 issues) from I.P.S., Georgetown Station, P.O. Box 25301, Washington, D.C. 20007.

Khalidi, Walid, **Before Their Diaspora: A Photographic History of the Palestinians, 1876–1948.** Washington, D.C., Institute for Palestine Studies, 1985. 323 pp. $27.50 (paper). Collection of nearly 500 photographs documenting Palestinian life, with comments by leading Palestinian historian.

Mattar, Philip, "The Critical Moment for Peace." **Foreign Policy,** Fall 1989, pp. 141–59. The U.S. must act now as a catalyst for peace and leave all issues, including statehood, open to negotiation.

Miller, Aaron David, "Palestinians and the Intifada: One Year Later." **Current History,** February 1989, pp. 73–76+. State Department analyst reviews developments during the first year of the intifada.

Peretz, Don, **Intifada: The Palestinian Uprising.** Boulder, Colo., Westview Press, 1990. 250 pp., $14.95 (paper). Excellent study of the uprising, including its origins, Israeli policies and international repercussions, by political scientist.

Quandt, William B., Jabber, Fuad, and Lesch, Ann Mosely, **The Politics of Palestinian Nationalism.** Berkeley, University of California Press, 1973. 234 pp. $10.95 (paper). Classic study tracing the growth of Palestinian nationalism from the mandate period until the early 1970s.

Spiegel, Steven L., "State of Confusion." **The New Republic,** April 10, 1989, pp. 15–18. The case against a Palestinian state.

For further in-depth reading, write for the Great Decisions 1990 Bibliography (see page 4).

8.

GLOBAL WARMING AND THE ENVIRONMENT

FORECAST DISASTER?

GLOBAL WARMING is a little like the weather: everybody talks about it. But, unlike the weather, more and more people realize that something must be done about it. For Americans, the reality of global warming was driven home by the drought of 1988. A seven-week heat wave left much of the U.S. gasping in record high temperatures; crops from Georgia to California withered and forest fires raged over millions of acres in the West. The record temperatures were not unique to the U.S.: it was the hottest year on earth since record-keeping began a century ago.

The earth has been warming up for the past century, but the pace has been accelerating in the last decade. Global warming is largely the result of the rapid buildup in the atmosphere of carbon dioxide (CO_2) and other "greenhouse gases" that trap the earth's heat. They are produced by car exhausts, the burning of forests and other sources. Switch on the light, heat coffee in the microwave and drive to work and you have helped raise the earth's temperature. The heat and drought combined with other problems—the unrelieved air pollution in many U.S. cities, the oil spill fouling Alaska's pristine waters and the discovery of a new large hole in the ozone layer over the Antarctic—have raised the public's alarm about the state of the environment.

Environmental issues transcend national boundaries: wind and rain need no passports. Increasing CO_2 emissions, the loss of forests and rapid population growth—all are critical problems and all contribute to the most urgent issue of all, global warming. Sen. Timothy Wirth (D-Colo.) has called it "a chal-

AP/Wide World Photos

The destruction of forests, by design or accident, as at Yellowstone National Park in 1988, is raising the earth's temperature.

lenge as compelling and as imperative as nuclear arms control." Others predict it may become the dominant foreign policy issue of the 21st century.

There is "growing scientific consensus that significant global warming due to greenhouse gas emissions is probable over the next century and that rapid climate change is possible," with disas-

trous consequences for planet earth, according to Environmental Protection Agency (EPA) head William K. Reilly. What is less clear is precisely how climate change will affect particular regions.

There is some agreement that the greatest change in temperature is likely to occur during the winter in the high latitudes of the northern hemisphere, where the Arctic ice would melt. This would ease navigation and facilitate oil exploration and human settlement.

In the middle latitudes, which include the U.S., Canada, Europe and parts of the U.S.S.R., winter temperatures would probably increase more than summer temperatures and the rain belt would shift northward. Forests would begin to die, agriculture would be less productive and the grain belt could shift northward to Canada and Siberia.

Third World countries in the southern latitudes would be hard hit. There is likely to be less rainfall in sub-Saharan Africa, which is already in the grip of a long drought; the humid tropical regions would get hotter and wetter; and warmer tropical waters could spawn more intense storms.

Global warming would raise the sea level because as the temperature rises, the surface of the ocean expands. The increase could be in the range of 1.5 to 6.5 feet, with a rise of 3 feet over the next century considered likely. This would displace a quarter of the world's population, which lives in coastal regions. The Eastern Seaboard of the U.S. would be severely damaged unless billions of dollars were spent to build a seawall defense. Major port cities, such as New Orleans, Louisiana, Amsterdam, the Netherlands, and Shanghai, China, would be endangered, and entire island nations like the Maldives could be inundated.

The economic and political damage of such an environmental catastrophe could threaten the very existence of Egypt, Bangladesh and other coastal states. For Bangladesh, one of the world's poorest countries, a seawall defense is out of the question. The same is true for Egypt. If the heavily populated delta area of Egypt were flooded, millions of people would have to flee, resulting in a huge refugee problem.

Because global warming would lead to major changes in rainfall, this would affect the availability of food, forests and wildlife. A change in rainfall patterns could be especially devastating to India, which would be parched without the summer monsoon, and, to a lesser extent, China.

Many plants—rice, for example—can only grow within a narrow range of temperature and humidity. If the temperature were to rise a few degrees, less rice could be grown, with disastrous consequences for the food supply of much of Asia. In North America, forests would begin to die during the first half of the 21st century, and wildlife, which is very sensitive to changes in temperature and rainfall, would migrate or die.

The scope of the global warming problem and its probable impact are expected to become clearer in the next decade, but action, many believe, cannot wait. At their summit meeting last July, the heads of the seven largest industrialized democracies called for "decisive action" on global warming. Top American and Soviet scientists, meeting in Sundance, Utah, last August, sent a joint letter to Presidents George Bush and Mikhail S. Gorbachev urging them to form an "environmental security alliance" to counter global warming. And in November, Prime Minister Margaret Thatcher of Britain, in an address at the United Nations, urged completion by 1992 of a treaty to regulate the production of greenhouse gases.

Already, planners in a number of countries are considering how to adapt to the effects of climate change if sea levels rise and agricultural zones shift.

How much is known about global warming? What steps have already been taken to halt it, and what steps can the international community, the U.S. government and individual citizens take in the future?

Global greenhouse

Global warming results from the so-called greenhouse effect. In a greenhouse, sunlight radiating through the glass heats the trapped air, which is blocked from mixing with the cooler air outside. The gases in the atmosphere, like the glass in a greenhouse, trap part of the heat the earth radiates and bounce it back to the earth's surface. If there were no gases or clouds to form the protective greenhouse blanket, the earth's average temperature would be closer to 0° F than 60° F.

The gases in the atmosphere absorb heat at different rates. Oxygen and nitrogen, the most abundant, absorb the least heat; the greenhouse gases, the most. Carbon dioxide accounts for about 50% of the greenhouse effect. It is produced by the burning of fossil fuels, primarily coal, oil and gas, that combined release about 6 billion tons of carbon into the atmosphere annually. (Most American cars generate their own weight in carbon in 12 months.) Deforestation, especially the destruction of tropical forests for agriculture or timber, adds another 1–3 billion tons of carbon to the atmosphere.

Chlorofluorocarbons (CFCs), found in car air conditioners, refrigerator coolants, insulation foams, aerosol products like hair sprays and deodorants, and in solvents to clean microchips and electronic equipment, account for another 25% of current greenhouse gas emissions. The balance of the greenhouse gases are methane, produced by decaying vegetation in waterlogged soil (such as wetlands and rice paddies), burning fossil fuels and ruminating cattle; nitrous oxide, released by nitrogen fertilizer and the burning of coal; and water vapor.

Because greenhouse gases tend to be long lasting, even if all production were stopped today, the gases already "in the bank" would continue to warm the planet. CO_2 remains in the atmosphere for 40 years; CFCs, for 100.

The ozone factor

CFCs do double damage to the environment. In addition to contributing to global warming, CFCs speed the breakdown of ozone in the stratosphere. At ground level, ozone is one of the main components of smog, which makes breathing difficult and which can be fatal. At 12 to 30 miles above the earth's surface, however, ozone shields the earth from the sun's ultraviolet radiation. This ultraviolet radiation causes skin cancer and cataracts, suppresses the body's immune system and reduces crop yields. It also may be destroying phytoplankton, microscopic plants found in Antarctic waters that are the base of the entire food chain in that region.

The extent of the depletion of the ozone layer only became apparent in the spring of 1985 when British scientists discovered a large hole over Antarctica. That discovery galvanized the scientific community to recommend international action to phase out the production and use of CFCs.

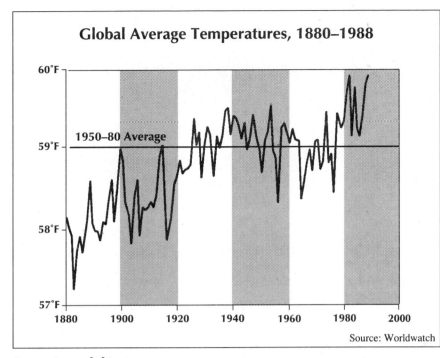

Global Average Temperatures, 1880–1988

1950–80 Average

Source: Worldwatch

A matter of degrees

Since the beginning of the century the temperature of the earth has warmed by approximately 1° F. That may not sound like a lot, but an increase or decrease of only a few degrees can have a significant impact on the earth. At the height of the last Ice Age some 18,000 years ago, the global temperature was only 6° F to 9° F colder than today. During the little Ice Age, from roughly 1500 to 1700, when temperatures were 2° F lower than at present, ice blocked the coast of Iceland for five or six months a year, compared with one to three weeks today. When the temperature was only 1° F to 2.5° F warmer than at present, enough sea ice melted to enable the Vikings to colonize Greenland and possibly reach northern America.

The global warming trend has coincided with the world's rapid industrialization. The U.S., with its energy-powered industries and gas-guzzling, air-conditioned cars, currently produces about 21% of the greenhouse gases; the Soviet Union, 14%; the European Community, 14%; China, 7%; and Brazil and India, 4% each.

If the present level of emissions continues, the amount of CO_2 in the atmosphere could reach double the pre-industrial level by the year 2050. The earth's surface would then be 3° F to 8° F warmer than today. This would mean that in Washington, D.C., the number of days per year with temperatures over 100° F would increase from 1 to 12; in Omaha, Nebraska, from 3 to 21; and in Dallas, Texas, from 19 to 78.

There are skeptics who believe the evidence on global warming is incomplete. Some analysts question whether there is in fact any connection between the increase of CO_2 and a rise in global temperatures; solar activity may be a better explanation. The doubters recall widespread predictions in the cool 1970s that the earth was entering a new Ice Age. For now, the skeptics are very much in a minority.

Global Circulation Models

Scientists base their projections about the effect of global warming on the climate on mathematical models, known as Global Circulation Models, or GCMs. These models take into consideration variables such as temperature, precipitation, humidity, evaporation, wind and cloud cover. The models are tremendously complex: it takes 10 hours of time on a supercomputer to calculate a year's weather.

The GCMs now in use are imperfect: the world's climate is far too complicated to make accurate forecasts. The main unknown factors are the "feedback effects" from rising CO_2 levels. For example, as the amount of CO_2 in the air increases, plants grow faster. As they grow, they remove carbon from the air and in the process slow global warming. On the other hand, vegetation decays faster in warmth, releasing more CO_2 into the atmosphere. As the earth warms, evaporation will increase, promoting the formation of clouds. Clouds trap heat energy from the earth, which warms it, but they also deflect solar radiation, which has a cooling effect.

On one important point, the models agree: if present trends continue, the world's average surface temperature could rise by as much as 10°F by the end of the next century, which will substantially alter the earth's climate—not only the temperature but the wind velocity and rainfall.

Going to the source

Can the momentum of global warming be slowed? Can greenhouse gas emissions be reduced?

Coal is the cheapest form of energy for many countries—and also the "dirtiest" in terms of CO_2 emissions. Burning coal releases twice as much CO_2 as natural gas and 50% more than oil to produce the same amount of energy. Synthetic fuels made from coal are the dirtiest of all. But countries that have plentiful supplies of coal will not easily

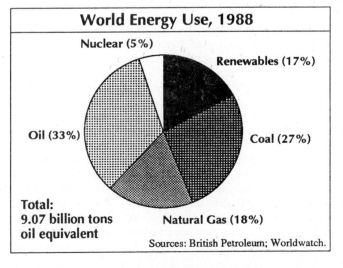

World Energy Use, 1988

Nuclear (5%)

Renewables (17%)

Oil (33%)

Coal (27%)

Natural Gas (18%)

Total: 9.07 billion tons oil equivalent

Sources: British Petroleum; Worldwatch.

be persuaded to stop burning it and to develop costly substitutes.

Burning oil is another major source of CO_2. As long as oil supplies seemed limitless and were cheap, there was little incentive for industrial powers to cut back consumption. Indeed it was assumed that economic growth depended on larger and larger consumption of energy. It was not until the oil shocks of 1973–74 and 1979, when the price of oil jumped from $2 a barrel to $35, that the U.S. and other oil importers took steps to conserve energy.

Since 1973 the production of goods and services in the U.S. has increased 40% while energy consumption has remained steady, thanks to conservation and improved efficiency. Japan, Italy and West Germany are even more energy efficient than the U.S.: West Germany uses half as much energy as the U.S. to produce a ton of steel, and Japan, one third as much.

Destruction of forests

Forests, by absorbing CO_2, help to reduce global warming. Their destruction, on the other hand, contributes significantly to CO_2 buildup. At present, some 28 million acres, an area the size of Pennsylvania, are being cleared annually to grow crops, graze cattle and provide fuel. Brazil, Colombia, Indonesia, the Ivory Coast and Thailand are the worst offenders.

Brazilian peasants have traditionally cleared the Amazon's rain forests by burning, in the belief that fire renews the soil and makes the next crop better. In fact, the soil becomes infertile in a few years and then more trees have to be cut down to make room for crops.

Because of the Amazon's vast size, Brazil has long regarded the region as an inexhaustible resource. In the past decade alone the government has provided over $1 billion in subsidies to ranchers and settlers to clear the rain forest and, as a further inducement, it taxes cleared land at lower rates than forested land. In 1989 there was a sharp drop in the amount of land burned in the Amazon region due to heavier rainfall and a suspension of tax incentives.

In Peru, farmers have destroyed an estimated 500,000 acres of tropical forests in order to plant coca, the source of three quarters of the cocaine entering the U.S. today. Coca offers growers a

UN Photo/John Isaac
Alternative energy: solar-powered pumps draw water from wells in Mali.

higher return than coffee and other traditional crops.

Intensive commercial logging has also denuded tropical forests. Japan's heavy demand for hardwoods, mainly for use in construction, resulted in the deforestation of vast areas of Thailand, Indonesia, the Philippines, Malaysia and Papua New Guinea. Indonesia has now banned the export of logs, the Philippines has banned tree cutting in most of the country, and Thailand, once a major supplier of teak, has outlawed all commercial logging.

Alternative energy sources

In addition to energy conservation, environmentalists see an urgent need to substitute clean energy for dirty energy—natural gas for coal and oil— and to develop alternative energy sources, that is, substitutes for fossil fuels. The effort to develop alternative fuels began in earnest in the 1970s, but slumped after oil prices fell in 1985. Fuels are divided into renewable sources, whose use when properly managed will not deplete supplies, and nonrenewable sources, such as oil and coal, that cannot be replenished. Today renewable energy sources—solar, hydro, wind and geothermal—provide about 4.5% of the energy consumed in the U.S., compared with about 20% of the energy used worldwide. Brazil, Is-

rael, Japan, the Philippines and Sweden are among the countries that make the most use of renewable energy. (California, in contrast with most of this country, gets about a third of its energy from renewable sources.)

The most promising yet problematic alternative (but not renewable) energy source is nuclear power, which supplies 17% of the electricity in the U.S., compared with 70% in France and 25% in Japan. But there is strong public resistance to nuclear energy plants on safety grounds as a result of the accidents at Three Mile Island, Pennsylvania, in 1979 and Chernobyl in the U.S.S.R. in 1986. Many people believe there is no such thing as a safe nuclear reactor. Since 1978 no new nuclear plants have been ordered in the U.S., and plans for over 100 were canceled, mainly because of their prohibitive costs.

Nuclear power advocates maintain that a new generation of simpler, safer and standardized reactors should allay public concern, and some environmentalists are now reconsidering their opposition. However, the problem of disposing of radioactive waste and the high cost have yet to be solved.

For most Third World countries, nuclear power is simply not an option. They cannot afford it, and they do not have the technical and managerial expertise to run the plants.

Solar power, which uses simple collectors to absorb the sun's heat and transfer it to water or air, is suitable for regions that receive large amounts of sunlight, like the Mojave Desert outside of Los Angeles, California, where seven of the world's largest solar thermal units provide enough power for 270,000 people. Israel uses solar energy extensively to heat water.

More-sophisticated photovoltaic cells, which convert the sun's rays directly into electricity and which were first used as fuel in spacecraft, are practical for powering communication systems in remote areas.

Hydropower, or the harnessing of the power of water, provides about 6% of the world's energy. It is widely used by industrial countries (for example, the Tennessee Valley Authority in the U.S.) and many Third World nations. Brazil, which lacks oil, has invested heavily in large hydroelectric plants. Its Itaipu project alone produces as much electricity as 24 coal-fired plants.

Not all large hydropower projects are environmentally sound. Small hydro installations tend to be less destructive in terms of the number of people displaced and areas lost to flooding.

Windmills supply some energy but they are only practical along coastlines, offshore or on mountains. Since 1973, 10,000 wind machines, most of them made in Denmark, have been installed around the world. The largest markets are China and India.

Other ways to keep cool

Despite mounting evidence of the devastating role deforestation plays in global warming, industrialized and developing countries alike continue to destroy their forests. Planting trees is not only necessary to replace depleted stocks, but also to absorb excess CO_2 from the atmosphere. (A tree can lock in CO_2 for 30 to 40 years.) To offset the amount of CO_2 that will be produced by its new plant, an electric utility company in Connecticut is contributing to the cost of planting 52 million trees in Guatemala.

Many environmentalists see tree planting as a politically palatable way to reduce global warming. Some countries, notably Israel and South Korea, have been leaders in reforestation. However, tree planting is labor-intensive and a long-term project, and it would be difficult even to replace the

trees that are currently being cut down, much less increase the forested areas.

Methane emissions constitute about 11% of greenhouse gases, and reducing them poses major hurdles. Some methane can be recovered from solid waste landfills and used to produce energy. Some emissions can be prevented by reducing leaks in the course of transporting natural gas, which has a high methane content. But other sources pose graver problems. Much of the recent increase in methane emissions has undoubtedly come from the tripling of rice production in Asia between 1950 and 1985. As long as large populations depend on rice, beef and milk to sustain them, there will continue to be methane emissions.

Banning CFCs, which would be technically feasible by the end of the century, would help save the ozone layer and decrease cases of skin cancer, as well as slightly reduce global warming. But there is resistance to phasing out CFCs—as there is to many other environmentally sound policies—on the grounds of cost and convenience to the consumer. Third World countries in particular are opposed to paying for substitutes unless the West contributes.

Global threat, global response

Our earth is one but the world is not.
—1987 Report of the World Commission on Environment and Development (Brundtland Report)

AS AN UNDERSTANDING of the greenhouse effect has grown in the past few years, the need for international collaboration to counter its effects has become more urgent. Progress has been hampered by sharp differences between the industrialized countries, which are mainly responsible for creating the problem, and the developing nations, which are contributing a growing share of greenhouse gases.

The Third World, which currently accounts for about 15% of CO_2 emissions, needs energy for building factories, schools, offices and houses, for industry, communication and transportation systems. Both China and India

are counting on coal to fuel their development, and the fact that coal emits more CO_2 than oil or gas is simply not a major consideration. China, with a population of over 1 billion, hopes to double coal production in 11 years. India, with a population of 835 million, expects to triple coal consumption.

In the past, Third World countries tended to regard pleas to curb their use of fossil fuels as a scheme to hinder their development. They claim that at a time when they are industrializing they cannot afford to replace or modify the coal- and oil-burning plants that produce much of their electricity. (They are also unenthusiastic about reducing CFCs. China alone plans to produce 300 million refrigerators.)

Developing countries resent outside meddling in their domestic affairs. Brazil, for example, has bridled at foreign

criticism of its destruction of the Amazon rain forest. Brazil asserts it has the right to develop the Amazon region as it sees fit. The U.S., Brazilians note, has not stopped destroying its own primal forest in Alaska and is cutting down more trees a year than it is replacing. Nevertheless, Brazilian President José Sarney, in an apparent concession to foreign and local pressures, announced in April 1989 a major program to save the Amazon by creating separate zones for economic development and ecological preservation.

Many environmentalists believe the burden is on the industrialized countries to demonstrate that they take global warming seriously. It is up to them to work out policies—in particular strategies for reducing the consumption of fossil fuels—and to apply them at home. Only by setting an example will

Scott Willis ©1989 San Jose Mercury News

they convince developing countries that it is in their own self-interest to reduce greenhouse gas emissions. Secondly, the industrialized countries should be prepared to give aid to the Third World, through the International Bank for Reconstruction and Development, or World Bank, and bilateral programs, to enable them to make the transition to alternate energy sources and new energy-saving technologies.

In spite of their deep-seated differences, industrialized and developing countries together, in meetings at the UN and elsewhere, have agreed on the broad dimensions of the global warming problem and are working out strategies to attack it.

International cooperation

The world's consciousness of the environment was first raised by the UN Conference on the Human Environment, held in Stockholm, Sweden, in 1972. Out of that meeting emerged the UN Environment Program, or UNEP, which helps promote sustainable development, that is, development that will not fatally damage or deplete natural resources.

In 1985 UNEP, together with the World Meteorological Organization (WMO), a UN agency that gathers weather and climate data, and the International Council of Scientific Unions organized a conference in Villach,

Austria, which produced the first scientific consensus on global warming. The conference recommended an early meeting between scientists and politicians to consider a strategy to deal with the problem. It also organized two workshops to study how climate change could affect various regions of the world and options for limiting or adapting to its effects.

The work begun at Villach is being carried on by the Intergovernmental Panel on Climate Change (IPCC), which is the main international body concerned with global warming. Founded in 1988 by UNEP and the WMO, the IPCC established three working groups that are to produce a report this year for consideration at a second major climate conference in Geneva, Switzerland. The first working group, chaired by Britain, is assessing scientific knowledge about climate change; the second, chaired by the U.S.S.R., is assessing the social and economic impact of global warming; and the third, chaired by the U.S., is weighing strategies of response.

A 70-nation conference on global warming met in the Netherlands in November 1989. There was agreement on the necessity of stabilizing CO_2 emissions but not on a specific timetable for curbing emissions. The U.S. and Japan objected to a timetable on the grounds that further study was needed,

and the Soviet Union, on the grounds that the cost of compliance would be prohibitive.

Global warming is expected to head the agenda of the UN environment meeting commemorating the 20th anniversary of the Stockholm conference. The conference, which will probably be held in Brazil in 1992, could result in the adoption of a climatic convention first proposed by Britain. It would do for global warming what the Montreal Protocol has done for protection of the ozone layer. (The Montreal Protocol of September 1987, considered one of UNEP's major achievements to date, provides for a 50% reduction in the industrialized countries' production and use of five of the most harmful CFCs by the end of the century, with developing countries granted a longer time to comply. In May 1989, 80 nations meeting in Helsinki, Finland, speeded up the timetable by calling for an end to the production of CFCs by the year 2000.)

World Bank

While international agreements may eventually counter the effects of global warming, in the developing countries it is the policies of large development institutions such as the World Bank that have potentially the most immediate impact. The World Bank, in deciding which development projects to finance, takes into consideration their environmental impact. Environmental soundness, however, is only one of the World Bank's criteria, and projects that are the most effective in promoting growth and alleviating poverty are not always good for the environment. For example, the bank spent half a billion dollars to build a dam in Brazil and in the process a rain forest the size of Britain was destroyed. World Bank President Barber Conable conceded that "the bank misread the human, institutional and physical realities of the jungle and the frontier" and promised that "if the World Bank has been part of the problem in the past, it can and will be a strong force in finding solutions in the future." In 1987 the bank formed a new environmental department. Critics charge that the bank's environmental officers have little power, and they believe the bank could do far more than it has to encourage energy efficiency and the development of renewable energy technologies.

The U.S. response

PRESIDENT BUSH came into office calling for a new attitude about the environment. As a candidate he had said, "those who think we are powerless to do anything about the greenhouse effect are forgetting about the 'White House effect.' As President I intend to do something about it."

Bush chose a prominent environmentalist, William K. Reilly, to head the EPA. And, in his first major policy address, Secretary of State James A. Baker 3d called for international action to combat global warming. Under the Global Climate Protection Act of 1987, the President is responsible for "developing and proposing to Congress a coordinated national policy on global climate change." He is advised by the Council on Environmental Quality as well as the EPA, which works closely with the Intergovernmental Panel on Climate Change. In a March 1989 report to Congress, the EPA suggested specific international measures to slow global warming. These included requiring all new autos to average at least 40 miles per gallon; stepping up research on solar power; taxing fossil fuel users; and reforestation. The recommendations must now be studied by the executive branch, Congress and the international community.

The action EPA recommends would require extraordinary international consensus. Yet the U.S. has had difficulty achieving such consensus at home. The Reagan Administration (1981–89) opposed environmentalists' efforts to impose antipollution requirements on industry.

It rolled back fuel-efficiency standards for automobiles and trimmed funds for research on alternative fuels, including solar power. Despite the pleading of Canada, Reagan delayed taking action against acid rain on the grounds that more research was needed. (Acid rain is formed when sulfur dioxide from burning coal combines with moisture in the atmosphere. It has destroyed life in lakes and forests hundreds or even thousands of miles from its point of origin.)

Bush recommended strengthening the Clean Air Act of 1970 by reducing acid rain, airborne toxic chemicals and ozone, the main components of urban smog. His proposal would have a sig-

nificant effect on energy policy, increasing the use of clean-burning fuels like natural gas at the expense of coal and gasoline. In addition, the President promised to seek an early accord with Canada on acid rain.

In another reversal of Reagan's policy, the Bush Administration tightened fuel-economy rules for 1990-model automobiles, this at a time when consumers once more favor larger cars that use more fuel. That trend began in 1985 with what environmentalists call the "third oil shock," the fall in oil prices resulting from an oil glut. The new rules require automakers to attain an average fuel consumption of 27.5 miles per gallon, one mpg above the 1989 standard. Bush also proposed requiring auto manufacturers to phase in cars powered by "clean fuels" like methanol, produced from natural gas.

The Administration is divided over how to act on evidence of climate change. The EPA is in the lead in favoring stronger steps to stabilize or reduce CO_2 emissions. The State Department has come under heavy pressure from other nations, especially in Europe, to reach an international accord on this issue. On the other hand, some White House officials are concerned about the economic impact of reducing CO_2 emissions and want more evidence before imposing stricter rules.

At the conference in the Netherlands early last November, U.S. objections were an important factor in preventing the adoption of an international accord on CO_2. After the Administration came under

"NAH — IT WOULDN'T BE PRACTICAL"

strong criticism in Congress for moving too slowly on global warming, Reilly, in a change of tone, told the Senate Foreign Relations Committee on November 20 that if other nations would agree to quicker action, the U.S. would also.

Congressional initiatives

Shortly after the heat wave of 1988, Senator Albert Gore (D-Tenn.) introduced one of two major bills addressing global warming. Entitled the World Environment Policy Act of 1989, the bill would require stricter fuel-economy standards for cars and would ban CFCs. It would also broaden the mandate of the White House Council on Environmental Quality to cover world environmental policy.

The second bill, the National Energy Policy Act of 1989, was introduced by Senator Wirth and had 35 cosponsors. The bill calls for energy efficiency; conservation; the conversion of gasoline-fueled vehicles to natural gas; clean coal and renewable energy; reforestation; and support for international family planning to stem population growth. The bill also provides for up to $500 million to be spent on research and development of a new, safer generation of nuclear reactors, an issue which has divided the environmental community in this country and elsewhere.

Public interest groups

Much of the pressure for U.S. action on global warming has come from the public. This is also true in Europe and Japan, where greens, as environmentalists and their parties are known, have become a significant political force. In this country, U.S. policy research and educational organizations and lobby groups have awakened public interest and conveyed their concerns to Washington. (See the list of organizations on page 89.) But they are not entirely satisfied with their results. "So far, the implications of the greenhouse phenomenon have not played the slightest role in long-term strategic planning by the government," laments David Wirth of the Natural Resources Defense Council. Most of the groups favor adoption of a national energy policy, a timetable for reducing CO_2 and other greenhouse gas emissions, and reforestation. They would like to see more Federal funds applied to basic research on global warming and the development of alternate energy sources. At a time when our economic competitors such as Japan and West Germany are spending more in this area, Federal funds are actually shrinking, notes the U.S. Export Council for Renewable Energy, a trade association.

Policy options

Some of the strategies to reduce global warming will be costly, others, inconvenient. Technologies exist that could cut U.S. energy use by as much as 50%, but they are not being applied because the incentive to conserve is lacking. Whatever the cost, most scientists agree that the price of not implementing energy-saving strategies will be far costlier, even catastrophic.

"The danger of crying wolf too soon, which much of the scientific community fears, is that a few cool years may discredit the greenhouse issue…A greater danger is to wait too long," according to James E. Hansen, a scientist with the National Aeronautics and Space Administration.

What policies can the U.S. carry out on its own and in concert with other nations to counter global warming?

Since 63% of the oil used in the U.S. is for transportation, reduction of CO_2 emissions from autos should come first, according to many environmentalists. They would like to see the fuel economy of new automobiles and light trucks increased to as much as 45 mpg and 35 mpg, respectively, by the year 2000. (Volvo and Toyota have developed cars that can get 70–100 mpg.)

Such high mileage standards are opposed by most auto manufacturers, who point out that fuel economy has already greatly improved. Before the oil shock of 1973–74, U.S. cars averaged 13 mpg; in 1989, by law they had to average 26.5 mpg.

Another strategy for reducing CO_2 emissions would be to tax the polluter. A boost in the gasoline tax (the Federal tax at present is 9.1¢ per gallon) to perhaps 50¢, according to environmentalists, would be easy to administer and environmentally sound. (Americans at present pay some of the lowest prices for gasoline of any country.) At the same time it would help reduce the Federal budget and U.S. dependency on imported oil.

Opponents include many motorists, oil companies and liberal groups who insist the tax increase would unfairly burden lower-income motorists, increase inflation and slow the economy. Auto manufacturers would prefer to see older, more-polluting vehicles retired and new models substituted.

Another solution would be to replace gasoline with cleaner-burning fuels, such as methanol and coal. The oil industry opposes provisions in Bush's clean air legislation that call for the increased use of alternative fuels, claiming that methanol, for example, is too expensive. It claims the answer can be found in reformulated gasoline.

Developing countries depend on biomass, or plant matter, mainly firewood and crop residues, for more than 40% of their energy needs. Much of the biomass, however, is burned so inefficiently that it provides little energy. **Adopting more efficient methods to use biomass,** for example converting the residue from processing sugarcane to gas to drive turbines and produce electricity, would add to the energy supply without adding significantly to the greenhouse effect.

There are many other existing technologies that would not only reduce fossil fuel consumption but cut costs. Insulating houses is one example. Another is replacing the typical frost-free refrigerator, which uses 1,200 kilowatt hours a year, with a state-of-the-art model using 200.

Local action

Many communities have already adopted ambitious environmental codes. In California, there are regional ordinances that will outlaw gasoline engines for lawn mowers, starter fluids for barbecues and even gasoline-powered automobiles by the year 2007.

Although these measures are aimed at improving air quality, not at reducing global warming, environmentalists are counting on activists at the local level to bring pressure on the government to help tackle the harder issues. Last October, a House subcommittee voted to apply California's stringent limits on auto emissions to the whole country beginning in 1994.

A leadership role?

Most environmentalists agree that the U.S., as the largest contributor to global warming, must take concrete steps on its own to slow the process. This could require the Federal government to set ground rules and regulate a broad range of activities that will impact on individuals and industries. Only then can the U.S. expect to enlist the cooperation of developing countries on global measures.

Skeptics counter that those who are pushing the U.S. to assert its leadership are in fact asking the U.S. to make unilateral sacrifices. They recommend waiting to act on global warming until more research is completed. Even if the evidence is conclusive, it is very difficult to get countries to cooperate on implementing solutions. For example, in October 1989, an international conference was unable to agree on measures to protect Antarctica's environment.

Price tag

The major obstacle to taking effective action to counter global warming is the cost. A decade of failed attempts in the U.S. Congress to strengthen the Clean Air Act illustrates the pitfalls ahead. According to one estimate, it could cost the U.S. as much every year to control CO_2 emissions as it spends on defense. Protecting U.S. coastal cities from a three-foot rise in sea level could cost up to $100 billion. Yet if the alternative is catastrophe, is that too high a price to pay?

Already the less painful steps, such as abolishing CFCs in spray cans, have been taken. But significant reductions in CO_2 emissions in the future would require a change in the lifestyles of everybody. As long as the evidence for global warming is not conclusive, there will be an excuse for postponing the hard decisions.

On the other hand, if forecasts are correct, the longer action is delayed, the worse the consequences will be. A principal obstacle is not the lack of evidence about the consequences of global warming but a lack of political will to take preventive measures. Even in the unlikely event that CO_2 buildup is not found to contribute to global warming, industries that have reduced their energy consumption will be more efficient

" I MISS THE OZONE LAYER...."

Schorr, *The Kansas City Star.* ©1988, Los Angeles Times Syndicate.

and more competitive with their European and Japanese rivals.

Much energy-saving technology is already available in the industrialized countries but not in the Third World. The latter cannot be expected to adopt environmentally sound policies without help from the U.S. and other developed countries. The U.S. Agency for International Development currently earmarks only a few tens of millions of dollars for programs to counter global warming. It could give a higher priority to encouraging energy efficiency and the development of alternative energy sources in the Third World. The U.S. could also use its muscle in the World Bank to assure that development assistance is reserved for environmentally sound projects.

Those who question this course of action note that the Third World countries receiving U.S. aid are responsible for only about 6% of the world's greenhouse gases. They can reduce those emissions without U.S. help, for example, by cutting off government subsidies for electricity and fuel that encourage waste, not conservation. Without sacrificing development, Third World countries can save a great deal of energy by leapfrogging outdated technologies.

Finally, no strategy to counter global warming is workable without addressing the issue of rapid popula- **tion growth, according to family-planning advocates.** U.S. funding for international population control programs has fallen by one third since 1985. Only by increasing funding for organizations that foster family planning, such as the International Planned Parenthood Federation and the UN Fund for Population Activities, can the pressure on the environment caused by rapid population growth and increased need for everything from food to energy be relieved.

Opponents of a population strategy maintain that the U.S., on moral grounds, should not provide funding for organizations that sanction abortion counseling or services. The problem is not population but devising a strategy for sustainable development that is environmentally sound.

★ ★ ★

According to Smithsonian Institution biologist Thomas Lovejoy, "most of the great environmental struggles will be either won or lost in the 1990s." By the next century, it will be too late. The 1990s could be a decade of decisions for the environment and the greenhouse we all share.

Opinion Ballot
||||➡ **on page 94** ||||➡

FOR DISCUSSION

1. "We do not have generations, we have only years, in which to attempt to turn things around," warns Lester Brown of the Worldwatch Institute. Why has the state of the environment worsened so dramatically?

2. Some predict that in the not-too-distant future global environmental problems will be the principal concern of many countries, eclipsing, for example, the East-West struggle. What do you think?

3. Most environmental problems are transnational. Is it fair to ask Third World countries to sacrifice development for the greater good?

4. Global warming is an issue politicians in the U.S. and Europe have been quick to adopt—after all, everybody is against harming the environment. But would they be prepared to support measures that hurt their constituents economically? Would you be willing to forgo air-conditioning in your car if effective substitutes for CFCs were not developed?

5. Saving the Amazon rain forest has lately become a fashionable issue, one for which rock stars are ready to stage benefit concerts. Why is it important to preserve the trees? Do Brazil and other countries have the right to dispose of their resources as they see fit?

6. The U.S. cannot solve the problem of global warming on its own, and solutions will be very expensive. Should U.S. foreign aid emphasize development of alternative energy sources, or do you think that at present only fossil fuels are practical in the Third World?

7. The future of nuclear energy is a question that has split the environmental movement. Do you think the benefits outweigh the risks?

8. If predictions of a global warming trend turn out to be exaggerated, what will be the effect of actions that have been taken to slow it?

SUGGESTED READINGS

Abrahamson, Dean Edwin, ed., **The Challenge of Global Warming.** Washington, D.C., Island Press in cooperation with the Natural Resources Defense Council, 1989. 358 pp. $19.95 (paper). Assesses the evidence for climate change and suggests policy responses.

Flavin, Christopher, "Slowing Global Warming: A Worldwide Strategy." **Worldwatch Paper** 91. Washington, D.C., The Worldwatch Institute, October 1989. 94 pp. $4.00. Increased energy efficiency is the key to reducing greenhouse gas emissions.

Goldemberg, José, et al., **Energy for a Sustainable World.** Washington, D.C., World Resources Institute, 1987. 119 pp. $10.00 (paper). Study of the demand for energy concludes that even if the world's population were to reach 7 billion, global energy use would only need to rise 10% from today's level.

"Inside the Greenhouse." **Newsweek,** July 11, 1988, pp.16–24. Special report explains what could happen if global warming is not slowed. Good illustrations.

Ray, Dixy Lee, "The Greenhouse Blues: Keep Cool About Global Warming." **Policy Review,** Summer 1989, pp.70–72.

"What the greenhouse debate needs most is a dose of healthy skepticism."

Schneider, Stephen H., "The Changing Climate." **Scientific American,** September 1989, pp.70–79. Global warming should be evident within a decade or so—but we should not wait that long to take action.

Shea, Cynthia Pollock, "Protecting Life on Earth: Steps to Save the Ozone Layer." **Worldwatch Paper** 87. Washington, D.C., The Worldwatch Institute, December 1988. 46 pp. $4.00. Documents the erosion of the ozone shield and urges a crash program to reduce CFC emissions.

"U.S. Policy and the International Environment." U.S.Department of State, Bureau of Public Affairs, Washington, D.C. 20520-6810. Public Information Series, June 1989. 4 pp. Available free. Outlines U.S. efforts to halt environmental degradation and emphasizes necessity for international cooperation.

Wirth, David, "Climate Chaos." **Foreign Policy,** Spring 1989, pp. 3–22. Implications for U.S. policy of worldwide climate disruption; author suggests the adoption of a multilateral treaty requiring reductions in greenhouse gases.

For further in-depth reading, write for the Great Decisions 1990 Bibliography (see page 4).

KEY TO ORGANIZATIONS

The following are a few of the many organizations that can provide additional background on the eight topics or information on opportunities for local involvement in these issues. Some of the organizations listed provide nonpartisan educational programs and materials, while others advocate a particular point of view. We encourage you to learn more about the eight topics in Great Decisions, make your policy choices known through the Opinion Ballots, and then become actively involved in the policy process at the local, state, national and international level.

General

Access: A Security Information Service, 1730 M St., N.W., Suite 605, Washington, DC 20036; (202) 785-6630.

Common Cause, 2030 M St., N.W., Washington, DC 20036; (202) 833-1200.

Educators for Social Responsibility (ESR), 23 Garden St., Cambridge, MA 02138; (617) 492-1764.

Freedom House, 48 East 21st St., New York, NY 10010; (212) 473-9691.

National Council for World Affairs Organizations (NCWAO), c/o Brenda Lei Foster, Pacific & Asian Affairs Council, 2004 University Ave., Honolulu, HI 96822; (808) 941-6066.

United Nations Association of the United States of America (UNA-USA), 485 Fifth Ave., New York, NY 10017; (212) 697-3232.

World Without War Council, 1730 Martin Luther King, Jr. Way, Berkeley, CA 94709; (415) 845-1992.

Topic 1. U.S.S.R. and Eastern Europe

American Committee on East-West Accord, 109 11th St., S.E., Washington, DC 20003; (202) 546-1700.

The Atlantic Council of the United States, 1616 H St., N.W., Washington, DC 20006; (202) 347-9353.

Campaign for Peace and Democracy/East and West, 155 West 76th St., New York, NY 10023; (202) 724-1157.

Citizen Exchange Council, 12 West 31st St., 4th Floor, New York, NY 10001-4415; (212) 643-1985.

Committee for National Security, 1601 Connecticut Ave., N.W., Suite 302, Washington, DC 20009; (202) 745-2450.

IREX (International Research and Exchanges Board), 126 Alexander St., Princeton, NJ 08540-7102; (609) 683-9500.

National Council of American-Soviet Friendship, 85 East 4th St., New York, NY 10003; (212) 254-6606.

Sane/Freeze, 711 G St., S.E., Washington, DC 20003; (202) 546-7100.

University of Maryland, Center for International Security Studies, 3106 Morrill Hall, College Park, MD 20742; (301) 454-4344.

Topic 2. U.S., Europe and Japan

American Enterprise Institute for Public Policy Research (AEI). 1150 17th St., N.W., Washington, DC 20036; (202) 862-5800.

Asia Society, Contemporary Affairs Department, 725 Park Avenue, New York, NY 10021; (212) 288-6400.

Consumers for World Trade, 1001 Connecticut Ave., N.W., Suite 800, Washington, DC 20036; (202) 785-4835.

Delegation of the Commission of European Communities, Press and Public Affairs, 2100 M St., N.W., 7th Floor, Washington, DC 20037; (202) 862-9500.

Emergency Committee for American Trade, 1211 Connecticut Ave., N.W., Suite 801, Washington, DC 20036; (202) 659-5147.

Topic 3. Nicaragua and El Salvador

Americas Watch, 36 West 44th St., New York, NY 10036; (212) 840-9460.

Amnesty International U.S.A., 304 West 58th St., New York, NY 10019; (212) 807-8400.

Committee in Solidarity with the People of El Salvador (CISPES), 1314 14th St., N.W., Suite 7, Washington, DC; (202) 265-0890.

Friends of the Americas, 912 North Foster Dr., Baton Rouge, LA 70806; (504) 926-5707.

Inter-American Dialogue, c/o Aspen Institute for Humanistic Studies, 1333 New Hampshire Ave., N.W., Suite 1070, Washington, DC 20036; (202) 466-6410.

National Council of Churches, Caribbean and Latin American Office, 475 Riverside Dr., New York, NY 100115; (212) 870-2460.

Network of Educators Committees on Central America (NECCA). P.O. Box 43509, Washington, DC 20010; (202) 667-2618.

Policy Alternatives for the Caribbean and Central America (PACCA), 1506 19th St., N.W., Suite 2, Washington, DC 20036; (202) 332-6333.

Topic 4. Vietnam, Cambodia & the U.S.

Asia Society. (See Topic 2.)

The Indochina Project, 318 Fourth St., N.E., Washington, DC 20002; (202) 547-5075.

National League of Families of American Prisoners and Missing in Southeast Asia, 1001 Connecticut Ave., N.W., Suite 219, Washington, DC 20036-5504; (202) 223-6846.

Refugees International, 220 Eye St., N.E., Suite 240, Washington, DC 20002; (202) 547-3785.

Social Science Research Council, 605 Third Ave., New York, NY 10158; (212) 661-0280.

U.S.-Indochina Reconciliation Project, 5808 Greene St., Philadelphia, PA 19144; (215) 848-4200.

The Vietnam Project, 2100 M St., N.W., Suite 607, Washington, DC 20037; (202) 955-0088.

The William Joiner Center for the Study of War and Social Consequences, 4th Floor, Wheatley Hall, University of Massachusetts, Boston, MA 02125; (617) 929-7864.

Topic 5. Third World Arms Bazaar

American Association for the Advancement of Science, Program on Science, Arms Control and National Security, 1333 H St., N.W., Arms Control Office, 11th Floor, Washington, DC 20005; (202) 326-6490.

Arms Control Association (ACA), 11 Dupont Circle, N.W., Washington, DC 20036; (202) 797-6450.

Five College Program in Peace and World Security Studies, c/o Hampshire College, Amherst, MA 01002; (413) 549-4600.

Stockholm International Peace Research Institute, Pipers vag 28, 8-17173 Solna, Sweden; (8) 55 97 00.

United Nations Department for Disarmament Affairs, United Nations, New York, NY 10017; (212) 754-1234.

U.S. Arms Control and Disarmament Agency, Arms Transfer Division, 320 21st St., N.W., Room 4734, Washington, DC 20451; (202) 647-3496.

World Priorities, P.O. Box 25140, Washington, DC 20007; (202) 965-1661.

Topic 6. United Nations

Campaign for UN Reform (CUNR). 418 7th St., S.E., Washington, DC 20003; (202) 546-3956.

Friends of the United Nations, 120 East 36th St., Suite C, New York, NY 10016; (212) 532-9289.

UNA-USA. (See "General.")

U.S. Committee for the United Nations Children's Fund (Unicef), 110 Maryland Ave., N.E., Washington, DC 20002; (202) 547-0204.

World Federalist Association, 418 7th St., S.E., Washington, DC 20003; (202) 546-3950.

Topic 7. Palestinian Question

American-Arab Affairs Council, 1730 M Street, N.W., Suite 512, Washington, DC 20036; (202) 296-6767.

American Educational Trust, P.O. Box 53062, Washington, DC 20009; (202) 939-6050 or (800) 368-5788.

The Institute for Palestine Studies, Georgetown Station, P.O. Box 25301, Washington, DC 20007; (202) 342-3990.

International Center for Peace in the Middle East, P.O. Box 20511, Dag Hammarskjold Center, New York, N.Y. 10017; (212) 288-2350.

The Middle East Institute, 1761 N St., N.W., Washington, D.C. 20036; (202) 785-1141.

National Council on U.S.-Arab Relations, 1735 Eye St., N.W., Suite 515, Washington, D.C. 20006. (202) 293-0801.

Topic 8. Global Warming

Environmental Defense Fund, 1616 P St., N.W., Suite 150, Washington, DC 20036; (202) 387-3500.

National Wildlife Federation, 1400 16th St., N.W., Washington, DC 20036-2266; (202) 797-6800.

Natural Resources Defense Council, 1350 New York Ave., N.W., Washington, DC 20005; (202) 783-7800.

World Resources Institute, 1709 New York Ave., N.W., Suite 700, Washington, DC 20006; (202) 638-6300.

Worldwatch Institute, 1776 Massachusetts Ave., N.W., Washington, DC 20036; (202) 452-1999.

Profile of Opinion Ballot Participants and How Their Opinions Differ

Results of 38,536 opinion ballots submitted by 4,694 participants in the Foreign Policy Association's nationwide Great Decisions study and discussion program offer special perspectives not only for Washington policymakers but for all those interested in foreign policy issues. The participants, who cast their ballots between January and July 1989, include a significant percentage of community leaders. Some 66 percent have college or advanced degrees. And they are from all regions of the country. The states that submitted the largest number of ballots are Oregon, California, Washington, Illinois, Arizona and Pennsylvania.

Nuclear deterrence, one of the cornerstones of American defense policy, is considered ethically acceptable—without reservations—by less than one third of respondents to the Great Decisions 1989 Opinion Ballots; only slightly more than a third consider it very effective in advancing U.S. interests.

The participants were virtually unanimous, however, in advocating a stronger role for the United Nations as a means of protecting U.S. interests in such spots of high international tension as the Persian Gulf and in favoring neutrality in relations with Iran and Iraq, whose war has now been ended.

Strong support was also expressed for transferring the management of Latin American debt from the U.S. Treasury to an international agency and for multilateral rather than unilateral U.S. actions in world politics. Many respondents favored a faster pace in the arms reduction negotiations between the United States and the Soviet Union, seeking deeper cuts of each side's military forces. There was little inclination to go slow in fostering ties with China, but the Chinese crackdown on the pro-democracy movement may have come after most participants had sent in their ballots. Regarding the problem of combating drug use, participants did not see U.S. military interdiction or aid to producer countries as highly effective.

The participants who mailed in their ballots are no cross section of the general public. Female participants outnumber males by a 3 to 2 margin. The majority is over 60 years old. Two thirds hold college degrees, with advanced degrees quite common. Many would be considered "opinion leaders": one in seven indicated they were often asked for their opinions on foreign policy and half said this happened sometimes. A majority of the participants had been abroad during the past four years. And more participants than not indicated that they had changed their opinions as a result of taking part in the Great Decisions program.

A. How many years have you participated in the Great Decisions program (that is, attended one or more discussion sessions)?

This is the first year I have participated	37%
I participated in one previous year	13%
I participated in more than one previous year	45%

B. Age

17 or under	3%
18–30	13%
31–45	7%
46–60	15%
61 or over	58%

C. Sex

Female	57%
Male	38%

D. Have you been abroad during the last four years?

Yes	51%
No	44%

E. What is the highest level of formal education you have completed?

Some high school	5%
High school degree	6%
Some college	19%
College graduate	31%
Advanced degree	35%

F. How often are you asked for your opinion on foreign policy matters?

Often	15%
Sometimes	50%
Never	30%

G. Would you say you have or have not changed your opinion in a fairly significant way as a result of taking part in the Great Decisions program?

Have	44%
Have not	28%
Uncertain	22%

Note: Percentages do not add up to 100 because not all respondents answered every question.

1989 Opinion Ballot Report Results

(An opinion survey of 4,694 participants)

Topic 1: Ethics in International Relations: Power and Morality

Issue A. The U.S. relies on a number of policy instruments, some of which are listed below. For each, check whether you agree, agree with reservations or disagree that the policy is ethically acceptable.

	agree	agree with reservations	disagree
Nuclear deterrence	32%	41%	27%
Armed intervention	9%	45%	45%
Covert action	13%	46%	41%
Economic sanctions	38%	48%	14%

Issue B. How would you rate the following policies in terms of their effectiveness in advancing U.S. interests?

	very effective	somewhat effective	not very effective	not effective
Nuclear deterrence	35%	41%	13%	11%
Armed intervention	8%	36%	34%	22%
Covert action	6%	36%	33%	24%
Economic sanctions	14%	44%	29%	13%

Topic 2: The Persian Gulf: Reassessing the U.S. Role

Issue A. When it comes to protecting American interests in the Persian Gulf, the U.S. should:

Be prepared to use force	61%
Sell advanced arms to moderate Arab states	24%
Strengthen the role of the UN	94%
Cooperate with the Soviet Union	86%

Issue B. With regard to relations with Iran and Iraq, the U.S. should:

Favor Iran over Iraq	2%
Stay neutral	93%
Favor Iraq over Iran	5%

Note: Percentages may not add up to 100 because of rounding.

Topic 3: Latin American Debt: Living on Borrowed Time?

Issue A. With regard to Latin American debt, the U.S. should:

Leave debt problem for the Latin American governments and their creditor banks to work out	12%
Continue the case-by-case strategy of debt management as outlined by the Baker Plan	40%
Transfer responsibility for debt management from the U.S. Treasury to an international agency under the auspices of the World Bank	48%

Issue B. Which of the following statements comes closest to your thinking?

Latin American debtors should be held responsible for all the debt no matter what the social and political costs	10%
Latin American debtors should service their debts according to their ability to do so	64%
Some or all of the region's debts should be forgiven	26%

Topic 4: Arms Agreements: Too Little Too Late, or Too Much Too Soon?

Issue A. On strategic arms, the U.S. should:

Proceed cautiously before concluding a START treaty	35%
Work toward rapidly concluding a START agreement	14%
Work toward deeper reductions than those called for by START	29%
Take unilateral steps toward nuclear disarmament	22%

Issue B. On conventional arms, the U.S. should:

Seek deep cuts in Warsaw Pact forces in exchange for modest cuts in NATO forces	28%
Seek deeper cuts in Warsaw Pact forces in exchange for deep cuts in NATO forces	43%
Build up conventional capability	10%
Make unilateral reductions in conventional forces	19%

Topic 5: China: Redefining the Revolution

Issue A. The primary goal of U.S. policy toward China should be:

Increase ties with China across-the-board	29%
Increase economic and cultural ties but limit defense cooperation	61%
Maintain the current level of relations	10%
Reduce ties to China	1%

Issue B. Do you consider the following constitute obstacles to improved U.S. relations with China?

U.S. protectionist trade policies	68%
The Taiwan issue	71%
China's treatment of Tibetans and other minorities	78%
China's arms sales to the Third World	80%
China's improving relations with the Soviet Union	22%
China's one-child policy	15%

Topic 6: Farmers, Food and the Global Supermarket

Issue A. On a scale of 1 to 10, where 1 is low in importance and 10 is high, how important, in your opinion, is:

The survival of the American family farm	6.8
The promotion of free agricultural trade	7.1
The elimination of hunger worldwide	7.9
Global population control	8.0
Global land management and environmental protection	8.3
Reasonably priced and plentiful food for America	7.3
Emergency food aid for countries in need	7.3
Long-term development assistance for Third World countries	7.3

Issue B. With respect to its domestic farm policy and international agricultural trade, the U.S. should:

Give farmers subsidies or other Federal support regardless of the effect on international trade	8%
Give farmers subsidies or other Federal support as long as that does not interfere with international trade	25%
Use subsidies as a bargaining tool to get other countries to relax their agricultural trade restrictions	33%
Eliminate subsidies and other Federal support for farmers	34%

Topic 7: Horn of Africa: Empty Cornucopia?

Issue A. On a scale of 1 to 10, where 1 is low in effectiveness and 10 is high, how effective, in your opinion, is each of the following in promoting U.S. interests in Ethiopia:

Provide development aid to Ethiopia	6.3
Buy more Ethiopian products	4.8
Impose trade sanctions against Ethiopia	2.8
Withhold food aid from Ethiopia	2.5
Condition development aid on improvement in human-rights situation	6.5
Support for Eritrean resistance	3.6
Seek Soviet cooperation to resolve Eritrean war	7.3

Issue B. What policy should the U.S. follow toward Somalia?

Continue to give aid to the Siad Barre government	12%
Condition future aid on improvement in human-rights situation	78%
Withhold aid	10%

Topic 8: International Drug Traffic: An Unwinnable War?

On a scale of 1 to 10, where 1 is low in effectiveness and 10 is high, how effective, in your opinion, is each of the following in combating illicit drugs:

Pressure on producer countries to halt supplies	5.8
U.S. military interdiction	4.2
U.S. aid to producer countries	4.3
Drug education and treatment programs in the U.S.	8.3
Legalization of drugs in the U.S.	4.2

Helmut Norpoth, a public opinion expert, is the author of the *National Opinion Ballot Report.* His analysis is based on a tabulation prepared by the Calculogic Corporation of New York City.

Dr. Norpoth is a professor of political science at the State University of New York at Stony Brook. He has served as a consultant for the New York Times/CBS News Poll and has been the recipient of a number of research and travel grants and awards. A scholar of European and U.S. party politics, Dr. Norpoth has published numerous articles in the United States and West Germany.

Opinion Ballots

HOW TO USE THE OPINION BALLOT: *For your convenience, there are two sets of ballots. Please cut out and mail your completed ballots (the entire page) before* __June 30__ *so they can be included in the national tabulation. N.B. If your group wants to discuss ballot responses after each meeting, we suggest you photocopy the ballot pages for your own use.*

Topic 1: U.S.S.R. and Eastern Europe

Issue A. Do you think that without Western economic aid the liberalization efforts in the Soviet Union and Eastern Europe will collapse?

- ❑ 1. Yes
- ❑ 2. No

Issue B. Should the U.S. offer the Soviet Union and Eastern Europe substantial loans and favorable trade terms? Check one choice only.

- ❑ 1. Without any conditions.
- ❑ 2. Only if free-market reforms are adopted.
- ❑ 3. Only if defense spending is cut.
- ❑ 4. Only if free-market reforms are adopted and defense spending is cut.
- ❑ 5. Not at all.

Other, or comment ....

....

Topic 2: The U.S., Europe and Japan

Issue A. At present, is the U.S. economy in good shape or in bad shape?

- ❑ 1. Good shape
- ❑ 2. Bad shape

Issue B. In the next few years, will the U.S. economy grow or decline?

- ❑ 1. Will grow
- ❑ 2. Will decline

Issue C. Do budget and trade deficits pose major problems for the nation's health?

- ❑ 1. Yes
- ❑ 2. No

Issue D. With regard to U.S. trade and investment policy, which of the following statements comes closest to your thinking? Check one choice only.

- ❑ 1. The U.S. should take steps to protect itself from foreign competition.
- ❑ 2. The U.S. should restrict investment from and trade with those countries that place restrictions on U.S. investors and exporters.
- ❑ 3. The U.S. should continue to work for more-open trade and investment policies worldwide.

Other, or comment ....

....

Topic 3: Nicaragua and El Salvador

Issue A. On a scale of 1 to 10, where 1 is low in importance and 10 is high, how important is it to you that the U.S. achieve each of the following in Central America?

- _____ 1. Stop the spread of communism.
- _____ 2. Topple the Sandinista government in Nicaragua.
- _____ 3. Promote economic and social development.
- _____ 4. Strengthen democratic institutions.
- _____ 5. Promote respect for human rights.
- _____ 6. Protect U.S. investments.
- _____ 7. Keep the Soviets and/or the Cubans out.

Other, or comment ....

....

Issue B. With respect to Central America, the U.S. should give highest priority to (check one choice only):

- ❑ 1. Increasing economic aid to the region.
- ❑ 2. Working more closely with governments in the region to settle conflicts peacefully.
- ❑ 3. Providing more military support.
- ❑ 4. Reducing the U.S. role in Central America across the board.

Other, or comment ....

....

Topic 4: Vietnam, Cambodia and the U.S.

Issue A. With regard to U.S. policy toward Vietnam, the U.S. should (check one choice only):

- ❑ 1. Normalize relations without preconditions.
- ❑ 2. Normalize relations only after there is a comprehensive settlement in Cambodia.
- ❑ 3. Normalize relations with Vietnam only after the present government is replaced by a democratic one.

Other, or comment ....

....

Issue B. With regard to U.S. policy toward Cambodia, the U.S. should (check one choice only):

- ❑ 1. Support a coalition government headed by Prince Sihanouk even if the Khmer Rouge are included.
- ❑ 2. Support a coalition government headed by Prince Sihanouk provided the Khmer Rouge are not included.
- ❑ 3. Support the Vietnam-backed Hun Sen government.
- ❑ 4. Adopt a hands-off policy, withholding U.S. support from present government and opposition groups.

Other, or comment ....

....

Topic 5: Third World Arms Bazaar

Issue A. For each of the policy options listed below, indicate whether you favor it strongly (1), favor it (2), oppose it strongly (3), oppose it (4), or have no opinion (5):

_____ a. Resume CATT talks with the Soviet Union.

_____ b. Expand CATT talks to include other countries.

_____ c. Tighten MTCR restrictions on technology transfers.

_____ d. Extend MTCR restrictions to more countries.

_____ e. Unilaterally tighten U.S. restrictions on weapons and weapons-technology transfers.

_____ f. Stop production of binary chemical weapons.

_____ g. Pursue a comprehensive nuclear test ban.

Other, or comment ....

....

Topic 6: United Nations

Issue A. Should the U.S. give the UN a higher priority in its foreign policy than it does at present?

❑ Should

❑ Should not

Issue B. Should the U.S., in conjunction with the Soviet Union, make the UN the principal forum for resolving conflicts and keeping the peace?

❑ Should

❑ Should not

Issue C. How effective, in your opinion, is the UN in settling issues of global security?

❑ Effective

❑ Not very effective

❑ Ineffective

Issue D. Would you say that on most international questions the interests of the U.S. coincide with those of the majority of member states?

❑ Yes

❑ No

In planning future GREAT DECISIONS programs, we would find it helpful to know more about participants and would appreciate your answers to the questions below.

A. *How many years have you participated in the GREAT DECISIONS program (that is, attended one or more discussion sessions)?*
   ☐ **1.** *This is the first year I have participated.*
   ☐ **2.** *I participated in one previous year.*
   ☐ **3.** *I participated in more than one previous year.*

B. *What is your age?*
   ☐ **1.** *17 or under* ☐ **3.** *31 to 45* ☐ **5.** *61 or over*
   ☐ **2.** *18 to 30* ☐ **4.** *46 to 60*

C. *Your sex?*
   ☐ **1.** *Female* ☐ **2.** *Male*

D. *Have you been abroad during the last four years?*
   ☐ **1.** *Yes* ☐ **2.** *No*

E. *What is the highest level of formal education you have completed?*
   ☐ **1.** *Some high school* ☐ **4.** *College graduate*
   ☐ **2.** *High school degree* ☐ **5.** *Advanced degree*
   ☐ **3.** *Some college*

F. *How often are you asked for your opinion on foreign policy matters?*
   ☐ **1.** *Often* ☐ **2.** *Sometimes* ☐ **3.** *Hardly ever*

G. *One final question. Would you say you have or have not changed your opinion in a fairly significant way as a result of taking part in the GREAT DECISIONS program?*
   ☐ **1.** *Have* ☐ **2.** *Have not* ☐ **3.** *Uncertain*

Your zip code: _____ _____ _____
                         (first three digits only)

Topic 7: Palestinian Question

Issue A. Which form of political structure would best resolve the Palestinian question? Check one choice only.

❑ 1. An independent Palestinian state.

❑ 2. Palestinian autonomy under Jordanian rule.

❑ 3. Palestinian autonomy under Israeli rule.

❑ 4. Israeli annexation of occupied territories.

Other, or comment ....

....

....

Issue B. In order to advance the peace process, the U.S. should:

	1 yes	2 no
a. Assume leadership in seeking a negotiated settlement.	❑	❑
b. Wait for a regional consensus to develop before pursuing a negotiated settlement.	❑	❑
c. Pressure Israel to make concessions.	❑	❑
d. Pressure the PLO to prove its policy changes are bona fide.	❑	❑

Other, or comment ....

....

....

Topic 8: Global Warming

Issue A. What actions should the U.S. government take to counter global warming?

	1 yes	2 no
a. Mandate cleaner fuel in automobiles.	❑	❑
b. Increase the gas tax to encourage conservation.	❑	❑
c. Support nuclear power.	❑	❑
d. Make foreign aid contingent on sound environmental policies.	❑	❑
e. Support an international convention to reduce CO_2 emissions.	❑	❑
f. Wait until there is more-conclusive proof of global warming.	❑	❑

Other, or comment ....

....

....

Opinion Ballots

How to use the Opinion Ballot: *For your convenience, there are two sets of ballots. Please cut out and mail your completed ballots (the entire page) before* **June 30** *so they can be included in the national tabulation. N.B. If your group wants to discuss ballot responses after each meeting, we suggest you photocopy the ballot pages for your own use.*

Topic 1: U.S.S.R. and Eastern Europe

Issue A. Do you think that without Western economic aid the liberalization efforts in the Soviet Union and Eastern Europe will collapse?

❑ 1. Yes
❑ 2. No

Issue B. Should the U.S. offer the Soviet Union and Eastern Europe substantial loans and favorable trade terms? Check one choice only.

❑ 1. Without any conditions.
❑ 2. Only if free-market reforms are adopted.
❑ 3. Only if defense spending is cut.
❑ 4. Only if free-market reforms are adopted and defense spending is cut.
❑ 5. Not at all.

Other, or comment ....
....

Topic 2: The U.S., Europe and Japan

Issue A. At present, is the U.S. economy in good shape or in bad shape?

❑ 1. Good shape
❑ 2. Bad shape

Issue B. In the next few years, will the U.S. economy grow or decline?

❑ 1. Will grow
❑ 2. Will decline

Issue C. Do budget and trade deficits pose major problems for the nation's health?

❑ 1. Yes
❑ 2. No

Issue D. With regard to U.S. trade and investment policy, which of the following statements comes closest to your thinking? Check one choice only.

❑ 1. The U.S. should take steps to protect itself from foreign competition.
❑ 2. The U.S. should restrict investment from and trade with those countries that place restrictions on U.S. investors and exporters.
❑ 3. The U.S. should continue to work for more-open trade and investment policies worldwide.

Other, or comment ....
....

Topic 3: Nicaragua and El Salvador

Issue A. On a scale of 1 to 10, where 1 is low in importance and 10 is high, how important is it to you that the U.S. achieve each of the following in Central America?

_____ 1. Stop the spread of communism.
_____ 2. Topple the Sandinista government in Nicaragua.
_____ 3. Promote economic and social development.
_____ 4. Strengthen democratic institutions.
_____ 5. Promote respect for human rights.
_____ 6. Protect U.S. investments.
_____ 7. Keep the Soviets and/or the Cubans out.

Other, or comment ....
....

Issue B. With respect to Central America, the U.S. should give highest priority to (check one choice only):

❑ 1. Increasing economic aid to the region.
❑ 2. Working more closely with governments in the region to settle conflicts peacefully.
❑ 3. Providing more military support.
❑ 4. Reducing the U.S. role in Central America across the board.

Other, or comment ....
....

Topic 4: Vietnam, Cambodia and the U.S.

Issue A. With regard to U.S. policy toward Vietnam, the U.S. should (check one choice only):

❑ 1. Normalize relations without preconditions.
❑ 2. Normalize relations only after there is a comprehensive settlement in Cambodia.
❑ 3. Normalize relations with Vietnam only after the present government is replaced by a democratic one.

Other, or comment ....
....

Issue B. With regard to U.S. policy toward Cambodia, the U.S. should (check one choice only):

❑ 1. Support a coalition government headed by Prince Sihanouk even if the Khmer Rouge are included.
❑ 2. Support a coalition government headed by Prince Sihanouk provided the Khmer Rouge are not included.
❑ 3. Support the Vietnam-backed Hun Sen government.
❑ 4. Adopt a hands-off policy, withholding U.S. support from present government and opposition groups.

Other, or comment ....
....

Topic 5: Third World Arms Bazaar

Issue A. For each of the policy options listed below, indicate whether you favor it strongly (1), favor it (2), oppose it strongly (3), oppose it (4), or have no opinion (5):

_____ a. Resume CATT talks with the Soviet Union.

_____ b. Expand CATT talks to include other countries.

_____ c. Tighten MTCR restrictions on technology transfers.

_____ d. Extend MTCR restrictions to more countries.

_____ e. Unilaterally tighten U.S. restrictions on weapons and weapons-technology transfers.

_____ f. Stop production of binary chemical weapons.

_____ g. Pursue a comprehensive nuclear test ban.

Other, or comment ....

....

Topic 6: United Nations

Issue A. Should the U.S. give the UN a higher priority in its foreign policy than it does at present?

❏ Should

❏ Should not

Issue B. Should the U.S., in conjunction with the Soviet Union, make the UN the principal forum for resolving conflicts and keeping the peace?

❏ Should

❏ Should not

Issue C. How effective, in your opinion, is the UN in settling issues of global security?

❏ Effective

❏ Not very effective

❏ Ineffective

Issue D. Would you say that on most international questions the interests of the U.S. coincide with those of the majority of member states?

❏ Yes

❏ No

In planning future GREAT DECISIONS programs, we would find it helpful to know more about participants and would appreciate your answers to the questions below.

A. *How many years have you participated in the GREAT DECISIONS program (that is, attended one or more discussion sessions)?*
   ☐ **1.** *This is the first year I have participated.*
   ☐ **2.** *I participated in one previous year.*
   ☐ **3.** *I participated in more than one previous year.*

B. *What is your age?*
   ☐ **1.** *17 or under*   ☐ **3.** *31 to 45*   ☐ **5.** *61 or over*
   ☐ **2.** *18 to 30*   ☐ **4.** *46 to 60*

C. *Your sex?*
   ☐ **1.** *Female*   ☐ **2.** *Male*

D. *Have you been abroad during the last four years?*
   ☐ **1.** *Yes*   ☐ **2.** *No*

E. *What is the highest level of formal education you have completed?*
   ☐ **1.** *Some high school*   ☐ **4.** *College graduate*
   ☐ **2.** *High school degree* ☐ **5.** *Advanced degree*
   ☐ **3.** *Some college*

F. *How often are you asked for your opinion on foreign policy matters?*
   ☐ **1.** *Often*   ☐ **2.** *Sometimes*   ☐ **3.** *Hardly ever*

G. *One final question. Would you say you have or have not changed your opinion in a fairly significant way as a result of taking part in the GREAT DECISIONS program?*
   ☐ **1.** *Have*   ☐ **2.** *Have not*   ☐ **3.** *Uncertain*

Your zip code: 2944 _____ _____ _____
                    (first three digits only)

Topic 7: Palestinian Question

Issue A. Which form of political structure would best resolve the Palestinian question? Check one choice only.

❏ 1. An independent Palestinian state.

❏ 2. Palestinian autonomy under Jordanian rule.

❏ 3. Palestinian autonomy under Israeli rule.

❏ 4. Israeli annexation of occupied territories.

Other, or comment ....

....

....

Issue B. In order to advance the peace process, the U.S. should:

	1 yes	2 no
a. Assume leadership in seeking a negotiated settlement.	❏	❏
b. Wait for a regional consensus to develop before pursuing a negotiated settlement.	❏	❏
c. Pressure Israel to make concessions.	❏	❏
d. Pressure the PLO to prove its policy changes are bona fide.	❏	❏

Other, or comment ....

....

....

Topic 8: Global Warming

Issue A. What actions should the U.S. government take to counter global warming?

	1 yes	2 no
a. Mandate cleaner fuel in automobiles.	❏	❏
b. Increase the gas tax to encourage conservation.	❏	❏
c. Support nuclear power.	❏	❏
d. Make foreign aid contingent on sound environmental policies.	❏	❏
e. Support an international convention to reduce CO_2 emissions.	❏	❏
f. Wait until there is more-conclusive proof of global warming.	❏	❏

Other, or comment ....

....

....